A Historical
Archaeology of the
Modern World

CONTRIBUTIONS TO GLOBAL HISTORICAL ARCHAEOLOGY

Series Editor:
Charles E. Orser, Jr., *Illinois State University, Normal, Illinois*

A HISTORICAL ARCHAEOLOGY OF THE MODERN WORLD
Charles E. Orser, Jr.

A Continuation Order Plan is available for this series. A continuation order will bring delivery of each new volume immediately upon publication. Volumes are billed only upon actual shipment. For further information please contact the publisher.

A Historical Archaeology of the Modern World

Charles E. Orser, Jr.

Illinois State University
Normal, Illinois

PLENUM PRESS • NEW YORK AND LONDON

Library of Congress Cataloging-in-Publication Data

On file

Cover illustration: 1551 French woodcut depicting the natives of Brazil, from *C'est la deduction du sumptueux ordre plaisantz* (printed by permission of the Houghton Library, Harvard University).

ISBN 0-306-45173-5

© 1996 Plenum Press, New York
A Division of Plenum Publishing Corporation
233 Spring Street, New York, N. Y. 10013

Printed in the United States of America

To Brian Fagan

Preface to the Series

The concept for this publication series on global historical archaeology developed out of my growing realization that it is no longer possible to study the post-1492 world as if it had happened in only one place. This perception is not unique to me; many scholars in the discipline have independently reached the same conclusion. For example, not long ago Kathleen Deagan wrote that it would be increasingly difficult for historical archaeologists to ignore a global perspective after the celebration and controversy of the Columbus quincentenary. Others have said much the same thing in other ways. I agree with them wholeheartedly. The year 1992 presented historical archaeology with exciting, promising vistas. Over the past few years, archaeologists around the world have awakened to the possibilities and potentialities of historical archaeology. They have responded to the field's challenges with gusto, making significant contributions to the storehouse of archaeological knowledge about our collective modern past.

But along with the excitement and the vitality of global historical archaeology come certain responsibilities. Historical archaeologists, because we study the modern world, must be sensitive to what is happening in the world around us. Prehistorians have shown in many wonderfully insightful studies that contemporary concepts, attitudes, and biases affect their perspectives on the past. They realize that they do not conduct their research behind the imposing walls of an ivory tower. Instead, they are fully entrenched in this world, facing it head on like everyone else.

Historical archaeologists are perhaps even more susceptible to the many challenges of today's world. Like all archaeologists, we study homes and cemeteries, places of work, and places of rest. At the same time, though, many of us also hold up our most recent ancestors to the harsh light of analytical examination. Historical archaeologists find it impossible to overlook many issues of vital concern today. Social inequality, feminism, racism and race construction, ethnicity and the retention of tradition, forced migrations, and the use of archaeology to construct notions of history and heritage are all topics with some longevity in this world. They did not emerge from thin air; they came from the past we historical archaeologists study.

Over the past few years, I have been fortunate enough to learn something about the exceptionally fine research being conducted by conscientious historical archaeologists outside North America. Much of their research is innovative and intriguing; some of it seems old-fashioned and traditional. But each piece of research, regardless of its theoretical direction, is one small frame in the developing picture of global historical archaeology.

It is my hope that archaeologists from outside North America will find this series to be a welcome and open voice. They have much to teach the world, and historical archaeologists located in other continents would do well to listen. I also hope that North Americans working outside their home continent will be encouraged to use this series as an outlet. Conducting research outside one's home country is challenging, eye-opening, and gratifying. The personal insights and lessons learned are inestimably useful and timelessly pertinent to scholars working both at home and abroad. Even historical archaeologists who never contemplate working outside North America will discover that they have much to learn by opening their intellectual eyes to the wide world around them. So many of the people we study went into the world with their eyes open. Can we not do the same?

Contributions to Global Historical Archaeology is a new series of publications focusing on the archaeological expressions of modern history and culture. The issues explored by the series' authors will be as many and varied as the men and women who left their homes in search of new lives and of those who stood on the distant shores to greet them. The thrust of the series will be to explore topical, methodological, and comparative questions in historical archaeology. We will consider monographs and edited volumes on all subjects. Historical archaeologists across the globe are encouraged to submit manuscripts to the series, even if their research may not be completely global in focus. Theoretical tracts obviously have wide use well beyond the region of their application. Authors examining one or two specific sites, however, should make every effort to cast their arguments and findings in the widest terms possible. Few are the sites that were truly isolated after 1492. But those that were isolated have much to teach us about the limits of globalization and they must not be ignored. We openly welcome manuscripts as well as suggestions for making Contributions to Global Historical Archaeology a series that meets the needs of all historical archaeologists and that proudly leads the discipline into the next century.

CHARLES E. ORSER, JR.

Preface to the Volume

This book has been in my mind for many years, but it only began to take final shape in Strokestown, Ireland, as I started my study of Irish tenant farmers. At first, my interest in Irish peasants merely seemed to be a fortuitous union of my longtime interest in Irish history and my long-standing fascination with the archaeology of postbellum farm tenancy in the American South. But as I read about Ireland, I became increasingly impressed by the relevance of what I already knew about African-American slavery. Even my most recent research on Brazilian maroons seemed to be oddly pertinent to my study of the Irish tenantry. Though the displaced Africans were vastly different in history and culture from the men and women who inhabited the stone cabins of central Ireland, the two peoples nonetheless appeared to be bound together. I became fascinated with the connection between them, and this book began as a personal search to understand how the archaeology of fugitive Brazilian slaves and poor Irish farmers fit together.

My research took many twists and turns, but I slowly began to realize that four historical forces provided the basis for the connection between seventeenth-century Brazil and early-nineteenth-century Ireland. Colonialism, Eurocentrism, capitalism, and modernity were the common denominators between the two places. I also came to understand that these historical forces were globally significant. Their widespread impact convinced me that historical archaeologists must pay explicit attention to them. This book is my effort to explain how the four forces—which I term "haunts" because of their all-pervasive character—can be studied by historical archaeologists. I focus specifically on artifacts, landscape, and social inequality, and use Palmares, Brazil, and Gorttoose, Ireland, as empirical examples.

My hope is that professional archaeologists and archaeological students alike will find interest in what I present here. Though my secret desire is that everyone will agree with what I have written, I know that this expectation is unreasonable. In any case, I hope that readers will come away from these pages challenged and invigorated.

Acknowledgments

One incurs many intellectual debts while writing a book of this sort. Perhaps my greatest debt is owed to Brian Fagan. I learned many things from Brian while we were writing *Historical Archaeology,* but perhaps the most important lesson was that archaeological writing should be readable and interesting. During the course of my archaeological training in the late 1970s, I became increasingly uncomfortable with the often confused language I saw coming from the pens of the discipline's most revered minds. Slowly, I tried to progress from the tortured language of "science" to the more relaxed flow of good, solid writing. The final step was provided by Brian. As gentle master to struggling apprentice, he encouraged me to write concisely and carefully. For this reason, I gratefully dedicate this work to him. Though I know that I am still far from his celebrated standard, I recognize this book as an honest start. I hope that he will agree.

While composing this book on global historical archaeology, I received the kind and generous assistance of archaeologists from around the world. I owe a truly special debt of gratitude to all those scholars in Brazil and Ireland who helped me to conduct fieldwork in their countries. In Brazil, I owe a huge and largely unpayable debt to Pedro Paulo Abreu Funari, professor in the Department of History, State University of Campinas. Pedro has been a close collaborator and friend for years and without him my research in Brazil would be impossible. Also instrumental in the research were Michael J. J. Rowlands, Department of Anthropology, University College London; Zezito de Araújo, Director of the Center for Afro-Brazilian Studies, Federal University of Alagoas, Maceió; José Alberto Gonçalves, Secretary of Culture, União dos Palmares; and Clóvis Moura, President of the Brazilian Institute of African Studies, São Paulo. My research in Ireland could not be conducted without the support and assistance of Luke Dodd, administrator of the Famine Museum, Strokestown; Kevin Whelan, Royal Irish Academy, Dublin; Lionel Pilkington, Department of English, University College Galway; and Terry Barry, Department of Medieval History, Trinity College, Dublin. I also received much appreciated assistance

from Don Mullan, Concern Worldwide; Conleth Manning, Office of
Public Works, Dublin; John Waddell, Department of Archaeology,
University College Galway; Angela Savage, Department of Chemis-
try, University College Galway; Ronald Cox, Department of Civil,
Structural, and Environmental Engineering, Trinity College, Dub-
lin; and Colette O'Daly, National Library of Ireland.

It would be far too difficult to list everyone who helped me to
shape the arguments in this book. Several archaeologists have gra-
ciously read and commented on parts of the manuscript. In the
United States, my principal readers and critics were Mark Leone,
William Marquardt, Paul Shackel, Neil Silberman, and James
Skibo. A student, Jeanne M. Schultz, also read the manuscript. In
Brazil, most of the book was read and commented upon by Pedro
Funari. In Ireland, my principal readers were Luke Dodd and Kevin
Whelan. I have also received invaluable comments and suggestions
from Anders Andrén, Department of Archaeology, University of
Lund, Sweden. In addition, Christopher DeCorse, Elizabeth Scott,
and Suzanne Spencer-Wood were kind enough to send materials and
to discuss with me the issues in this book. I would also like to thank
Jerome S. Handler, for drawing my attention to the pipes from Santo Domingo and Cuba, and David Austin in Wales, Nicholas Brannon in Ireland, and Jorge Miranda in Portugal, for sending me useful, hard-to-find publications from their countries. Each one of these
scholars has helped to shape my thinking, though none is responsible for anything that appears here.

I also wish to acknowledge the support and encouragement of
Eliot Werner of Plenum Press. Not only did he show enthusiasm for
this book, but he was also amenable to starting an entire series on
global historical archaeology. All historical archaeologists can be
encouraged by his faith in their field.

As always, I cannot adequately express my thanks to Janice,
Erin, Emily, and Christine for their moral support during the writing of this book. They encourage my work and willingly make sacrifices for it. Though not an archaeologist by training, Janice has a
sense of what is important about the past and she urges me to
search for it in everything I do.

Contents

A Crisis in Historical Archaeology

"It is with theories as with wells: you may see to the bottom of the deepest if there be any water there, while another shall pass for wondrous profound when 'tis merely shallow, dark, and empty" (Allibone 1890:698). Jonathan Swift, the celebrated author of *Gulliver's Travels,* penned these words in 1726 during his tenure as dean of the majestic St. Patrick's Cathedral in Dublin. Many of today's best literary scholars applaud Swift for his insightful social commentaries, and generations of schoolchildren learn the fine art of satire by reading his essays and poems. Though sometimes biting and often obscure, Swift always gave freely of his now timeless wisdom.

In his fanciful tale of Lemuel Gulliver's curious encounters with Lilliputians, Houyhnhnms, and Yahoos, Swift used symbols and metaphors to teach us about ourselves. Swift's observation about wells and theories even offers subtle insights for today's archaeologists. Swift implied that like wells, several theories can exist at the same time, often occurring side by side. Unlike wells, however, theories are not passive. They do not sit and wait for us to use them. Instead, theories attract us; they beckon to us and compete for our attention. Theories pull us toward them and evoke desire. Archaeologists are often like thirsty travelers emerging from a desert only to behold a fountain.

But Swift revealed that theories have a dark side. They can be deceptive and false, dark and empty. They can be polluted fountains. A theory that at first may seem enlightening, may eventually appear shallow and dry. But Swift found hope in this world of competing theories. Shafts of light penetrate the dark recesses of ignorance as scholars search for understanding and enlightenment. Even the most profound theory, like the deepest well, can be explored and interpreted. Theories dot the intellectual landscape like wells across a colonial countryside. But like many wells, some theories may reveal their secrets only hesitantly after much probing and searching. But their secrets can be revealed because theories, like wells, are the conscious creations of thoughtful men and women.

This book is about the wellsprings of knowledge in historical archaeology. Historical archaeologists are well known for their curiosity about old, abandoned wells. Ivor Noël Hume (1969:10), the renowned excavator of Colonial Williamsburg, Virginia, said that wells are "time capsules buried deep in the earth." Few archaeologists would dispute his wisdom. The sunken wells of the past are known often to contain the discarded belongings of bygone generations. As a result, archaeologists eagerly anticipate excavating within a well's circular confines. This is as it should be.

My perception, however, is that historical archaeologists generally have not inspected the wells of archaeological theory with the same enthusiasm they have shown toward the abandoned well shafts of the past. Antiquated wells are important places for archaeologists to investigate, but historical archaeology will only mature as a serious pursuit when its practitioners tackle the deep theoretical issues that accompany their interpretations of the past. Historical archaeologists should be just as impatient to study the wells of theory as they are to probe the mysteries of brick-lined wells. In thinking theoretically, historical archaeologists should pretend they are approaching an unexcavated well for the first time.

WELLS OF ARCHAEOLOGICAL KNOWLEDGE

Archaeologists have always thought about theory. In fact, so extensive is the library of theoretical thought in archaeology that a list of references would fill pages (but see Trigger 1989). With the development of the New Archaeology in the mid-1960s, much of Anglo-American archaeology became explicitly theoretical. Progressive archaeology professors required their thirsty students to pour through dense tomes, probing the wells of theory for sustenance and survival. Much of what these eager students read was written not only by men and women steeped in archaeological knowledge but by prominent philosophers of science. Though many of these philosophers could not distinguish between a potsherd and a curved, flat stone, they did understand how scholars dug wells of theory. Archaeologists regularly visited these philosophical fountainheads to take the thought-provoking water. So electrified was the atmosphere in the late 1960s and early 1970s that most middle-aged archaeologists today would probably admit to having thought about archaeological theory at some point in their professional careers.

The widespread, almost pervasive interest in theory has perhaps waned a bit since the heady, quasi-religious days of the New Archaeology, but theory is still an integral part of archaeological research. So ingrained is the understanding of theory's role that most archaeologists readily accept that *all* archaeological activity— even identifying a piece of stone as a an arrow point—includes theory to some extent (Gibbon 1984:45). Most contemporary archaeologists would probably agree with philosopher of science John Kemeny (1959:89) when he wrote: "I doubt that we can state a fact entirely divorced from theoretical interpretations."

If the commonplace act of identifying a piece of chipped stone as an artifact incorporates theory, then we may well say that theory is irrevocably linked to archaeology. Expanding this thought, we may easily imagine the importance of theory when it comes to framing larger interpretations about past societies. Gordon Willey and Philip Phillips (1958:1), perhaps the two leading archaeological theorists in the United States in the 1950s, put the situation plainly and unambiguously: "integration and interpretation without theory are inconceivable."

But interpretations of the past are never easy to formulate. In fact, they are usually contested and often—perhaps usually—hotly debated. Controversies between archaeologists arise because the past is neither straightforward nor simple. Also, because interpretation rests on theory, competing views can easily exist side by side, as do Swift's wells. Because the past is not completely knowable, we can never be certain that our interpretations are correct. More importantly, several competing interpretations, resting on different theories, may be true at the same time. Each may serve to explain the past in a slightly different manner. The earthen ringforts that dot the landscape of rural Ireland provide an example. Driving through the Irish countryside, we could find, with little difficulty, reasonable men and women who interpret the ringforts as defensive works built by fairies. Reinforced by ancient myths and legends learned as children, these men and women are convinced that their interpretation is true. Professional archaeologists, of course, would disagree, arguing instead that the ringforts were fortified, defended farmsteads built by real men and women during the Late Iron Age (Flanagan 1992:93). Nonetheless, both interpretations coexist today, each resting on clear-cut, though often unstated—perhaps even unrealized—theoretical assumptions.

Different theories of the past are possible because "sincere intelligent people can disagree" (Gibbon 1989:7). As Bruce Trigger (1989) said, the highest-level theories are like languages, because one can express any idea using them. Like languages, however, theories can be unintelligible. Also, translations can vary, leading to widespread disagreement. In fact, disagreements have been so commonplace in archaeology that by the early 1980s, Merrilee Salmon (1982:140), a philosopher of archaeology, wrote: "Widespread agreement exists that archaeology lacks well developed theories that command acceptance." In other words, archaeologists could only agree that they could not agree on one another's theories about the past. This widespread lack of consensus led two archaeologists to identify a "malaise" among their colleagues (Moore and Keene 1983:3). Many archaeologists seemed lost and confused about theory, not knowing from which well to drink. Many sampled several wells, indiscriminately drawing theoretical water first from one, then from another. This rampant malaise, rather than constituting a deadly disease, only showed "that archaeology is not the straightforward and progressive study of the past that textbooks would have us believe" (Gibbon 1989:7).

Archaeologists have not been alone in finally realizing the deep complexity of their field. Historians, for instance, have recently retackled their "objectivity crisis" and have delved further in trying to understand how they know the past (Kloppenberg 1989; Lowenthal 1985; Novick 1988).

We may easily imagine why theory and interpretation are so contested in prehistoric archaeology. After all, no one remembers prehistory; no one left any written accounts of the period; no one drew maps or took photographs. Cave paintings and other ancient messages are often ambiguous sign posts, defying easy interpretation. Some cannot be deciphered at all. Thus, the archaeological interpretation of prehistory is infinitely arguable because no one really knows what happened. Competent archaeologists base their interpretations on careful research and scholarly conjecture—and they disagree. The distance in years between a modern archaeologist and the prehistoric people under study ensures unknowability, no matter how innovative or sensible a particular interpretation may appear. As a result, much of the ongoing theoretical debate in prehistoric archaeology concerns the simple, though frustratingly complex question, "How do we know what we know?" How do we really know that Irish ringforts were not built by fairies?

If this is true about prehistoric archaeology, what about historical archaeology? Does theory fare any better among archaeologists interested in the more recent past? Are the interpretations rendered in historical archaeology any better documented, any more plausible or reasonable than those of prehistory?

In 1977, no less an archaeological thinker than Lewis Binford (1977:13) prophesied that historical archaeologists one day would be in "the forefront in theory building" in archaeology. In his view, historical archaeologists would be theoretical pathfinders, shining lights down Swift's wells so that their archaeological colleagues with other specialties might see what had been otherwise obscured. Binford was in a position to know his subject. Almost 20 years earlier he had served as Moreau Maxwell's field assistant at Fort Michilimackinac, a colonial French and British stronghold on the northern tip of Michigan's lower peninsula (Maxwell and Binford 1961). Binford, who certainly knew prehistoric archaeology, also was intimately familiar with historical archaeology. But was he right? Could historical archaeologists be in the forefront of archaeological theory building? Could they help prehistorians peer down the wells of the past?

Regrettably, Binford's prophecy was not immediately fulfilled. In fact, his vision remained unrealized 10 years later. Perhaps in answer to Binford's optimism, historical archaeologists organized the 1987 plenary session of the annual meeting of the Society for Historical Archaeology specifically to assess their field's theoretical health. Many historical archaeologists faced the dim reality that Binford had been wrong. More importantly, perhaps, some historical archaeologists felt a sense of urgency. Rather than being a leader, the unthinkable had happened: historical archaeology had developed a malaise. Nicholas Honerkamp (1988:5), the session's organizer, boldly stated what many historical archaeologists already knew: that historical archaeology was "distinctly atheoretical." So profound was the malady, so deep was the wound, that Honerkamp confessed to feeling a "theoretical angst." As he assessed the situation, "someone seems to have declared a moratorium on thinking about and discussing the reasons that underlie historic sites research" (Honerkamp 1988:5). The patient was not simply ailing; the illness was critical, the diagnosis bad. Historical archaeology was, in terms of theory at least, very sick.

Honerkamp's position was a strong one, but he was not alone in
his opinion. Charles Cleland (1988:13), who had been involved in
theoretical issues in historical archaeology since the 1960s, said
plainly: "It must be concluded that historical archaeologists in general are simply not interested in or concerned with theory." It
seemed undeniable that by the 1980s, most historical archaeologists
had taken to heart John Combes's (1968:164) entirely pessimistic
view of 20 years earlier: "Discussions concerned with methods and
theory in historical archaeology are for the most part a waste of
time."

The juxtaposition of Binford's optimism in 1977 and Honerkamp's and Cleland's pessimism in 1987 is striking. How could the
once-bright future of historical archaeology have tarnished so quickly? Had something terrible happened in those years to subvert the
field? Had a diabolical terrorist sabotaged the field to the point of
trivializing it? What caused historical archaeologists to abandon
theory?

The answers to these important questions undoubtedly lie in
many places, but perhaps one key place to start looking for them is
in the discipline's past itself. The history of historical archaeology is
not one of my central topics in this book, but certain of its aspects
are important enough to demand attention. As such, we must take a
brief detour into the history of theory in historical archaeology. I
could start my tour almost anywhere, but an excellent starting point
is with Lewis Binford, the optimist of archaeological theory.

A BRIEF DETOUR INTO
ARCHAEOLOGICAL HISTORY

In 1975, Binford was charged with writing a paper for the plenary session of the Society for Historical Archaeology's annual meeting. The overall goal of the session was to bring together prominent
scholars to discuss the role of material culture in historical archaeological research. Binford's central role in the session was not an
accident. Not only was he a prominent archaeological thinker—
some would say he was *the* leader in the field—he also had personal
experience with historical archaeology. Historical archaeologists eagerly sought his comments for both reasons. For his part, however,
Binford was not convinced that he had any wisdom to offer. In fact,
he was rather perplexed by the prospect of speaking to his eager

audience. I can imagine him sitting at his desk staring at an empty page, impatiently waiting for his thoughts to emerge in coherent form. Rather than guess at his dilemma, though, I believe Binford himself best described his situation:

> It's New Year's Day 1975. I am trying to prepare a paper for presenta-
> tion at a conference on historical archaeology. Do I have anything to say?
>   This was the setting and my thoughts as I began preparation of this
> paper. Then I began to think along the following lines. If this was a
> conference on archaeology I would have no problem. I have unpublished
> material relevant to many subjects of general archaeological interest.
> Obviously my problem arose from the "historical" orientation of the
> conference. Why? Why should I be uncomfortable and indecisive as to an
> appropriate subject or way of treating a problem. I continued to be
> uneasy with "historical." Clearly I felt that persons doing "historical"
> archaeology were different from myself with different interests. Why?
> Certainly it is not because of specially relevant or technical information
> which is part of the "information pool" of persons working at sites of
> relatively recent age in North America. I can talk creamware and kaolin
> pipes with the best of them. Why? That word "historical" again! (Binford
> 1977:13)

Many of us, reading Binford's comments in the mid-1990s, may be shocked. Why would such a prominent archaeologist, with a long-standing association with historical archaeology, be so concerned about the word "historical"? What precisely was the problem? Did Binford sense Honerkamp's angst long before most others had felt it?

I cannot pretend to know what Binford was thinking as he struggled with his paper. I perceive in his quandary, however, an intellectual legacy cast over historical archaeology by the American archaeologist Walter Taylor (1948). Binford's confusion in 1975 indicates that he had fully adopted Taylor's views on history and anthropology. Because Binford (1972:8) openly admired Taylor, we must continue our quest with him. Taylor, it seems, was the source of Binford's deep-seated angst.

Binford admired and was perhaps at bit awed by Taylor's doctoral dissertation, *A Study of Archaeology,* completed in 1943, but delayed in publication until 1948. Most of the work is a meticulous critique of American archaeology, and Binford and a generation of New Archaeologists voraciously drew wisdom from it like water from a well (Binford 1972; Deetz 1988). Though Taylor dealt specifically with the practice of American prehistoric archaeology, his work holds a peculiar, behind-the-scenes place in the history of thought in historical archaeology. Its importance lies in Taylor's willingness to address in detail the knotty issue of the relationship between history and anthropology. Though the subject had interested British archaeologists for many years (see Hogarth 1899), here was an American archaeologist rattling the gates of archaeological orthodoxy by juxtaposing history and anthropology.

Taylor attacked the very foundations of archaeological research. He was bold and direct and much of his text is unmistakably blunt. If Taylor found a dry well of archaeological thought, he said so. He named names and pointed fingers, and in doing so, Taylor inadvertently confronted several issues of importance to historical archaeologists. Addressing one of the most basic, "What has history to do with cultural anthropology?" Taylor worked like a watchmaker, taking the back off both history and anthropology to examine their inner workings and to see whether their parts were interchangeable.

Taylor decided that both historians and cultural anthropologists incorporate a four-step analytical method that guides them through the gears and springs of human existence. Both kinds of scholars begin their research by defining a research problem or a subject of study. Once this often difficult task is completed, they both collect and evaluate information that will help them to understand the problem. Both historians and anthropologists then impose order on the collected information and begin the process of synthesis and interpretation. In this last, interpretive step historians and cultural anthropologists paint their pictures of human existence, building their ideas of everyday life from the information they choose to collect. Taylor figured that anthropologists and historians use this four-step method because neither can engage in experimentation. Neither historians nor anthropologists can go into a laboratory and reproduce the French Revolution or re-create the Crow kinship system. Information about both subjects, and all similar subjects, can be collected and interpreted, but neither can be re-created with test tubes or laboratory mice.

Taylor's analysis to this point was not controversial. The four-step method aptly described the way most historians and cultural anthropologists conducted research. Few members of either discipline could disagree. Both devise problems for study and then set about collecting information that will permit them to compose a plausible interpretation using that information. Controversy arose, however, with Taylor's fifth level of analysis. It was here that Taylor saw the pursuits of history and anthropology diverging in significant and telling ways.

Taylor (1948:38) imagined that only anthropologists show an interest in "the study of the nature of culture, of cultural constants, or processes, or regularities, and of chronological development." He believed that the writing of history is typically idiographic, or focused on unique circumstances, notable men and women, and specific sequences of events. For Taylor, historians do not concern themselves with the broader processes of life in the same way as do anthropologists. But, anthropologists can also cease their work at the fourth level of analysis whether their subject matter is "18th century England, Blackfoot Indians, or an industrial community in Indiana" (Taylor 1948:41). Anthropological vigilantes did not require them to consider broad cultural processes. For archaeology, Taylor concluded that the lack of disciplinary enforcement was best because most archaeologists had not reached the fifth level. As far as he was concerned, archaeologists could be either historians or anthropologists. The "critical test is what the archaeologist does with his discoveries, not his subject matter" (Taylor 1948:43). The central question for Taylor was an easy one: "Will the archaeologist cease work at the fourth level—historical reconstruction—or proceed to the fifth level, attempting to understand the larger processes of human existence?" The choice was personal, but it determined whose wells the archaeologist would inspect, the historian's or the anthropologist's.

The controversy Taylor's work sparked in prehistoric archaeology has been addressed before (see, for example, Gibbon 1989:61–117). Most of the resultant debate need not concern us here. What is decidedly pertinent, however, is that Taylor's opinion about history and anthropology gained prominence in historical archaeology. In fact, Taylor's impact on the field is so great that it cannot be ignored. His dissertation was republished in 1967, just as historical archaeology was being formally organized in both the United States (Jelks 1993; Pilling 1967) and Great Britain (Barton 1968). Binford had used the first edition of Taylor's book, but after 1967, the text was readily available to a new generation of eager archaeological thinkers. Many of these thinkers were historical archaeologists.

Whether Taylor's work created the confusion or, more likely, it was already present in archaeological circles is unimportant. The significance of his book stems from his explicit handling of an issue that deeply concerned historical archaeologists—one that confused and perplexed them. Were they historians who insisted on crawling around in the dirt looking for broken ceramics, or were they anthropologists who simply chose to use archaeology in their study of recent history? John Cotter (1967:15) gave succinct voice to the rampant confusion when he referred to the historical archaeologist as the "anthropologist-turned historical sites archaeologist or the historian-americanist-turned archaeologist." This comment was published the same year that Taylor's dissertation was reissued. Cotter, the long-respected excavator of Jamestown and probably the first person in the United States to teach a regular university course in historical archaeology (Cotter 1977:100, 1994:22), did not even know what term to use when referring to what he did for a living. Perhaps Cotter's confusion is the clearest indication of the theoretical malaise that had settled over historical archaeology.

The debate over who should excavate historical sites—historians or anthropologists—furiously raged in historical archaeology during the field's formative years. Those engaged in the controversy generally held one of three positions. Some argued that historical archaeology was essentially a "historical" discipline and that anthropological training was not beneficial to the investigation of historic sites (see, for example, Harrington 1955; Noël Hume 1964; Walker 1967, 1968, 1970). Others argued that historical archaeology was really a kind of anthropology dedicated to the recent past (Cleland and Fitting 1968; Fontana 1965; Mrozowski 1988; Schuyler 1970; South 1977). A third group proposed that history and anthropology should be united because it was pointless to segregate two such obviously related disciplines (Deagan and Scardaville 1985; Dymond 1974; Jelks 1968; McKay 1976; South 1968). For the last group, historical archaeology was a separate, unique discipline.

Proponents of the various viewpoints carried on a long, sometimes fruitful, often painful exchange as they attempted to control the hearts and minds of historical archaeologists. Though the debate at times grew vicious and personal, the groups were not armed camps. The proponents never held rallies to convince their non-aligned colleagues of the righteousness of their position. They issued no propaganda and took no full-page advertisements in local newspapers. They had no great plans, and organized no concerted conspiracies. Instead, each group was composed of scholars convinced that their perspective was best for studying the past.

Many historical archaeologists today find the history–anthropology debate to be vacuous and uninteresting. In fact, a common consensus for the 1990s was predicted by Bernard Fontana (1968:78) during the height of the debate in 1967. Fontana said that historical archaeology "will not be promoted by ill-considered debates between historians and anthropologists or by accusations that others are doing mayhem to their sites because of their departmental brand of training." Since 1967, several highly qualified non-archaeologists have moved effortlessly between history and anthropology, visibly demonstrating Fontana's wisdom (see, for instance, Breen 1989; Mintz 1986). No less a scholar than Margaret Mead (1951:5) realized as early as 1951 that the distinction between history and anthropology was "fast becoming obsolete." Today we may say that for many scholars the two fields are distinct only in a "trivial, academic specialization sense" (Gailey 1983:241; also see Gutman 1976:xii; Zinn 1970:11).

In the 1990s we may easily dismiss the history–anthropology debate in historical archaeology as trivial. Using the gift of hindsight, we may see that it resolved nothing. After the dust from the debates had settled, many historical archaeologists still thought of themselves as historians, while others called themselves anthropologists. Each group continued to produce competent and sometimes even brilliant archaeological studies. Still, we cannot ignore that the history–anthropology controversy was dangerous because it created the camps, no matter how loosely organized. Instead of working together to define and refine their field, the more committed proponents of the three positions frequently disagreed vehemently, often using unflattering and even embarrassing epithets to refer to one another (see, for example, Demmy 1968; Dollar 1968; Howard 1974; Thurman 1974). These vitriolic exchanges indicated that the participants thought the stakes were high, that historical archaeology mattered, and that they believed in their perspectives. But the debate served in a very real way to retard the theoretical maturation of historical archaeology. In fact, the scars from the debate have not entirely healed, even after years of malaise. As Barbara Little (1994:30) recently observed: "the attitude may still be found that historical archaeology is something of a junior varsity where simple confirmation of historical 'fact' is the main goal." Little does not say precisely where she thinks this attitude prevails, but my perception is that it is to be found within archaeology itself. Historical archaeologists may not be considered to be real players in the great archaeological game. At best, they may be called in as substitutes now and then.

Many historical archaeologists found the debate to be intellectually exhausting. And it may have convinced more than one archaeologist that the history–anthropology debate was the only valid theoretical concern of their discipline. Mindful of the verbal violence occasioned by the debate, many historical archaeologists had to confront the inescapable fact that the debate spent their creative efforts. If thinking about theory in historical archaeology meant confronting the history–anthropology issue, then perhaps the deeper issues of historical archaeology were better left alone. As a result, many historical archaeologists may have been ready to accept Iain Walker's (1967:31–32) assessment that too much archaeology is "cluttered with irrelevant theory." Perhaps this was the source of the malaise that Honerkamp, Cleland, and others sensed in 1987.

The significance of the view that historical archaeology is atheoretical should not be downplayed. Even so, this perspective is distinctly peculiar in the context of archaeology. If we can agree that all archaeology involves theory to some degree, how can it follow logically that historical archaeology is overtly nontheoretical? In other words, why do prehistorians regularly think about theory, while far too many historical archaeologists do not? Why are so many historical archaeologists interested in less intellectually taxing subjects like the size and shape of cannonballs and the bore dimensions of smoking pipe stems? Many historical archaeologists focus exclusively on the minutiae of the past, ignoring the often complex theoretical issues that may affect that minutiae. In their effort, in John Goggin's words, to "get down to brass tacks" (South 1964), many historical archaeologists have focused intently on the brass tacks, forgetting all else.

My perception that most historical archaeologists simply grew weary of the history–anthropology debate and therefore ignored theory altogether is somehow unsatisfying. It begs the question of "why?" Rather than simply to admit that a problem exists, we must be called upon to understand what it is about historical archaeology that seems to make theory unnecessary.

WHY THEORY SEEMS UNNECESSARY

The exact reasons for the lack of theorizing in historical archaeology may be difficult to discover. Some ideas, however, may be found outside archaeology. Daniel Boorstin (1987), the prolific historian and librarian of the United States Library of Congress, may have inadvertently identified part of the problem in his essay "Why a Theory Seems Needless." Boorstin's essay, which focuses on American political thought, has nothing overtly to do with archaeology. Still, his comments are suggestive and enlightening.

In Boorstin's lifetime of reading and writing about American political life, he was increasingly struck by an interesting paradox. On the one hand, no people on earth have been so committed as Americans to the belief that their country was founded on a perfect theory of governance. Most Americans accept that the Founding Fathers deeply believed in the political theory they put into operation with the Constitution, one of the finest documents in political history. At the same time, however, no people have ever been so oddly disinterested in political philosophy as Americans. Americans simply do not have a tradition of thinking about their government in intellectual, theoretical ways (though it must be said that they think about it in several other ways). This paradox troubled Boorstin and he sought to find a reasonable explanation for it. While conducting the research to unlock this American puzzle, Boorstin landed on the idea of "givenness." It seemed to him that most Americans readily accept that the values and beliefs of the United States are "given" by "certain facts of geography and history peculiar to us" (Boorstin 1987:76–77). The United States is the way it is because it is the United States. For most Americans, the explanation bears no further investigation because it is self-evident.

This quasi-explanation was not good enough for Boorstin. Delving deeper, he found buried within the idea of "givenness" three "faces" that account for the paradox. First is the idea that America's Founding Fathers supplied the United States with a perfect political theory right from the start. So complete is the theory that further discussion is unnecessary. The Founding Fathers were smart men, they knew what they were doing, and that is that. The second face holds that Americans receive their national values from the present. And because the founding political theory is always implicit in the present, Americans have no need to wonder about their values or to suggest the need for wholesale governmental change. When contemplating their nation's ills, most Americans accept that somehow the citizens have strayed from the way the Founding Fathers wanted things to be. If a problem exists in America, it results from how far we have strayed from the Fathers' original theory, not from the theory itself. The flaw lies with Americans, not with America. Finally, the third face is based on the idea of continuity. Most Americans envision the nation's past to merge with the present in one uninterrupted flow of history. Though significant and potentially revolutionary events have occurred in American history—the Civil War, the Great Depression, antiwar and civil rights protests—there is enough coherence to provide a sense of unity for most Americans. The country they honor and respect is much the same place that Thomas Jefferson and George Washington honored and respected 200 years ago. Nothing drastic enough has happened to distance us from these wise and thoughtful men and the time in which they created the great experiment in democracy.

Boorstin's ideas are strictly about American history as seen from his undoubtedly unique vantage point. He did not even hint that his ideas involve archaeology in any way, and we can be reasonably certain that archaeology never crossed his mind. Nonetheless, several ideas in Boorstin's intriguing essay have relevance to historical archaeology. In fact, his ideas can be used to suggest possible reasons why a theory seems needless in historical archaeology.

Historical archaeology has always been something of a poor cousin to prehistoric archaeology—Little's (1994:30) "junior varsity." Robert Schuyler (1988:36) was bold enough to suggest that most historical archaeologists suffer from a "P-P-P-P-P Complex," or the "Pseudo-Processual Progress Proffered by Prehistorians." This malady is an inferiority complex that includes "the self-defacing belief that prehistorians use more sophisticated methodology" than historical archaeologists and "more importantly, have successfully issued processual statements." Many historical archaeologists have floundered on the minutiae of archaeology—Goggin's "brass tacks." Stanley South (1977:8–12) identified the focus on the often tiny "facts" of the past as "particularism." As an expression of how much historical archaeology leans on its prehistoric colleague, Kathleen Deagan (1988:10) rewrote Noël Hume's (1964) "handmaiden to history" to read "handmaiden to prehistoric archaeology." It thus appears that the few historical archaeologists who were interested in theory in the discipline's beginning generally borrowed their ideas from the "founding fathers" of archaeology. Since historical archaeology is such a young field, we can readily accept that these founding fathers (and a few founding mothers) were prehistorians. So, rather than being in the forefront of theory building as Binford thought, historical archaeologists have been on the trailing edge, picking up whatever theoretical refuse they thought they could use. To avoid this crass imitation, Deagan (1988:11) and others (Cleland and Fitting 1968; Mrozowski 1988; South 1977) have been quick to point out that historical archaeologists should develop their own theories.

Boorstin's second and third points—that theory is implicit in daily American life and that continuity exists in American history— are much more difficult to address. I explore both ideas in various ways in the rest of this book. At this point, it may suffice to say that another reason why a theory seems needless in historical archaeology stems from the artifacts and sites historical archaeologists study. Many of the things and the places from the modern past can be easily and readily recognized today. Of course, this is not universally true, and numerous examples of unrecognizable objects and baffling structures are constantly being found by historical archaeologists. But what I mean here is that the "things" of historical archaeology—glass bottles, shell buttons, iron mouth harps, brass door knockers, ceramic bowls, copper coins, limestone foundations, wooden fence lines—*appear* to be easily and readily understandable today. As a result, many historical archaeologists often feel little need to "explain" the function and use of the objects they excavate. For example, when Stanley South (1977:68–71) explored the distribution of straight pins at the eighteenth-century Public House and Tailor Shop in Brunswick Town, North Carolina, he did not need to explain straight pins. He could justifiably assume that straight pins had much the same function they have today in a tailor shop—even one from a century ago. As such, South could simply say "straight pins" and leave it at that. A theory seems needless. Some historical archaeologists, however, have discovered, as Greek philosopher Phaedrus said in A.D. 8, that things—even physical things—are seldom what they seem. Like Swift's wells, the meaning of historic "things" can be hauntingly deceptive and decidedly troublesome (see Chapter 5).

The issue of historical continuity also has important significance to historical archaeology. We may well argue that the past is of one piece. Year follows years in a never-ending flow of events. Of course, the linear view of history is a Western notion not necessarily accepted by members of other cultures (Zimmerman 1987:46; also see Leone 1978). Though we cannot argue that history does not unfold year by year, I believe that the modern era incorporates important disjunctions with what came before, particularly prehistory. As a result, the subject matter of historical archaeology is inherently different from that studied by other archaeologists, especially prehistorians. This idea requires careful explanation, and so it is the subject of Chapter 3. As a preview, though, my perspective on the past can be easily stated. I believe that history was a vastly different "place" than prehistory. As a result, the study of each time requires a slightly different set of ideas and concepts, and if not new ideas entirely, at least an innovative slant on old ideas. In this important sense, historical archaeologists are unlike prehistorians. I thus reject Stephen Mrozowski's (1988:21) idea that "enough structural properties may have been common to allow for comparisons to be drawn, albeit cautiously" between "British colonial America, Mesopotamia, and Mesoamerica." I believe, and historical archaeology shows, that only the most basic similarities inherent in urbanism can be found between colonial Boston, Ur, and Tenochtitlán. As places with different histories and diverse populations, these three urban centers were quite dissimilar.

So, Boorstin's essay can be used to suggest why some, and maybe even most, historical archaeologists find theory needless in historical archaeology. I have only shown the relevance of his ideas to historical archaeology in the briefest possible way because a full critique of archaeological history is not my intent. My comments could easily be expanded tenfold. Rather than doing this here, I now turn to my research program, leaving the more complete study of archaeological history to future analysts.

THE RESEARCH PROGRAM, THE SITES, AND THE PERSPECTIVE

Though to this point I have repeatedly used the word "theory," I have been careful not to explain precisely what I mean by the term. I have been overt and open about several other topics, but curiously quiet on my use of this important word. I can now say that I have only used the word "theory" because it has archaeological relevance. Archaeologists are not surprised by the term and readily accept its presence, though they may not agree so readily to its precise meaning. The *Oxford English Dictionary,* a definitive source on Standard English, defines "theory," among other ways, as "a scheme or system of ideas or statements held as an explanation or account of a group of facts or phenomena." This definition is consistent with how most archaeologists understand the term.

In his overview of the history of archaeological thought, Bruce Trigger (1989:20–22) said that theories exist on three levels. Low-level theories involve artifact classifications, demonstrations that one archaeological deposit is earlier than another, and observations that men and women in a particular culture are buried in distinct ways. Middle-level theories are generalizations that strive to account for the regularities in human behavior, and for example, may involve the relationship between population pressure and the need for more food production. High-level theories consist of abstract rules that explain the major propositions that permit the understanding of complex phenomena. Darwinian evolution, historical materialism, and ecological determinism are all examples of high-level theories. As Trigger (1989:23–24) pointed out, archaeologists have filled the shelves of modern libraries with ideas about the relationships between high, middle, and low theories. Some archaeologists choose to focus their attention on low-level theories, while others wish only to study the more general theories of the upper level. And examinations of whether the middle level is created from the lower or the upper level have become something of a growth industry in archaeology.

Much of the discussion about theory is confusing. In fact, it may be the miasmic atmosphere that hovers over understanding precisely what theory is that has driven many historical archaeologists to the hinterland of archaeological thought. To overcome this problem, and to bring historical archaeologists back to the dais of theoretical discussion, I prefer to abandon the term "theory" at this point and to speak in terms of a "research program."

My understanding of a research program derives from Guy Gibbon's (1989) explanation is his well-crafted critique of the New Archaeology. Gibbon (1989:2–5) rooted his conception of the research program in the ideas of philosophers of science. Though perhaps a formidable term, a research program is simply a framework for organizing the underlying principles and assumptions of research. Scientists use research programs to structure and organize their efforts and to make explicit the underlying assumptions they build into their findings and interpretations. We may conceptualize a research program as an interconnected network of ideas and concepts used in a particular research project. Research programs define what entities or processes can be said to exist, they define the limits and validity of knowledge about these entities and processes, and they define the appropriate methodology for gaining the knowledge.

Scholars accept a research program as long as it seems to explain the way the world works, and discard it when it stops making sense. Thus, I intend to use a research program in the sense meant by the Greeks with their word *theoria,* from whence we get "theory." *Theoria* comes from the root *thea,* meaning "seeing, looking at." *Theoria,* therefore, literally means "looking at the world."

The idea of developing a research program precisely defines my intent in this book. Rather than to focus on the methods of historical archaeology as South (1977) did so brilliantly in the first true theoretical book in the field, I propose to construct a research program for historical archaeology. In accomplishing this task, however, I do not intend to explore "airless theory" without some connection to actual archaeological material. As such, I use two archaeological sites—Palmares, Brazil, and Gorttoose, Ireland—to anchor my research program in the reality of the past.

Palmares and Gorttoose at first seem so dissimilar that my combined use of them here may seem a bit odd, and perhaps even idiosyncratic. Stark differences between the two settlements are readily obvious. Runaway slaves, fleeing the coastal sugar plantations of northeastern Brazil, created Palmares around 1605 and lived there until 1694. Peasant farmers first lived at Gorttoose in County Roscommon from about 1780 until 1847. The sites are similar in that both ceased being occupied on dates that are historically known, but the reasons for termination are different though related. The Portuguese, after 20 years of annual assaults, finally hired mercenaries to destroy the capital of Palmares, which they did on the night of February 5–6, 1694. The Portuguese attackers scattered the men and women in the nine other villages as well. In 1847, at the height of the Great Irish Famine, the owner of the Strokestown estate, on which Gorttoose was situated, ordered the eviction and assisted emigration of its starving tenants. Beginning on May 27, thousands were shipped to America, with many dying along the way. Gorttoose and Palmares are also geographically distinct, being about 8,000 km (5,000 mi) apart (Figure 1). Whereas Palmares was discretely set into the mountainous, South American coastal backlands, Gorttoose was in Europe, nestled in the rolling hills and broad flatlands of central Ireland. In addition to distinctions in history and geography, important cultural characteristics differentiate Palmares from Gorttose. The residents of Palmares were a mix of central African Bantus, native Brazilian Tupinambá Indians, dissatisfied Portuguese colonists and outcasts, and perhaps a few

Figure 1. The geographic locations of Palmares, Brazil, and Gorttoose, Ireland.

Dutch rebels. The residents of Gorttoose were Irish farmers with ancient Celtic roots.

Given the historical, cultural, and geographic distinctions between Palmares and Gorttoose, how can these two sites be useful in this book, particularly since neither has been excavated yet? This question is infinitely reasonable because it initially would appear that my use of two such disparate sites would work to diffuse my argument, watering down the impact of my message. However, it is precisely the sites' distinctions that intrigue me. Their very dissimilarities fit perfectly into my research program. While working on both sites almost simultaneously has been physically taxing and logistically difficult, research on two distinct sites on two different continents has not been intellectually unnerving or contradictory. On the contrary, my work at Gorttoose has helped me to understand more about Palmares, just as learning about the rebel slaves of Palmares has taught me more about the social conditions of the impoverished tenants at Gorttoose. How this can be true is what this book is about.

My eagerness to take American historical archaeology outside the United States perhaps requires some explanation. My goal is not to promote an imperialist program, in which I try to demonstrate the righteousness of American historical archaeology to the rest of the world. Rather, my idea is simply to address issues that interest me as a historical archaeologist living in America and "growing up" in American archaeology. The fugitive slaves of Palmares and the poor, landless peasants of Gorttoose interest me as an anthropologist. During the course of researching both projects, I discovered that I kept coming back to the same issues. Sometimes I found them hidden in the Brazilian backcountry; sometimes they were propped up against the wall of a peasant's one-room cabin. Occasionally, they were given voice by a Portuguese soldier who, upon seeing Palmares for the first time, worried about its growing power. Often I found the issues expressed by an English traveler who, while riding through early nineteenth-century Ireland, wondered how people could live with the conditions faced by peasant men and women. In many cases, I gained insights about the past by the comments of living, Brazilian and Irish men and women.

Neither Palmares nor Gorttoose are situated in an archaeological vacuum, because both Brazil and Ireland have developing traditions of historical archaeology. Brazilian historical archaeologists have focused much of their attention on the earliest period of contact between Portuguese colonists and native inhabitants (Andrade Lima 1993; Funari 1989, 1991a, 1991b, 1994; Prous 1991:543–562). Recently, however, a growing number of archaeologists in Brazil have shown interest in slave life, urbanization, and other topics not directly related to cultural contact (see, for example, Chahon 1995; Guimarães 1990; Guimarães and Lanna 1980; Marins 1995; Zanettini 1988, 1990). The Palmares research occurs within the growing effort to know more about the realities of slave life in Brazil and to add to the increasing interest in anthropological historical archaeology there (Orser 1992). Ireland has no tradition of historical archaeology as such, though some archaeologists work in "postmedieval archaeology." Irish archaeologists generally think of the postmedieval period as terminating around A.D. 1700, or well before the establishment of Gorttoose (Ryan 1991). As a result, postmedieval archaeological research throughout Ireland typically occurs at sites dating before 1750 (see, for example, Blades 1986; Brannon 1984, 1990; Klingelhofer 1992; Lacy 1979). Faced with an impressive embarrassment of prehistoric riches, Irish archaeologists have yet to focus major attention on the postmedieval period, and particularly on the nineteenth century.

This book is about neither Palmares nor Gorttoose. This is not an extended site report detailing the precise findings at either place. I also make no effort to compare Palmares and Gorttoose. Instead, my focus is on developing a research program for historical archaeology that can incorporate findings from diverse places like Palmares and Gorttoose. I use these two sites only to illustrate and explain my arguments and to ground my ideas in archaeological reality.

My perspective in this book is mutualistic. My understanding of mutualism derives from the work of cultural anthropologist Michael Carrithers (1992). I explore his perspective in detail in Chapter 2. For now, suffice it to say that mutualism is a perspective proposing that individuals and their social relationships are "the basic stuff of human life" (Carrithers 1992:11). Men and women create and maintain numerous social relationships, juggling and expressing each depending upon the setting and the circumstances. An understanding of these relationships reveals much about cultural and social life, regardless of whether our focus is, as Taylor (1948:41) said, "18th century England, Blackfoot Indians, or an industrial community in Indiana."

Any social scientist can study social relationships. Political historians of ancient Greece, sociologists of medieval France, and cultural historians of colonial Boston can all examine the complex web of relationships that existed within those societies. Archaeologists can also study relationships. Prehistorians and historical archaeologists can and do study relationships all the time. In this sense, Mrozowski (1988) was correct that all archaeologists of complex societies, including historical archaeologists, share a common interest. Where historical archaeology and the archaeology of, say, ancient Sumer part company is in the overarching influence exerted on these relationships by what I term historical archaeology's "haunts." The haunts are historical processes that underlie all historical archaeological research whether or not the archaeologist realizes it. The haunts are colonialism, Eurocentrism, capitalism, and modernity.

Scholars from many disciplines have poured their hearts into understanding each one of the haunts. We may imagine that on Swift's landscape each haunt has several wells devoted to it. We may also imagine that many of these wells are quite deep. Nonetheless, the haunts are part and parcel of historical archaeology and to understand them we must not be frightened by the prospect of probing so many deep, dark wells. An archaeologist confronted with several undisturbed real wells (and an adequate budget) would be anxiously impatient to begin his or her investigation of them. As Noël Hume (1969:10) observed, abandoned wells can "provide more archaeological information about their colonial owners than any other source." Historical archaeologists should feel the same sense of anticipation when they approach a landscape of theoretical wells in which the haunts await discovery and analysis.

The haunts have a place on the stage of all historical archaeological research. Sometimes an archaeologist will push one of them to center stage and shine the spotlight of analysis upon it. Global colonialism and capitalism are often given the nod because they are sometimes overbearing hams that refuse to be ignored. The haunts often feign shyness and hide in the background, silently waiting to be called forth as needed. But we should not be fooled. Global colonialism, Eurocentrism, capitalism, and modernity are always present in historical archaeology. Given their significance to historical archaeology, I explore each in detail in Chapter 3.

My identification of the haunts of historical archaeology carries a hidden message. By now, careful readers have realized that I have a particular perception of what historical archaeology is, but that I have not expressed it. Though I am not impartial in my definition of the field, I have hidden it from view. Since one may well suppose that my conception of the field plays a central role in this book, I must make my position explicitly clear.

PRECISELY WHAT IS HISTORICAL ARCHAEOLOGY?

One may wonder why this section is necessary. After all, I have repeatedly referred to historical archaeology, and we should reasonably expect by now that archaeologists agree on what the field studies. Regrettably, however, the precise purview of historical archaeology is not always completely agreed upon, and the term "historical archaeology" is not without controversy.

Over the past several years, historical archaeologists have defined their field in three ways: as the study of a time period, as a research method, and as the study of the modern world (Orser and Fagan 1995:6–14). Each definition is in a sense correct, though only the last one unlocks the power of the field.

Historical Archaeology as the Study of a Time Period

When archaeologists established the now-defunct Conference on Historic Site Archaeology at the University of Florida in 1960, their expressed goal was to study something called "the historic period" (South 1964). In America, this historic period stood in contrast to the prehistoric period, and surprisingly, American archaeologists knew more about prehistory than history. For many of them, writing represented the clearest way to distinguish between prehistory and history. James Deetz (1977:7) expressed this view with characteristic clarity: "The literacy of the people it studies is what sets historical archaeology apart from prehistory." Thus, archaeological time can be divided into two broad categories: pre- or nonliterate (prehistoric) and literate (historic).

The idea of segmenting the past on the basis of writing is an old one in archaeology (see, for instance, Woolley 1937:15). This division—outwardly so straightforward and conservative—actually caused a crisis of self-confidence among historical archaeologists. After all, archaeologists around the world studied literate cultures from Sumer to Mexico City. Did this mean that historical archaeology had been around for years? This puzzling question led Robert

Schuyler (1977) to postulate that historical archaeology had at least five different "subfields." He defined each subfield according to its period of interest. "Classical archaeology" begins with the Minoans around 3000 B.C. and ends with the later Roman Empire at about A.D. 527. "Medieval archaeology" focuses on the A.D. 400–1400 period, while "postmedieval archaeology" concentrates on the period from A.D. 1450 to 1750. "Historic sites archaeology" concentrates on the period from A.D. 1415 to industrialization, and "industrial archaeology" studies complex technologies that first appeared around A.D. 1750. Though nicely set forward, these temporal divisions were not cast in stone. For example, the postmedieval period in Scotland is said to extend from 1488 to 1609 (Crawford 1968). But quibbling over whether the year 1488 was medieval or postmedieval is unimportant and uninteresting. What is important is that history is distinguishable from prehistory, and that historical archaeologists study history.

If we take the idea literally that history equals literacy, then we may well propose that the period of interest to historical archaeologists extends from about 3000 B.C. to the present depending upon where the archaeologist is standing. Every culture that used written communication is a legitimate subject for historical archaeology. China's Shang Dynasty (beginning around 1600 B.C.), ancient Sumer and Egypt, the pre-Columbian Maya, and any other literate culture can be the subject of the historical archaeologist's probing shovel. Howard Carter, famed discoverer of King Tutankhamen, Heinrich Schliemann, who sought to "prove the truth of Homer" in Mycenae, and Henry Layard, the pioneer in Assyria, were all historical archaeologists under this definition.

Historical Archaeology as Method

The idea that historical archaeology constitutes a method for studying the past is implicit in the view that the field focuses on literate cultures. Heinrich Schliemann, after all, poured over the Homeric texts in his efforts to locate Troy. Equating historical archaeology with a method gives an intellectual nod to Taylor's (1948:43) argument that archaeology is only a technique. For historical archaeology, the technique simply includes the careful use of several sources, many of which may be considered "nonarchaeological." As the name of the field indicates, the most frequently used nonarchaeological sources are historical, though others obviously can be used as well. Historical archaeologist William Adams (1977), in his pioneering study of the late nineteenth- and early twentieth-century town of Silcott, Washington, adopted an approach that was explicitly multi- and interdisciplinary. He used excavated archaeological materials, written historical texts, and even the remembrances of living men and women to cast light on the town's history, society, and people. Through the course of his research, Adams (1977:132) became convinced that, as a method, historical archaeology was no different from Mayan, classical, or Egyptian archaeology.

The idea that historical archaeology is a multi- and interdisciplinary method for examining the past was pushed to the limit by Peter Schmidt (1978) when he studied the ancient Buhaya kingdoms of Tanzania, East Africa. Schmidt termed his work "historical archaeology," even though he was interested in the Iron Age of the Lake Victoria region, dating roughly from 500 B.C. to A.D. 500. Though he used many sources of information, including traditional archaeological materials, Schmidt used one startling and decidedly nonarchaeological kind of information: the local peoples' rich oral traditions. Schmidt learned how to evaluate the stories they told him of ancient cultural origins and migrations and discovered how to use these accounts to locate ancient iron smelting sites.

Schmidt's research clearly demonstrated the interpretive potential when archaeologists are open-minded about what sources can be legitimately used to study the past. Archaeology that opens itself to all sources of information—written, oral, cartographic, botanical, zoological, chemical—is simply more powerful than archaeology that is narrow and restrictively focused.

These two conceptions of historical archaeology are not wrong. Historical archaeologists *do* study a particular period and *do* use a wide variety of sources, many of which may be described as historical. Both of the above definitions of historical archaeology, however, are a bit deceptive. Both appear to be unrestrictive—almost unstructured—and seem to permit the widest possible perception of historical archaeology. They summon us to call within our fold all those archaeologists, from Greece to Central Mexico, who use many different sources of information to examine the literate past. Historical archaeology defined as a method or as the study of a particular literate period seems open, inviting, and friendly.

Though not intending to be misanthropic, I believe that to identify historical archaeology with literate history or to relegate it to a methodology does the field a disservice. In my understanding, the simple act of using several diverse sources of information does not make one's research historical archaeology. As indicated by Schmidt's innovative research, the unbiased use of sources leads to creative research, but not necessarily to historical archaeology. Both perspectives can lead to good archaeology, but I believe that historical archaeology will only assume prominence in the minds of both scholars and the public when its practitioners openly accept that they study the modern world.

Historical Archaeology as the Study of the Modern World

Robert Schuyler (1970) was probably the first archaeologist to draw attention to the idea that historical archaeology is about the study of modern life. As I noted above, Schuyler envisioned the broad field of historical archaeology as composed of numerous subfields. Schuyler (1970:84) defined one of these subfields, "historic sites archaeology," as "the material manifestations of the expansion of European culture into the non-European world starting in the 15th century and ending with industrialization or the present depending on local conditions." Most historical archaeologists liked Schuyler's definition, and they afforded it a lasting place in the field when James Deetz (1977) used it, in a slightly revised way, in his much-read introduction to historical archaeology. Deetz (1977:5) defined historical archaeology as "the archaeology of the spread of European culture throughout the world since the fifteenth century and its impact on indigenous peoples." Judging by its widespread use, we may conclude that this definition has become accepted by historical archaeologists.

What is important about the Schuyler–Deetz view of historical archaeology is that it gave the field a clear and obvious mission. It boldly declared that the field was about a particular topic (modernity) in a particular place (the world). More importantly, perhaps, Deetz and Schuyler offered a way out of the malaise, the atheoretical haze, of historical archaeology. Historical archaeology could develop a sense of self-worth by focusing on the modern world. Kathleen Deagan (1988:8) summarized this realization succinctly: "Historical archaeology's obvious niche as a modern, synthetic field of inquiry is in the study of the processes and interrelationships by which human social and economic organizations developed and evolved in the modern world." Here again—stated in 1988 by Deagan as it had been in 1970 by Schuyler and in 1977 by Deetz—was the key for historical archaeology. Historical archaeologists had a way to solve their crisis of identity, to find their theoretical legs within the archaeological universe. Historical archaeology, though it uses many different sources of information and focuses on a literate past, is actually the study of the world in which we now live. In keeping with this idea, we may define historical archaeology as a multi- and interdisciplinary field that shares a special relationship with the formal disciplines of anthropology and history and seeks to understand the global nature of modern life.

I am not the first historical archaeologist to propose that historical archaeology should have a global focus. In a central article that helped to define the field, Robert Schuyler (1970:87) said that the global presence of Europeans creates a perfect laboratory for anthropological historical archaeologists interested in culture contact. Many years later, at the meeting where Honerkamp expressed his angst, Stanley South (1988) called for historical archaeologists to study "world cultural systems." A couple of years later, James Deetz (1991) expressed the view that historical archaeologists should adopt an "international comparative approach." And in the same volume, Kathleen Deagan (1991:97) noted the "irreversibly global nature of world society after 1500," and said that historical archaeologists would find it difficult to ignore this historical reality "after 1992," the 500th anniversary of Columbus's first voyage. Each of these authors points historical archaeology in the right direction. Unfortunately, none of them provide an explicit research program for making historical archaeology truly global in focus as I do in this book.

I propose that historical archaeologists should not be interested in all literate cultures, but only those that inhabited a time I broadly term "modern times." In this sense, I do view historical archaeology to be the study of a time period. This period began sometime around 1492 and extends until today, as I write these lines and as you read them. But historical archaeology as I see it is not simply about literacy, for my modern times includes global colonialism, Eurocentrism, capitalism, and modernity. These haunts did not simply exist in the world, floating above living men and women, waiting to be plucked down as needed. And, they did not depend on literacy, though it was a definite aid to each. The haunts pervaded modern life, changing the way people interacted with one another in complex, multifaceted ways. Real people in the past created and enacted colonialism, Eurocentrism, capitalism, and modernity through their interactions with other living, breathing men and women. I must now turn to the haunts and explain them in ways that have clear relevance to historical archaeology. I also must show why they are important to all archaeological investigations of modern times. Before doing so, however, I must set the stage by explaining my mutualist perspective.

Men, Women, Nets, and Archaeologists

2

"Man is thus nothing by himself; he owes what he is to society; the greatest Metaphysician, the greatest philosopher, if he were abandoned for ten years on the Isle of Fernandez, would come back transformed into a brute, dumb and imbecile, and would know nothing in the whole of nature" (cited in Gerbi 1973:53). The Abbé Cornelius de Pauw expressed this sentiment in 1768 in his *Recherches philosophiques sur les Américains ou mémoires intéressants pour servier à l'histoire de l'espèce humaine.* The learned father was referring specifically to the famous story of Alexander Selkirk. Selkirk's story is a minor though intriguing footnote in history. In 1704, while on a trip to the South Seas, Selkirk fell into an acrimonious argument with his captain. So violent was their disagreement that Selkirk asked to be released from the ship. The captain happily agreed and left him on a tiny Pacific island about 640 km (400 mi) west of Chile. Selkirk remained on the island, totally alone, for the next four years. Captain Woodes Rogers rescued him in 1709, and it was in Rogers's autobiographical account that Europe first learned Selkirk's compelling story. As history would have it, Selkirk did not become famous because of Rogers's literary efforts. Instead, he entered the annals of history as the main character in *Robinson Crusoe,* which Daniel Defoe published 10 years after Selkirk's rescue. One of the ironies of history is that the island of Selkirk's self-imposed exile is today named Róbinson Crusoe.

Abbé de Pauw's goal in *Recherches* was not to explain Selkirk's exile. The Abbé had a much more serious and far-reaching intention, for he sought nothing less than to discredit the native inhabitants of North America. He wanted to demonstrate that Native North Americans were animals, savages, and degenerates. They were not simply unlike Europeans, they were much worse (Gerbi 1975:53).

In the midst of the Abbé's misguided eighteenth-century racist reasoning, however, he touched upon a key idea of this book: that men and women need other individuals with whom to have social relations. The relations were what Selkirk was denied during his

29

sojourn on the deserted island, and it was this denial, this weird social aberration, that intrigued de Pauw. So serious was the loss of companionship that Defoe could not subject his readers to its cruelty. Thus, he allowed Crusoe what Selkirk lacked: a man Friday, someone with whom to interact.

For all of his apparent bluster, de Pauw was only one voice within a larger chorus of scholarship that resonated through the halls of Europe at the time of the "Great Discovery." As intellectuals in the European elite came to realize that the Americas not only existed but also were populated with decidedly non-European folk, they struggled to explain what was for them a "New" World. The debate over the Americas, both its natural and human faces, would eventually draw to it many of the brightest minds in intellectual history, including Descartes, Rousseau, Jefferson, Voltaire, and Hegel. The debates took decades to play out and before they were finished they rocked the very foundations of anthropological thought (Gerbi 1973; Voget 1975:1–90). What interests me most is de Pauw's insistence that people must be connected to one another to have some sense of the world and to find their place within it. This is the basis of mutualism (Carrithers 1992), and it is at the root of the historical archaeology I envision.

NETS AND PEOPLE

The idea that people interact is not new. The *Oxford English Dictionary* traced to 1563 the meaning of the word "society" as "association or intercourse with or between persons." The term derives from the Latin *societas,* meaning "fellowship, association." Its root, *socius,* is Latin for "a fellow, partner, companion." Generally, we may imagine that these associations or intercourses refer to those interactions that occur on a daily basis. Most of us generally accept that a society is composed of men, women, and children who interact with other men, women, and children whom they know. Perhaps we may expand our understanding to include people not known personally but who live in a familiar manner. We may well imagine that any individual's circle of acquaintances is, for practical purposes, fairly limited. The individual's acquaintances are limited to those people in his or her society. When Abbé de Pauw vociferously attacked the Society of Jesus as "ever untrustworthy," we understand that he meant the entire group of Jesuits, whether or not each one of them knew every other Jesuit. While certainly the name "society" in reference to the Jesuits has a special meaning, it still portrays a proper sense of the term. The Jesuit fathers are a group of people who interact and have a common purpose—scholarship and missionary activity. We may also assume that Jesuits share a fairly similar outlook on life. Using the Jesuits as an example, we may well suppose, perhaps because of our own limited experience in the world, that a society is a bounded universe of people. We may understand that societies are discrete, finite, and geographically manageable.

Social scientists have learned, though, that commonly held notions about what constitutes a society are often too confining. By identifying a group of people as a society we may be unfairly restricting our world view (Wolf 1982:3). In 1915, the great French sociologist Emile Durkheim (1915:426) made what we can take to be a somewhat startling statement: "There is no people and no state which is not part of another society, more or less unlimited, which embraces all the peoples and all the states with which it first comes in contact, either directly or indirectly." Durkheim—often called the "father of modern sociology"—is telling us that the little, tightly bounded societies we might imagine to exist are in fact unbounded, broad, and far-reaching. A society of interacting individuals is much larger than initially may be supposed.

Cultural anthropologists who took Durkheim seriously began to see the study of connections between people as the goal of their profession. Many envisioned the relationships between people as more important than some foggy notion of "culture." No less an intellectual power than A. R. Radcliff-Brown shared Durkheim's view. In his presidential address to the Royal Anthropological Society of Great Britain and Ireland, Radcliffe-Brown (1940:3) said: "A particular social relation between two persons (unless they be Adam and Eve in the Garden of Eden) exists only as part of a wide network of social relations, involving many other persons." Radcliffe-Brown, without doubt a major anthropological thinker, concluded that networks of interaction should be the very object of anthropological research. Twenty years later, American anthropologist Alexander Lesser reaffirmed the Durkheim–Radcliffe-Brown perspective in even stronger terms. Lesser (1961:42) argued that a proper understanding of human life could only be achieved

if we conceive of human societies—prehistoric, primitive, or modern—
not as closed systems, but as open systems; if we think of any social
aggregate not as isolated, separated by some kind of wall, from others,
but as inextricably involved with other aggregates, near and far, in
weblike, netlike connections.

Several anthropologists found the social network perspective
compelling, and many of them went forth into the world to observe
these "weblike, netlike connections" in action. What they discovered
should not surprise us; the webs, the nets of interaction, were finely
woven and intricately intertwined. Also, the nets came in various sizes. For example, in his study of a small Norwegian fishing
community, J. A. Barnes (1954:44) discovered that the nets had
different-sized meshes. He said that the "mesh" of a small population was tighter than that of a large group. People expressed relationships more often and in a more personal manner in small groups
because these interactions involved the same people over and over
again. Contacts were less frequent in larger groups and involved
a wider circle of people. Other social scientists have since refined
Barnes's understanding of how social networks operate, discovering
that social connections can link individual men and women across
time and space in limitless ways. Connections can incorporate kinship, relations of power, class loyalties, environmental perceptions,
economic strategies, and several other elements of daily life (Knoke
and Kuklinski 1982:15; Larrain 1986; Wolf 1984:397). Given this
body of research, we may envision a social network to be a multi-
dimensional web of people who are tied together through their relationships. What makes social networks even more complicated, and
infinitely interesting to archaeologists, is that these social networks
also create physical networks that gain expression in actual landscapes (Chapter 6).

Cultural anthropologist Michael Carrithers (1992) borrowed
the term "mutualism" from social psychology to describe the view
that the relationships of interacting men and women have primary
significance in group dynamics. In essence, a mutualist believes
that people act and react in relation to one another not in response
to hazy abstractions we may wish to call "culture" or "society." For
those who believe in the primacy of culture, "people do things because of their culture" (Carrithers 1992:34). In the mutualist perspective, people "do things with, to, and in respect of each other,
using means that we can describe, if we wish to, as cultural."

When we put our analytical magnifying glass on the relationships people maintain rather than on their culture, we soon realize
that people have an amazing potential. Other social animals—ants
and wolves, for instance—tend to live in relation to one another.
Humans, however, produce relationships *in order* to live (Godelier
1986:1). Because as Carrithers (1992:29) said, "human life is meta-
morphic"; the warp and weft of humans' interactive nets are constantly being changed as if by an overly fussy weaver. The changeable character of human life means that people "produce culture and
create history" (Godelier 1986:1).

The idea that men and women create history is not new to
archaeology. V. Gordon Childe (1951), the great British-trained Aus-
tralian, said long ago that men and women "make themselves"
through their actions. But how do archaeologists recognize past social relations? How do they identify the existence of long-distance
connections, the "other society" relationships Durkheim mentioned?
If we can accept that no web of people is ever truly isolated—like
Selkirk on his island—then we must wonder about peoples' connections with other webs, with other people who may live far away and
be quite different from them.

NETS AND ARCHAEOLOGISTS

Archaeologists have been interested in large-scale, intercul-
tural connections for many years. With painstaking care, they have
documented several, extremely broad webs of interaction, including
connections between the American Southwest and Mesoamerica
(Mathien and McGuire 1986; McGuire 1980; Riley and Hedrick
1980), across the ancient Near East (Edens 1992; Kohl 1987a,
1987b; Lamberg-Karlovsky 1972; Larsen 1987), and throughout prehistoric Europe (Cooter 1977; Dietler 1989; Haselgrove 1987).

Archaeologists cannot directly observe the actions of the people
they study, so they must learn to recognize the presence of past
interaction by the things people left behind. Artifacts become the
symbolic surrogates of netlike connections. As Robert Adams
(1974:240) said, the broadest relations are "tied to the spatial distribution of imperishable objects." In addition to portable "things,"
archaeologists can also use buildings and other features to identify
and chart long-distance interaction. In ancient Mesopotamia, for ex-

ample, C. C. Lamberg-Karlovsky (1975) used the distribution of steatite objects as a marker of long-distance trade. In the prehistoric American Midwest, Joseph Caldwell (1964:137) relied on multiple burials in log tombs, designs cut from copper sheets, drilled bear's teeth, and finely carved human figurines to argue that the Native American "Hopewellians" maintained intercontinental contacts (also see Struever and Houart 1972). In Scotland, William Cooter (1977) used dry-stone towers and earthen hill forts to document cultural interaction.

Each one of these archaeologists demonstrated that people in the past—and often in the far distant past—maintained regular, long-range interactions with other peoples. The documentation of these ancient networks confirms Durkheim's (1915) view that all people are connected. Other examples of long-range interactions could be easily cited, for they populate the past in profusion (see Schortman and Urban 1987). In prehistory, though, archaeologists face serious obstacles in unequivocally demonstrating past contacts and interactions. The problem is well illustrated by the case of the pochteca.

The pochteca were a powerful class of Aztec merchants, whom the Aztec people treated like nobility (Coe 1994:168). They were vanguards of the Aztec empire, and ambassadors of the divine power that emanated from the grandiose Mexican cities. The pochteca doubled as spies, carefully noting the activities of the empire's enemies, but basically they were merchants. As archaeologist William Sanders (1992:285) noted, the pochteca were not "primarily an arm of the state, but rather a class of urban professional middlemen." Thus, we may think of the pochteca as the yuppies of Middle America. Spanish Father Bernardino de Sahagún, who was with the Aztecs in the midsixteenth century, left us a list of the items the pochteca traded to the surrounding peoples: embroidered skirts and capes, jade objects, turquoise mosaic shields, large red seashells, yellow parrot feathers, black ocelot hides, and yellow tortoise shell cups (Sahagún 1959:17–19).

Scribes like Father Sahagún tell us much about the activities of the pochteca within the confines of the Aztec empire. He was explicit, in a confusing sixteenth-century way, about where the merchants went and what they did once they got there. What is not known today is how far the pochteca actually traveled in their commercial rounds. How far outside the boundaries of the Aztec homeland did they actually go?

This question has intrigued archaeologists for many years. Some experts believe that the pochteca traveled into the American Southwest, boldly entering a new environment and bringing with them exotic objects and strange ideas from far away (Wilcox 1986:17–29). Many believe that the pochteca—lugging precious cargo and expressing foreign notions—acted as agents of cultural change among the ancient peoples of the American Southwest (Mathien 1986:220–221). To support this contention, archaeologists have singled out objects found in the Southwest that are not native to that region. These exotic objects include macaw burials and mass-produced, straight-sided cylindrical jars (Washburn 1980). Some archaeologists even say that the elongated skulls of some Southwestern burials represent the cultural influence of the Aztecs (Brooks and Brooks 1980).

The pochteca were clearly important actors within Mesoamerica (Blanton et al. 1981:235–236). However, their precise influence outside Middle America is still a source of great debate. Not everyone is convinced that the pochteca had an impact outside Mexico, particularly on the indigenous peoples of the American Southwest. One problem with solidifying the connection between the Southwest and Central Mexico is that evidence has yet to come from the land between the Aztec homeland and the American Southwest. Archaeologists have usually looked at Mexico and the Southwest, overlooking the important land in between. As a result, one archaeologist said that assuming pochteca influence in the Southwest has "the happy advantage of allowing us to leap a thousand miles in a single bound without worrying too much about all that archaeologically unknown territory in between" (Pailes 1980:24).

Someday prehistoric archaeologists will better understand the exact role the professional Aztec merchants played in the prehistory of the American Southwest. Some are already looking at the region in between Mexico and the Southwest. For now, however, the controversy that surrounds the pochteca shows the problems prehistorians face when attempting to understand large-scale contact. The march of the pochteca toward the pueblos of the desert Southwest cannot be unambiguously documented without a huge amount of future research. The artifacts suspected of taking part in the exchange are not talking.

The archaeologist's task of understanding long-distance interaction is made considerably easier when abundant documentation exists to support the contacts. In the ancient Near East, for instance, clay tablets found at Kanesh in modern-day Turkey help to confirm extensive trading networks and societal interactions throughout the region (Giorgadze 1991:269). Many archaeologists in the Near East were once reluctant to use such "nonarchaeological" sources (Oppenheim 1957:27–28), but today most archaeologists recognize the added interpretive power that results from their use. The value of texts is particularly obvious when it comes to documenting large-scale nets of interaction. Historical archaeologists, of course, have never had to be convinced about the power of texts when interpreting the past. Their willingness to study long-distance interactions is another matter, however.

ARCHAEOLOGISTS, ANTINETS, AND ISOLATION

My comments in Chapter 1 suggest that historical archaeology is perfectly suited to the study of large-scale interactions for a number of reasons. Historical archaeologists are unabashed about using several kinds of sources. They study a past so recent that living men and women can sometimes remember it, and they investigate subjects that have global importance. Having defined historical archaeology as the study of the modern era, it is only natural for me to envision the field as global in focus. But not every historical archaeologist agrees. In fact, the strongest opponent to the investigation of large nets in historical archaeology comes from a surprising voice: Robert Schuyler. Schuyler's (1970) disapproval is unexpected because it was he who first identified historical archaeology's global potential.

In his paper delivered as part of the 1987 Society for Historical Archaeology plenary session, Schuyler (1988) wondered why historians usually ignore historical archaeology. As if this were not serious enough, Schuyler said that what was more wounding to the historical archaeologist's pride was that even cultural anthropologists overlook them. Schuyler's most damning piece of supporting evidence came from a prominent source: Eric Wolf's (1982) prize-winning *Europe and the People without History*.

Though not without its critics (Asad 1987), Wolf's book received much critical acclaim when it first appeared in 1982. Wolf's main point was to show the intricate ways in which disparate and often widely separated peoples forged lasting, global connections after A.D. 1400. To prove his point, he visited Portuguese slavers, West African kings, native North American fur trappers, English colonists, Chinese tea traders, Bombay textile industrialists, and Brazilian rubber tappers. Carrithers (1992:23) summarized Wolf's magnum opus well when he characterized it as a "Super Deluxe pizza: it has as much as you can get on a pizza, it is the best in town so far, it's a meal in itself and if you want something special this is it, but it's got anchovies."

The anchovies are those parts of the book that were destined not to meet with everyone's approval. Schuyler discovered one of the anchovies. In the over 400 pages of text and notes, Wolf (1982) entirely ignored historical archaeology. Astonishingly, one of the greatest anthropological thinkers of the late twentieth century only mentioned archaeology once in passing. On page 4 of the "Introduction," Wolf mentioned the presence of European trade goods on Iroquois sites in New York State. Though Wolf has admitted to having been influenced by archaeologists in his early training (Ghani 1987:357), he completely ignored archaeology in the remaining pages of his influential book. In Wolf's defense, he is not an archaeologist and we must not expect him to spend his time poring through archaeological journals and slogging through the often tortured, passive-voiced texts of most archaeological site reports. Still, Wolf is a well-read anthropologist and we could expect him to give historical archaeology a nod, even if it is a patronizing one. Wolf's total failure to mention it particularly bothered Schuyler, and to say the least it was disconcerting to most practicing historical archaeologists.

For Schuyler, Wolf's ease in overlooking historical archaeology was only symptomatic of a much larger problem. This problem can be neatly summarized: "How could Wolf, in his sweeping survey of life throughout the world after A.D. 1400, so effortlessly sail right past the one field whose practitioners were deeply concerned with the same issues?" Schuyler (1988:41) concluded that one answer to this question is painfully simple and insurmountable: historical archaeologists "do not excavate on a global level." Like all archaeologists, historical archaeologist focus their energies on one site or at most on a single, fairly small region at a time. Thus, historical archaeologists should not be surprised that their findings have limited application outside archaeology, particularly in a work with the magnitude of *Europe and the People without History*. Schuyler argued that instead of perceiving this interest-in-the-local as a weakness, historical archaeologists should see it as a strength. For him, "historical archaeology will always make its major contributions at the site level of analysis" (Schuyler 1988:41). Thus, in Schuyler's opinion, historical archaeologists should not worry about charting the material aspects of the worldwide connections identified by Wolf (1982). Instead, they should spend their energies on creating "historic ethnographies."

It is in the historical ethnography that we see Schuyler in his most antimutualist, antinet stance. In essence, Schuyler envisioned the archaeologist's ethnographies to be like those of the cultural anthropologist. And to write these ethnographies, Schuyler proposed that historical archaeologists should adopt a view of culture that is directly antimutualist; they should approach culture as if it actually exists. He imagined that "culture comes to us in history in the form of 'packages,' functional units with temporal and spatial boundaries, not as disembodied variables or processes" (Schuyler 1988:40). The temporal and spatial boundaries represent communities. Because archaeologists cannot excavate on a global level, Schuyler said that they would be best served by focusing on what they know best: individual sites, or even small groups of sites that may be described as communities. Only through detailed, localized research would historical archaeologists ever impress cultural anthropologists, historians, and other social scientists. For Schuyler, tight, thorough site reports would advance the field more than broadbrush, globally focused flights of archaeological fancy.

Schuyler made a number of points archaeologists would be well advised to remember. He was correct that no single archaeologist can ever hope to excavate an entire network. Anyone who would attempt such an enormous task would be quickly frustrated, his or her enthusiasm killed by the lack of time, the scarcity of funds, the logistical demands, or simple human fatigue. At the very least, our optimistic archaeologist would quickly realize what geographer Peter Haggett (1990:28) found when he started to think about global issues: the "problem posed by any subject which aims to be global is simple and immediate: the earth's surface is so staggeringly large." Schuyler was also correct that historical archaeologists are well suited to provide detailed interpretations of the sites they excavate. All historical archaeologists should be able to use the available sources, of whatever kind, to present thorough, interesting site reports. The site report—whether or not the archaeologist presents it as a community study—will always constitute archaeology's heart and soul. Site reports contain the detailed nuts and bolts of serious archaeological research and it would be ridiculous to deny their significance. Still, Schuyler's focus on the community raises an intriguing question. Keeping mutualism in mind, we may well ask: where does one community begin and another end?

In Chapter 1 I made reference to William Adams's research at Silcott, Washington, a tiny, late nineteenth-century town situated on the southern bank of the Snake River near the Idaho state line. In this study, Adams (1977:31) spoke in a language with which Schuyler, at least initially, would probably agree. He perceived Silcott "as it might have been, a community of people, not a collection of sites or artifacts to be viewed by and for archaeologists' own and singular enlightenment." Adams specifically focused on the ways in which the people of Silcott were connected to one another within their little community. Adams soon discovered, however, that the Silcott "community" was indeed far-reaching. The men and women who once lived there maintained several different levels of interaction. Inside Silcott, they kept in close contact with their immediate neighbors and they regularly purchased goods from the local general store. In the immediate region, they traveled by buggy, train, and boat to larger towns to buy the things they could not procure at home. Even these levels of interaction did not complete the Silcott "community," however, because the residents of the town were part of larger networks. When they obtained objects from Portland, San Francisco, Spokane, and Seattle they became participants in a still-larger regional network. As part of another, even larger network, they purchased objects made in Milwaukee, New York, and Providence. Even more remarkably, the residents of Silcott—living quiet lives in rural Washington State—obtained products made in England, Germany, and Poland (Adams 1977:78–97; see also Riordan and Adams 1985).

Historians do not mention Silcott in their histories of America or even of the Pacific Northwest. Cultural anthropologists have never flocked to the town to learn how its citizens lived. History has largely passed Silcott by. It was simply a small town in southeastern Washington where people lived their daily lives with little fanfare. Nonetheless, Adams's research shows that even on the edge of the Snake River in rural Washington, people had a "window on the world." Though far from New York, Boston, Berlin, and London, the men and women of Silcott were not truly isolated.

Even more startling evidence that residents of rural towns were not isolated comes from an amazing source: the American Ozarks. The mountainous Ozarks, spreading across northwestern Arkansas and into southwestern Missouri, are famous for being isolated. The region is widely regarded as a place inhabited by self-sufficient, gun-toting, individualistic mountain folk who received their education under the open sky and who openly reject outside interference. They are often portrayed as stubborn, relying only on their immediate kin group for support and aid.

This picture of life in the Ozarks is undoubtedly stereotypical. Leslie Stewart-Abernathy (1986, 1992), after excavating the Moser farmstead in northwestern Arkansas, developed quite a different perspective on life in the region. He discovered that the farmers at the Moser site were in constant contact with the outside world, much like the people of distant Silcott, Washington. One of the most fascinating artifacts Stewart-Abernathy found was a white metal badge impressed with the words "Columbia Exposition Chicago 1893." This remarkable find, unearthed in the supposedly isolated Ozark Mountains, reminds me of a medallion my research team found at Millwood Plantation, a nineteenth-century tenant plan-tation situated in a remote part of northwestern South Carolina. In the charred remains of a poor tenant farmer's cabin that had burned to the ground sometime around 1910, my excavators found a small medal reading "Souvenir of the 1887 Ice Carnival" (Orser 1988a:218–220). The Ice Carnival has been held in Saint Paul, Minnesota—a long way from Millwood Plantation—every year since 1886.

Stewart-Abernathy's Columbia Exposition badge and the Mill-wood Ice Carnival souvenir provide ample proof of outside connec-tions at these two apparently remote sites. We will never know whether the Sharps (residents of the Moser site from 1882 to 1904) or the Walkers (who lived in the Millwood tenant cabin) traveled to Chicago and to St. Paul, respectively, to procure these precious mementos. Perhaps someone sent the tokens to Arkansas and South Carolina. Maybe a widely traveled neighbor even brought them as gifts from afar. These details, though interesting to contemplate, are largely unimportant here (but see Chapter 5). What is now im-portant is that these two objects, and all the other artifacts brought in from someplace else, are symbolic representations of webs of interaction. The presence of these webs, and the very idea that simple farmers in remote corners of the American South could be full members in them—regardless of the actual details of their membership—suggest that Schuyler's communities were vast in-deed.

Skeptics may argue that my examples from Arkansas and South Carolina are contrived. After all, people lived at both sites as late as the early twentieth century. By this time, profit-hungry entrepreneurs had vigorously established extensive commercial networks across much of the world. Also, both sites are after all in the United States, a nation that has worked especially hard to bring material things to its people, whether they live in the mountainous Ozarks, the cotton belt of South Carolina, or rural Washington State. Perhaps the cases I present are not all that startling. Maybe it would be more surprising if the residents of Silcott, Millwood Plantation, and the Moser site were *not* connected to the large commercial networks the business world had set in motion.

But what about sites of more antiquity? Or even sites that are far outside the mainstream of American commercialism? Perhaps such sites better fit Schuyler's model of the community. Can we not imagine such sites to be communities in the restrictive sense of the term, bounded in space and time, including only the most tightly knit webs? I can answer these important questions by turning to one of my sites: Palmares in northeastern Brazil. Palmares, created in the seventeenth century and situated in what is, even in the 1990s, a somewhat remote corner of the world, provides a perfect example of why historical archaeologists must not overlook the importance of extremely broad webs of interaction in their research. I could hardly argue that Palmares was historically or culturally similar to Silcott, Millwood Plantation, or the Moser site. Still, it was connected to a vast network just as were the other three sites.

THE NETS OF PALMARES

We may easily imagine that Palmares represents a perfectly bounded community, a place set aside, isolated from the rest of the world. Escaped slaves are famous for having situated their rebel settlements in the world's out-of-the-way places. In fact, it was precisely the fugitives' quest for isolation that plagues today's archaeologists wishing to find their villages. Fugitive slave settlements are notoriously difficult to locate. Archaeologist Elaine Nichols (1988), for example, was largely empty handed when she finished her search for the renowned runaway villages in the Great Dismal Swamp of North Carolina and Virginia. The residents of the Great

Dismal Swamp were like all fugitives from slavery. Not wishing to return to bondage, they built their settlements in remote places. Surprisingly, however, evidence suggests that maroon communities were not truly isolated. Most were well connected to the outside world in a whole series of complex connections. For Palmares specifically, it can be demonstrated that its links to the outside world ensured its survival for almost 100 years.

Sebastião da Rocha Pita (1950:294), a contemporary of Palmares, stated that "about forty Negroes of the People of Guiné" created the maroon settlement around 1605. Unfortunately, the name "Guiné" is meaningless. The seventeenth-century Portuguese grandly referred to all Africans as "Guinean," meaning only that the people had come from the west coast of Africa (Hall et al. 1987:57; Kent 1965:165–166). Regardless, by 1612, colonial leaders in Brazil acknowledged the presence of Palmares and sent their first military raid against it. They undoubtedly figured that the early removal of the maroons would solve the runaway problem once and for all. Their raid was unsuccessful and Palmares continued to exist, and in fact to grow, for another 82 years.

The fugitives of Palmares chose as their new home the hills that parallel the coast of northeastern Brazil in what are today the states of Alagoas and Pernambuco. The seventeenth-century Portuguese colonial government referred to this region as the Captaincy of Pernambuco (Southey 1822:52). Northeastern Brazil had become an important sugar-producing region shortly after the Portuguese landfall in 1500. In 1584, colonial planters operated 26 sugar mills in the captaincy. In 1612, the date of the first armed assault on Palmares, sugar planters owned 170 mills. By the mid-1620s, the number of mills had grown to 230 (Boxer 1973a:192). Sugar was clearly king in colonial Brazil. In 1618, when Ambrósio Fernandes Brandão wrote his engaging *Dialogues of the Great Things of Brazil,* he reported that the production of sugar was the quickest way to acquire wealth in Brazil (Hall et al. 1987:132). A young, well-connected gentleman from Portugal could go to Brazil, establish a sugar plantation, and soon become a millionaire based on the labor of African slaves. Palmares and other maroon settlements were a clear obstacle in the path to Portuguese colonial wealth and well-being.

Portuguese planters operated their sugar mills—their producers of personal wealth—along the Atlantic Coast. Brandão said that they penetrated no more than 56 km (35 mi) into the rugged and heavily forested Brazilian interior. The people who organized, settled, and maintained Palmares were fugitives from these coastal sugar plantations, or, as they are called in Brazil, *fazendas.*

The Portuguese came to call the maroon settlement Palmares, because several prominent palm trees grew within its territory. The fugitives, though, looking toward their homeland, named their settlement Angola Janga, or "Little Angola" (Freitas 1984:44; Schwartz 1985:342). I use the colonialist term "Palmares" only because that is the name most recognized today. Since Latin was the *lingua franca* of the day, most contemporary observers referred to maroon settlements as *res publicae,* or polities. *Res publicae* was soon translated into modern languages as "republics" or *repúblicas.* Only later did writers use terms like "maroon" (Funari 1995:3). Though Angola Janga refers to the homeland of most of Palmares' residents, no one is absolutely certain what African cultures gained expression there. Still, contemporary Portuguese slavers looked so strongly to Angola for potential chattel that most would have concurred with Antônio Vieira's comment of 1648 that "without Angola there are no Negroes" (Boxer 1973b:137).

The Dutch, who gained a foothold in northeastern Brazil in 1630, worried about the growing power of Palmares (Boxer 1937b:98–100). As a result, in 1640 they sent a scouting party to investigate it. The leader of the expedition, Bartholomeus Lintz, was the first European to describe the fugitive villages. Lintz wrote that two settlements existed, a Great Palmares and a Lesser Palmares. Great Palmares contained about 5,000 people who lived in cabins scattered throughout the interior valleys. About 6,000 people lived in Lesser Palmares, which Lintz described as a village with three streets and huts made of "straw twisted together, one near another" (Barleus 1923:315–316, 1974:253–254, 304–305). The people of Palmares, the so-called Palmaristas, grew dates, coconuts, potatoes, beans, barley, and sugarcane in the broad fields surrounding their homes. They also domesticated "tame-fowl" and consumed large amounts of fish (Nieuhoff 1813:707–708; see Figure 2).

Palmares continued to attract runaway slave men and women in the early 1640s as conditions on the coastal estates continued to be harsh and even inhuman. The Dutch, though they were the worldwide rivals of the Portuguese, wanted to see Palmares destroyed as much as did their colonial rivals (see Chapter 8). Their murderous desire had the unintended benefit of providing an important glimpse of Palmares in the mid-1640s, just as it was beginning

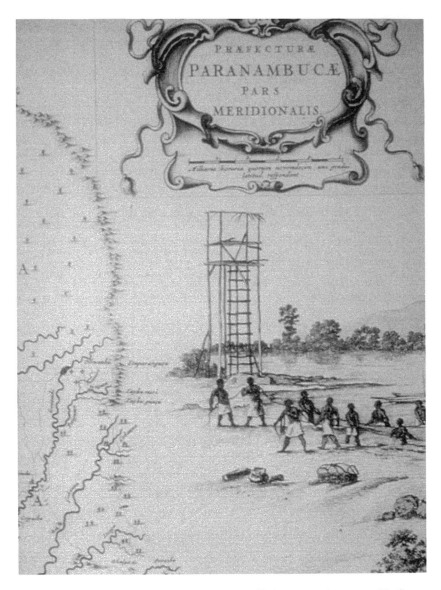

Figure 2. The only known contemporary image of Palmares, as it appeared in Caspar Barleus's *Rerum Per Octennium in Brasilia* (1647). Photo courtesy of the Edward E. Ayer Collection, The Newberry Library, Chicago.

to assume the character of a large and powerful force in colonial Brazil.

Dutch lieutenant Jürgens Reijmbach, who led an armed assault on Palmares in 1645, returned with a fascinating account of the place. He learned that the two Palmares settlements mentioned by Lintz had been moved about three years earlier, or about two years after Lintz's unwelcomed visit. The two "old" Palmares villages were once about 5 km (3 mi) apart. Two new villages were situated about 11 to 13 km (about 7–8 mi) away from the old site. The two new settlements were about 14 km (8.5 mi) apart, but to reach them, Reijmbach's column had to traverse land bristling with smaller camps of fugitives. Palmares was growing.

Reijmbach's description of one of the two settlements is a priceless piece of historical reporting. He observed that the Palmaristas had surrounded their village with a double palisade made of sticks. Between the sticks they had placed large beams. Inside this dense palisade line was "a trench full of pointed sticks." He remembered these sticks well because both his buglers had fallen against them, wounding themselves in the process. In fact, so enraged was one of them that he "cut the head of one Negro woman." The village was large, containing 220 houses, a church, four forges, and a large council house. Remarkably, Reijmbach identified this town as the seat of the king of Palmares. This monarch, whom the runaways called Ganga Zumba, or "Great Lord," also had a house 2 miles outside the town (Carneiro 1988:58; Carvalho 1902:92).

The attacks by Dutch and Portuguese forces had no lasting effect on Palmares and the kingdom continued to grow. The account left by Fernão Carrilho in 1677 reported that by this time Palmares included 10 major villages and several smaller outposts (Carneiro 1988:202–204). The king's village was called Macaco—either Portuguese for "monkey" or the Portuguese understanding of the African word "Makoko"—though the Portuguese also knew it as the "Royal Stockade" (Kent 1965:169). The other towns had equally exotic-sounding names: Osenga, Subupira, Dambrabanga, Arotirene, Tabocas, Zumbi, Amaro, Aqualtune, and Andalaquituche (Drummond 1859:304; Rodrigues 1945:131). Many of these towns were tied to Macaco by kinship. Gana Zona, who ruled Subupira—the "second city of Palmares"—was the brother of Ganga Zumba. Andalaquituche, for whom the village was named, was the nephew of Ganga Zumba and brother to Zumbi, the last, ever-defiant king of Palmares. Aqualtune was Ganga Zumba's mother (Carneiro 1988:57–58).

This picture of Palmares, or more accurately Angola Janga, implies that the Palmaristas lived a secluded life. They built ingenious, well-fortified towns to fend off Dutch and Portuguese invaders, they grew rich fields of crops, and they harvested fish from the rivers. Even Reijmbach seemed to admire—albeit perhaps grudgingly—the Palmaristas' ingenuity. He seemed particularly impressed by their ability to use the palm trees that dotted their lands. According to him, the people of Palmares used palm leaves to make houses, beds, and fans to tend their fires; they ate the insides of the coconuts, and cut smoking pipes from their woody shells. They even used coconuts to produce oil, butter, and wine (Carvalho 1902:92). Reijmbach also acknowledged that his troops found "gourds, straw baskets, and earthen pots" in the Palmaristas' abandoned homes. Palmares even had royalty who, like most established monarchs, found their power rooted in kinship.

Surely we can conclude from this evidence that Palmares, a great fugitive slave kingdom in the remote forests of northeastern Brazil, constituted a "community." Thus, it seems a perfect place to produce Schuyler's (1988) historic ethnography. If we take a closer look at Palmares, however, we can see that even this remote place, inhabited so long ago, was not isolated. The Palmaristas maintained complex connections with colonizing Europeans, with native South American Indians, and even with their ancestral homeland, Angola.

Palmaristas and Europeans

We may logically conclude that the Palmaristas and the colonial Europeans—the Portuguese, and from 1630 to 1654 the Dutch—were sworn enemies. After all, these Europeans sent armed expeditions against Palmares starting in 1612. After about 1670, they annually sent armies against Palmares until 1694 when they finally succeeded in destroying it (Ennes 1948; Freitas 1984:139–165). John Nieuhoff (1813:707), who spent from 1640 to 1649 in Brazil in the employ of the Dutch West India Company, reported that the "business" of the Palmaristas was "to rob the Portuguese of their slaves." In the light of this comment and other evidence, we may comfortably conclude that the Palmaristas represented a triple threat to the colonizing Europeans. They were an economic threat because they robbed the coastal sugar planters of their valuable work force and because the task of fighting Palmares cost the Portuguese colonial government a small fortune (Ennes 1938:195). The

Palmaristas represented a political threat because they presented an obstacle to expansion. And they posed a social threat because they constantly demonstrated the inherent weakness of the slave regime.

Still, historical records contain tantalizing references to Europeans assisting the men and women of Palmares. Contemporary chroniclers never dwelt upon these passing references, probably because they would tell a whole new story of Palmares, a story colonial authorities would rather have ignored. When these references are acknowledged, however, we can see that the Palmaristas maintained strong ties to colonial European networks.

Caspar Barleus (1974:252), a contemporary of Palmares, cryptically noted that Bartholomeus Lintz, who led the Dutch attack of 1640, "lived among them [and] after staying with them [knew] their places and mode of life." Barleus was puzzled as to why Lintz chose to betray his "ancient companions." Thirty years later, after Dutchmen like Lintz had largely abandoned Brazil, references to European support of Palmares continued to appear. Fernão de Souza Coutinho, colonial governor of Pernambuco, was furious with the local Portuguese settlers who passed firearms to Palmares "in disregard of God and local laws" (Carneiro 1988:227–228). The situation had not changed 17 years later, in 1687, when governor João da Cunha Souto Mayor threatened to imprison any settler even suspected of giving support to Palmares. Imprisonment would result regardless of the offender's social position or "noble birth" (Ennes 1938:240).

The Palmaristas are also known to have regularly bartered with European colonists, trading "their cane, bananas, and beans for such articles as utensils, arms, and ammunition" (Ramos 1939:64). More daring Portuguese colonists are said to have supplied the Palmaristas with vital—and treasonous—information about impending attacks (Kent 1965:171). That Reijmbach and other assailants seldom found the Palmaristas at home suggests that the received information was well-heeded and much appreciated.

What exactly do statements about European involvement in Palmares mean? At this point in the research, I can offer no definitive statements. What I do know, though, is that some Portuguese settlers—*moradores* in Portuguese—may have felt that they had closer links to the Palmaristas than to their countrymen, the coastal plantation owners, and the governmental elite. Seventeenth-century Portuguese society was stratified into at least four classes, expressed androcentrically as: men of letters, a roughly homogeneous class of educated scholars; the nobility, composed of knights, squires, and the so-called rich men; the clergy; and citizens—farmers, merchants, serfs, and others (Marques 1971:9–10). Outside the royal line, the merchants, artisans, and rich men realized the greatest profit from global exploration and colonization, because they had the opportunity to become sugar planters (Livermore 1973:69). The citizens who faced the greatest dangers in colonialism, the soldiers, sailors, and frontline settlers, often expressed bitterness about their inability to reap the benefits of colonization (Moser 1985:97–98). Thus, we may easily imagine that not every individual *morador* shared the plantation owners' vision of Brazil. *Moradores* may well have seen greater advantage, even if intermittent and short-lived, in defying the colonial government by throwing their support to the Palmaristas. Whatever their reasons, some *moradores* did maintain important connections with Palmares.

Palmaristas and Native South Americans

The land that would become Palmares was not uninhabited when the first people of "Guiné" fled there in 1605. The Brazilian northeast was a landscape of diverse cultures at the time the Portuguese made their first landfalls on the coast. Thousands of indigenous peoples lived in the northeast just as had their ancestors for centuries. European explorers who ventured along the Brazilian coast in the sixteenth century often applied the name "Tupinambá" to all those native men, women, and children who spoke the Tupí-Guaraní language, and who lived along the Atlantic from the mouth of the Amazon to São Paulo (Métraux 1948:95). Colonial chroniclers often used another term, "Tapuya," to refer to many other native peoples.

Sir Richard Burton, one of the first Europeans to reach Lake Tanganyika in East Africa in 1858, was in Santos, Brazil, from 1865 to 1868. Though Burton had the title of "His British Majesty's Consul for the Santos," he described his time in Brazil as "exile" (Burton 1874:i). But his time was not entirely wasted. An explorer himself, Burton soon became fascinated with the accounts of Brazil's earliest explorers. In pouring over the reports made by the intrepid adventurers who probed Brazil's mysterious countryside, Burton concluded that the chroniclers had identified "great divisions" among its many indigenous peoples. Encapsulated within these divisions were "a multitude of clans, a list of whose names would fill pages"

(Burton 1874:lxii). Faced with an immense number of native groups, many of whom the explorers identified with similar names, Burton (1874:lxiii) decided that the list could be distilled to just two major groups: the "Wild Indians—the Tapuyas—and the "Tame Indians." This last group included the Tupinambá, as well as the Tobayara, Tupynaqui, Tupigoare, Tupyminó, Amoigpirá, Araboyára, Rarigoára, Potigoare, Tamoyo, Carijó, and Goayaná. Burton included within the Tapuya the Aimoré, Potentin, Guaiatacá, Guaramomí, Goarégoaré, Jeçaruçú, Amanipaqué, and Payeá.

After reading these partial lists, can we blame the European explorers for failing to identify the precise differences between the natives of Brazil? Renowned anthropologist Robert Lowie (1946:556) concluded that the term "Tapuya" should be erased from anthropological memory because colonial reporters had so widely misapplied the term. In any case, Burton's compilation and Lowie's professional assessment show that northeastern Brazil, the land to which fugitive Palmaristas fled, was populated with several groups of natives, each of which had its own separate cultural identity.

The Portuguese, of course, did not care about the ethnographic details or the subtle divisions between the native groups. Missionaries sought to convert heathens, plantation owners to transform "unproductive" natives into workers. Colonizing Portuguese quickly set about to enslave the indigenous inhabitants of Brazil by whatever means necessary (Hemming 1978:152). By the late sixteenth century, Portuguese sugar producers had committed hundreds of Tupinambá to bondage in the steamy sugar mills, or *engenhos*. These natives, unaccustomed to the demands of inhuman labor, were soon either overcome by work or dead from unfamiliar European diseases (Cardoso 1983:66–67; Thornton 1992:140). One colonialist incredulously observed in 1583 that "no one could believe that so great a supply [of indigenous slaves] could be so quickly exhausted" (Scammell 1981:248). Brazil only revoked the laws allowing Indian enslavement in October 1831 (Conrad 1986:82).

The precise role played by native South Americans at Palmares is now largely a mystery. Seventeenth-century chroniclers did state that Europeans used them as allies in several assaults against Palmares. The Dutch expeditions of Rodolfo Baro in 1644 (Barleus 1923:370) and Jürgens Reijmbach in 1645 (Carvalho 1902) employed native allies in their attack forces. Domingos Jorge Velho commanded a force that included native Brazilians during his devastating, final assault on Palmares in 1694 (Ennes 1948:208; Southey 1822:26).

Other clues in the documents, however, suggest that many native people maintained strong and amiable contacts with the Palmaristas. In fact, the names of three of Palmares' villages— Arotirene, Tabocas, Subupira—are undoubtedly Tupi (Funari 1995:33–34; Kent 1965:169). Also, since Baro reported capturing "seven Brazilians" in his attack of 1644, we may conclude that native peoples lived in some of the Palmarista villages (Barleus 1923:370).

The Tupinambá are known to have fought the Portuguese throughout colonial history (Hemming 1978; Métraux 1948), and we may easily imagine that their goals corresponded with those of the Palmaristas. Also, we should not be surprised that the Tupinambá would have different attitudes, outlooks, and traditions than the surrounding Tupuya. The Tupuya were typically mentioned as the natives who accompanied the Europeans in their attack forces. The coexistence of native allies and enemies in the Brazilian northeast demonstrates the cultural complexity that existed at the time the Palmaristas forged their rebel kingdom.

Palmaristas and Africans

Though it at first appears that Palmares represents the perfectly isolated, inward-looking community, my comments so far should indicate that the Palmaristas maintained long-standing and possibly even daily contacts with other peoples in the Brazilian northeast. The majority of the connections were forged both with European colonists new to the area and with native peoples whose ancestors had lived in Brazil for centuries. As remarkable as these connections were, the Palmaristas maintained still another set of connections that were more far-reaching and somewhat more dramatic. These ties, these nets of interaction, were woven with people from their homeland, the place from which the men and women of Palmares had originally come. This place, of course, was Africa, and specifically, Angola.

No study of Palmares could be complete without considering seventeenth-century Angola. Angola's cultural situation was exceedingly complicated at the time the Palmaristas were creating their faraway kingdom in the dense forests of Brazil. A full explanation here would take me too far afield (but see J. C. Miller 1976, 1982; Thornton 1992), but a brief explanation will suffice to demonstrate why the historical archaeology of Palmares cannot ignore the Angolan homeland.

Many distinct peoples lived in central Africa at the time of Portuguese contact. When Diego Cão nudged his boat along the west coast of Africa in the early 1480s, the Kingdom of Kongo was "the undisputed leader among all the coastal states of Central Africa" (Vansina 1966:37). Portuguese traders and ambassadors quickly hammered out alliances between themselves and this powerful kingdom. It was not long before Kongolese kings were baptized as Christians, and sending their sons to Lisbon for "proper" Portuguese educations (Balandier 1968). The precise motives for the Angolan kings' actions can be debated. Either they were truly converted to European notions or else they simply pretended conversion in order to bring advantages to themselves and their people. Their precise reasons are unimportant here. What is pertinent is that the colonial Portuguese and the Kingdom of Kongo created firm links between themselves. In 1512, to flex their colonial muscles, the Portuguese threatened to cease all trade with the Kongo unless the Africans continued to supply slaves to the Portuguese (Saunders 1982:20–21). An absence of slaves meant a cessation of trade in European goods, so the African kingdom continued to hand over slave captives to the eager Portuguese.

During the early years of Portugal's involvement in Angola, the interior Jaga, or Imbangala (Vansina 1963), helped to speed the final disintegration of the Kingdom of Kongo. When this happened, the Portuguese were not willing simply to abandon central Africa. Instead, they turned their attention to the interior, a region they called "Angola" after the Mbundu king known as "Ngola" (Birmingham 1965:8; Boxer 1973b:237). So interwoven were the relationships between the Portuguese and the indigenous peoples of west central Africa that in 1556, when the Kingdom of Kongo attacked the Kingdom of Kdongo, Portuguese troops fought on both sides (Henderson 1979:82). The Portuguese construction of the colonial outpost Luanda in 1575 signalled their commitment to Angola.

Angola remained culturally diverse during the Palmaristas' rise to power. From about 1605 to 1654, the Portuguese toiled to maintain and even to stimulate the transfer of slaves from Angola to Brazil. From 1654 until at least 1683—just when the Palmaristas were strengthening their grip over the interior of Pernambuco—the Portuguese moved to cement their control over Angola (Birmingham 1965:24). The eventual Portuguese domination of Angola was one of the most brutal chapters in colonial history anywhere in the world (Bennett 1975:34–35).

Complex connections always characterized Angola's cultural history (Thornton 1992:188). Part of the reason for the cultural entanglements was simple: several diverse peoples lived in close proximity. The same may be said for many regions around the globe, but in Angola, another contributing factor to the complexity is extremely important: the European slave trade. Many of the slaves shipped out of Angola were war captives, and Portuguese merchants were not above starting a local war in order to increase the supply of slaves (Duffy 1962:60). The prisoners of war were the men and women who arrived in Brazil, destined by and large for the coastal sugar plantations. These people, in turn, were those who ultimately ran away to join the rebels in Palmares. We may well imagine, therefore, that the cultural traditions of Angola played a significant role in shaping Palmares. After all, historians figure that about 4,400 slaves arrived annually on the docks of northeast Brazil (Hall et al. 1987:181). This figure may be as large as 13,000 per year (Conrad 1986:29). These slaves did not come from a void; they were individuals imbedded in African networks. And it did not take them long to become enmeshed in a new set of networks. We may well assume, though, that the old networks were not forgotten. On the contrary, they were reaffirmed every time Palmares received new fugitives (Kent 1965:173).

At least one cultural institution from Angola may have played a powerful role in Palmares. This was the Angolan "kilombo" (J. C. Miller 1976:161–241). *Ki'lombo* is a word the Angolan Kimbundu use for "house" (Megenney 1978:152). Seventeenth-century Italian Capuchin missionary Giovanni Antonio Cavazzi used the word to refer to a Jaga, or Imbangala, war camp. The kilombo, however, was not simply the camp itself. Rather, the term referred to an organization of men brought together in comradeship and for ritual observances (J. C. Miller 1976:167). In any case, the members of Angolan kilombos fortified their camps with multiple palisades similar to those described by the attackers of Palmares (Ravenstein 1967:29; Schwartz 1970:331).

No one knows today whether Africans took the kilombo organization to Brazil and recreated it at Palmares. But since both the Angolan camps and the Brazilian fugitive villages were contemporaneous, we may reasonably assume that members of kilombos were captured, sent to Brazil, and escaped to Palmares. In this sense, then, the Palmaristas were part of the network that contained the kilombos from faraway Africa. Palmares was not a kilombo camp in the strict sense of the term, but it could not have existed without the kilombos of Angola. Rather, the two organizations were united as closely related kin.

THE IMPLICATIONS OF A MUTUALIST POINT OF VIEW

Our brief visit to Palmares has been enlightening. We have learned that even this out-of-the-way place, originally settled specifically because of its remote location, was not isolated at all. The people of Palmares had long-standing connections with European colonists from two powerful nations, Portugal and the Netherlands. They maintained relations with the surrounding native peoples, men and women who had learned to live in the Brazilian northeast from generations of their ancestors. The Palmaristas also had constant contact with their former homeland through the influx of new runaways. The newly enslaved men and women from Africa brought with them the rich traditions of the homeland (Figure 3).

Palmares provides a dramatic example of the need for historical archaeologists to think broadly, to incorporate a mutualist perspective in their repertoire of analytical and interpretative skills. I could just as easily have visited Gorttoose or any one of a thousand other archaeological sites inhabited in the modern era. In the mutualist perspective, all peoples have connections with others; all men, women, and children are embedded within the multiple nets created through interaction.

Our look at Palmares—and we have only glimpsed a small corner of its complexity—brings to the forefront at least three important implications of mutualism. These implications should be borne in mind by historical archaeologists, for each weighs heavily on our understanding of the past. Each also figures prominently in the rest of this book.

The first implication involves technology. Archaeologists are generally fond of both thanking and blaming technology for large-scale societal change. We can easily single out the iron plow, the automobile, the arrowhead, or a thousand other revolutionary inventions as catalysts of social and cultural change. The mutualist perspective downplays this technological point of view by arguing that change occurs, not strictly because of technology, but because of the relationships forged by technology (Carrithers 1992:28). Instead of supposing that the Palmaristas' acquisition of guns made them better able to defend their kingdom, we should concentrate on the

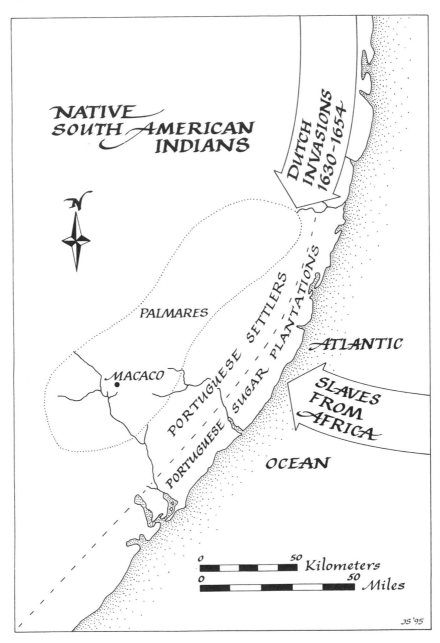

Figure 3. The diverse cultural context of Palmares.

relationships that allowed the Palmaristas to need, acquire, and use guns. These relationships are more telling and infinitely more interesting than the firearms themselves.

The second implication of mutualism is that relationships occur on both large and small scales. Wolf (1982:195–231) is correct in saying that the Atlantic slave trade tied together people from various parts of the globe, including Palmaristas, Portuguese frontier settlers, Dutch slavers and soldiers, native South Americans, and Angolan warriors, but none of these relationships would have been possible without fine-grained relationships between individuals. Here, Schuyler (1988) was correct. According to Carrithers (1992:31), contacts between individuals create "mutual attitudes, mutual intentions, and mutual understandings—or misunderstandings" about both parties.

The third implication is methodological. As Wolf (1982:3) stated in the first sentence of *Europe and the People without History,* historical researchers falsify reality when they disassemble the interconnectedness of the world's people and then fail to reassemble it. When we choose to perceive a group of people—the Palmaristas, for instance—as a distinctive "culture" or "nation" disconnected to the wider world, we seriously undervalue the people's creativity and ingenuity. Archaeologists make a serious mistake when they perceive an abandoned village as a disassembled set of old pottery sherds and pieces of glass. Most archaeologists already know this, but only through the intellectual process of reassembly can a people's past connections be constructed. This understanding in turn leads to views of how past peoples made history. Archaeologists do the past a disservice when they fail to envision humans as "inventive and profoundly social animals, living in and through their relations with each other and acting and reacting upon each other to make new relations and new forms of life" (Carrithers 1992:32–33).

We must keep well in mind, however, that the relations were not forged between equal partners in contact. The broad sweep of history clearly shows that some humans were more equal than others. Men and women had always created social inequalities, but the social distances between certain kinds of people generally became more pronounced in the modern era. The reason for the dramatic change is easily stated, if not so easily explained: The cosmic chalkboard that was used to chart the relationships between people was stored in a room that included four powerful, though shadowy, forces. These forces were global colonialism, Eurocentrism, capitalism, and modernity. Each one is central to historical archaeology.

The Haunts of | 3
Historical Archaeology

Colonialism, Eurocentrism, capitalism, and modernity—can there be four more hotly contested words in present-day scholarship? Each word, with its myriad facets, angles, and expressions, provokes images, sparks controversy, and raises passions. Each subject is rife in meaning and rich in historical detail. Experts from many disciplines have spent long hours pouring over each one, holding it to this light and that to see what is reflected, to discover what may be learned when it is held in a slightly different way, perceived from a new side, looked at from a new angle.

The breadth of writing and debate about colonialism, Eurocentrism, capitalism, and modernity means that I cannot do any one of them justice here. I feel vindicated, however, because this book is not specifically about any one of these difficult subjects. Still, each one is an integral part of historical archaeology, and I cannot turn my back on them. All of them haunt historical archaeology, trailing the field like four quiet shadows. They exist at every site, on every laboratory table, within every map and chart made. Sometimes one is pushed to the forefront to be the subject of analysis. At other times, they all may hang back like ghostwriters, ever present but unacknowledged and unnamed. Regardless, each subject pervades historical archaeology and so must be acknowledged, understood, and challenged.

Given the great size, multiple dimensions, and diverse historical peculiarities of the four haunts of historical archaeology, I would be foolhardy to attempt a thorough analysis of each, though each is central to the field. My plan here is merely to reach an understanding of each topic, to demonstrate how each fits into historical archaeology. To accomplish this task, I have only two goals. First, I must define each one of the haunts so that it has relevance to historical archaeology. It would do little good for me to develop, for example, a view of capitalism that only makes sense to political scientists or to economists; historical archaeologists would still be called upon to discover how capitalism is meaningful to their research. Second, I must put my understanding of each haunt into language that is consistent with the mutualist perspective. Both tasks are made easier in that colonialism, Eurocentrism, capitalism, and modernity are not vague, mystical things that float around above our heads. Instead, each one incorporates a complex set of relations between real men and women.

COLONIALISM: HISTORICAL ARCHAEOLOGY'S CONSTANT COMPANION

Historical archaeology has never been without colonialism. When Frank Setzler (1943:218) summarized archaeological research in the United States between 1930 and 1942, he made reference to what he termed "historical-archaeology." Writing before his colleagues formalized historical archaeology in the late 1960s, Setzler was uncomfortable with his newly coined term. To assuage his distress, he suggested (in a tiny, self-conscious footnote) that "perhaps Colonial-Archaeology would be a better term."

In using the term "historical-archaeology," Setzler traversed the spongy ground later trod by so many historical archaeologists who attempted to define their field. In equating historical archaeology with colonialism, he was not really off terra firma, because many archaeologists would forever associate historical archaeology with colonialism. J. C. Harrington (1952), writing in an influential overview of American archaeology, legitimized the connection by identifying colonial archaeology to be a "major subdivision" of historical archaeology. Harrington's (1952:336) definition of colonialism was so benign and noncontroversial that it could be accepted by even the most radical historical archaeologist. For Harrington, colonialism merely involved the transplantation of "a group, or community, having a common European culture," to "a new and unfamiliar environment." The so-called parent culture continued to exercise control over the colony "by political ties, visits to the homeland, and immigration." Because the subject matter of colonial archaeology was the colony, colonial archaeology was simply the archaeology of European places outside Europe.

Since Setzler's and Harrington's day, most historical archaeologists have accepted the idea that historical archaeology and colonialism are inexorably linked. The idea also has reached the general public, and people today do not find it startling to hear about archaeologists conducting research at colonial sites around the world. Colonial archaeology has become commonplace, accepted, and uncontested. At the same time, colonial archaeology has become routine, taken for granted, and even potentially boring. Thus, it is possible to publish a book on the archaeology of French colonialism in Illinois (Walthall 1991), for example, and never once have colonialism itself explored, examined, or taken apart. The book's many authors simply considered colonialism to be a historical category, an accepted and unquestioned part of the modern era. They segmented colonialism into periods, but left behind the character, scope, significance, and mutability of colonialism as a process. Their abandonment of colonialism tells readers that the topic is so well understood that discussion is unnecessary. Historical archaeologists know that colonialism refers to the transplantation of Europeans to new lands, and that it involves the interaction of Europeans with non-Europeans. Deetz's (1977:5) well-heeled, almost universally accepted definition of historical archaeology supports this viewpoint (see Chapter 1).

Colonial archaeology is typically devoted to the study of Europeans who ventured forth into the world. Archaeologists study their buildings and their ways of wresting subsistence from unfamiliar environments. They find particular interest in the kinds of artifacts Europeans made and used. Many historical archaeologists use their research to study acculturation (Rubertone 1989:33). These studies, however, often stand in marked contrast to colonial studies per se. In colonial studies, researchers focus on the European's adaptation to their new surroundings. Because these surroundings comprised both natural and cultural landscapes, historical archaeologists often emphasize the European responses to their new situations. Their research begins with the Europeans and expands outward. Conversely, investigators interested in acculturation typically concentrate on native responses to the European invasion. Their research begins with the aboriginal residents of a site or region. Significantly, though, acculturation studies also require Europeans. The indigenous peoples are usually seen as reacting to European encroachment.

Colonial studies may ignore the natives altogether. It is enlightening that the book on French colonialism (Walthall 1991) I mentioned above derived from a symposium entitled the "Conference on French Colonial Archaeology in the Illinois Country." The conference participants who explored Native American topics had their papers collected into a second volume, unattached to the first and distributed by a different publisher (Walthall and Emerson 1992). The effect of this separation is to remove the natives from the colonialists, to segregate the archaeology of European colonials from that of non-Europeans, an artificial separation that mimicks John Muir's (Wolfe 1938:320) description of most people: "undiffused, separate, and rigidly alone like marbles of polished stone, touching but separate."

For years, archaeologists believed that acculturation, as a measure of the impact of European colonialism on native peoples, could be understood simply by examining the natives' artifacts (Quimby and Spoehr 1951; White 1975). The idea was simple. If you excavated a native village occupied after the residents had met Europeans, you would find several artifacts that reflect the Europeans' influence. If you spread the artifacts across a laboratory table, you would notice that some of them looked like traditional native objects—chipped stone arrowheads, ground stone axes, baked clay potsherds, and one or two drilled shells. You also would notice that some of the things looked as if Europeans had manufactured them. This group might include silver bracelets, brass kettle fragments, brightly colored glass beads, and iron knife blades. If you looked closely, you might also observe that several objects seem to contain elements of both native and European cultures. Tubular clothing ornaments fashioned from brass kettle pieces, triangular arrowheads expertly chipped from green bottle glass, and triangular pendants made from melted glass beads would all fall into this category. The specific artifacts and the methods of manufacture and modification would vary depending upon the region and the date, but generally, these three kinds of artifacts can be identified at sites throughout the colonial world. The general similarity of artifact categories suggested that they could be used to chart the progress of acculturation. In this manner, archaeologists could contribute to the anthropological understanding of acculturation, with their angle being the physical side of the process.

Several archaeologists worked on acculturation, but George Quimby and Alexander Spoehr (1951) created its most famous archaeological model. As modified by John White (1975:161), a few of the artifact categories in the Quimby–Spoehr model are:

A.1. New types of artifacts received for which there is a native
       counterpart.

A.2. New types of artifacts received where there is no native counterpart.
A.3. New types of artifacts made from native materials but copying introduced models:
    A.3.a. Where the techniques are introduced along with the new artifacts.
    A.3.b. Where the techniques come from within the recipient group.
A.4. New types of artifacts where the introduced model is decorated after the native manner.

Using this framework, the possibilities for quantification are endless. Any archaeologist can add more categories to produce finer distinctions, and some categories can be dropped (Fontana 1978). In either case, the model is seductive. It says that archaeologists can gain immense interperative power about complex cultural processes by separating artifacts into categories. The categories can tell us something profound about the speed and degree of a native people's acculturation. In essence, the categories measure the "effectiveness" of colonization. Quimby (1966:3) himself used the scale to measure the Europeans' destruction of the native cultures in the western Great Lakes. When they finished, what remained was "only an empty shell of what had existed at the time of discovery." For Quimby (1966), the Native Americans who lived during the "Early Historic Period, 1610–1670," were much less acculturated—much less changed by European colonialism—than those men and women who were alive during the "Late Historic Period, 1760–1820." The artifacts unearthed at sites in the western Great Lakes show this steady advance of colonialism-in-the-form-of-material-things. Quimby's quantification of artifacts presented a frightening, though efficient, view of European influence. To witness their all-pervasive power, all archaeologists need do is to create the categories, separate the artifacts, and then sit back and measure the acculturation.

What the Quimby–Spoehr acculturation model professes to reveal about the native condition may partly account for the general unwillingness of most historical archaeologists to dwell on the process of colonization itself. The model tells us that colonization is easy. The artifacts represent the way in which native peoples—wherever they may be found—were incorporated into European ways of technology and eventually into European ways of thought, action, and being. The more native artifacts found in an archaeological collection, the more "traditional" the people. The greater the percentage of European objects at a native village, the greater the acculturation. The artifacts are visible, tangible reminders that native men, women, and children felt the very real effects of colonialism. This apparent ease in interpretation may be why most historical archaeologists do not often write explicitly about colonialism: there is no need to; it is a straightforward and relatively simple process to understand.

But is that all there is to the archaeology of colonialism? Europeans move in, set up towns, forts, and trading posts, and begin to influence the natives. The natives may try to resist, and often do for a while, but the artifacts imply that true resistance is pointless. Native men and women inexorably become acculturated. Given this scenario, played out throughout the colonial universe, it would seem that only the smallest, particular details of individual colonial situations remain to be written: How did acculturation happen to a certain group of people, how long did acculturation take, and what finally happened to the acculturated people?

If these questions summarized colonialism, then historical archaeologists would be the intellectual stars of colonial study. Historians, economists, political scientists, and others would hungrily flock to historical archaeology's doorstep. We would not be able to keep these thirsty scholars away. However, since nonarchaeologists are usually not found filling the seats at archaeological conferences and eagerly buying site reports, we can assume that this is not the case. Historical archaeologists, as Schuyler (1988) so ruefully observed, are not sought out by scholars in other disciplines, not even by colonial historians. We must imagine, therefore, that colonialism involved more than the simple transfer of material objects.

This conclusion is not new and I cannot take credit for offering any great insight here. Years ago, for example, archaeologist Ian Brown (1979) studied the eighteenth-century contacts between Native Americans and French colonials in the Lower Mississippi Valley. Brown argued that the Quimby–Spoehr model assumed too much historical continuity. In order for the scheme to work, we must be willing to assume that the function of an object remained the same over many years. A brass kettle, for instance, was a European import natives could use to cook corn (one Quimby–Spoehr category). In a couple of years, however, that same kettle could be cut up and made into ornaments for clothing (another Quimby–Spoehr category). Acculturation, if it could be seen at all in the artifacts, could only be observed at the precise moment the native man, woman, or child lost or discarded the kettle pieces or, for that matter, the brass kettle ornament.

Though Brown's practical criticisms of the Quimby–Spoehr model showed its severe weaknesses, his comment about the model's assumptions was most important. Brown (1979:118) said that the Quimby–Spoehr model assumed that all native peoples reacted in the same manner to European contact. If you can make the model work among the Chitimacha of Louisiana, then you can use it for the New Zealand Maoris, the Alaskan Inuits, and the Tasmanians. Acculturation is acculturation. In making this comment, Brown identified the key problem hidden within the Quimby–Spoehr model.

In another Native American example, focused on the seventeenth-century Narragansetts, Patricia Rubertone (1989) lit the way for historical archaeologists studying colonialism. The Narragansetts, farmers and hunters living in what is today Rhode Island, felt the brunt of English colonialism beginning in 1620 when they met their first Puritans (Nassaney 1989:79). Rubertone turns on its head the conceptual foundation of the Quimby–Spoehr model by exploring the meaning of wampum, a common colonial artifact. Tiny cylindrical beads cut from shells, wampum was a small but immensely powerful object in the fabric of colonial New England. Seventeenth-century Native Americans traditionally used wampum to cement political alliances and to pay tribute. As English strength grew in the land they boldly dubbed "New England," they adopted the native tradition of requiring tribute from their less powerful neighbors. The English quickly developed an interest in getting tribute from the Narragansetts. When the Narragansetts learned of the English designs on them, they realized they had several courses of action available. They could attack the English settlements in open and obvious defiance. They could try to create alliances with the other tribute-paying native groups, thereby presenting a united front against English domination. They could even try to talk their way out of paying. When viewed archaeologically, it would seem that the Narragansetts decided to pay, because their seventeenth-century village sites contain few pieces of wampum. In the light of these findings, we can only assume that the place to find Narragansett wampum is at English colonial sites.

This tale of English domination rings true. We know that the English were powerful in "New England" and that the Narragansetts faced the same dilemma as natives around the world when

confronting the Europeans' deadly technology. They could accultur-
ate or die. Rather than accepting this facile version of colonialism,
however, Rubertone (1989:41–42) looked at a Narragansett cemetery instead of a village site. The cemetery told another story. There
she found over 2,000 wampum beads, with 95 percent of them coming from just 4 of the 56 burials. In contrast, archaeologists excavating an earlier Narragansett cemetery unearthed only 52 wampum
beads in 59 graves. The difference in the presence of wampum at the
two sites is striking. Following the "rules" of acculturation, we
would expect that the presence of a "traditional" item like wampum
would decrease over time, not increase. The earlier cemetery should
contain more wampum, not less. What can the difference mean?

Rubertone (1989:42) interpreted the increase in wampum at
the more recent cemetery to be an indication of native resistance,
the antithesis of acculturation. The presence of the wampum in the
cemetery used at the time the English had increased their demands
on the Narragansetts may be perceived as a tangible statement of
political strength. Narragansetts deposited the wampum with deceased members of their village—possibly revered leaders—and in
doing so they also took the valuable shell beads out of circulation.
Wampum in graves could not be used for wampum-as-tribute. According to Rubertone (1989:43), the Narragansetts' ritual use of
wampum "challenged the role of colonial authority in Native New
England." Rubertone turned the tables on acculturation studies and
colonial archaeology by looking at artifact distributions in a different light.

It would be inaccurate to imply that historical archaeologists
universally employ the Quimby–Spoehr model to understand colonial times. I do not wish to misrepresent or to oversimplify the field.
Though some researchers did use the model in the past, it serves
today more as a teaching tool. The Quimby–Spoehr model is a mechanism to demonstrate the seductive appeal of overly simplistic
methods of interpreting complex historical connections and interactions between culturally diverse men and women. Rubertone's study
of the Narragansett cemetery is useful because she demonstrated
that colonialism is ultimately a mutualist endeavor. Colonialism,
seen through the archaeological lens, is neither straightforward nor
easy to comprehend. The Narragansetts devised an innovative way
to use their wampum within their historical milieu. By honoring
their deceased companions, they kept the valuable little shells out of
English hands. The new use for wampum was not enacted because

of a change in the natural environment or because of some technological innovation. Narragansetts did not learn how to make wampum beads just in time to put them in the more recent cemetery. The
increase in wampum cannot be technologically explained. On the
contrary, the Narragansetts consciously created a use for wampum
in response to the English colonizers who had stretched their net
across the Atlantic. The modified use of wampum was mutualist to
the core. It represented interactions among Narragansetts, between
Narragansetts and their dead ancestors, and between Narragansetts and Europeans.

Rubertone's study showed that colonialism is not a one-sided
process. Colonialism cannot be understood strictly as the transfer of
ideas and objects from Europeans to non-Europeans, from "us" to
"them." Algerian scholar Frantz Fanon (1968:102) expressed this
view most clearly and unambiguously in his famous line: "Europe is
literally the creation of the Third World." Europeans could not have
built their massive empires and perceived themselves as masters of
the world without the labors of the many non-Europeans who inhabited the world.

Even the notion of "culture" has colonialist overtones (Dirks
1992:3). In traversing the world, colonialists had to believe that
individual clusters of peoples existed as discrete cultures in order
that they might be easily set aside as "other." Exotic peoples had to
be categorized as "foreign" in order to be available for what were
often the horrors of colonization. Dominican father Bartolomé de
Las Casas (1992:6), in his chilling *A Short Account of the Destruction
of the Indies,* first published in 1542, refers to the work of the Spanish as "the atrocities which go under the name of 'conquests.'"

Colonialism is merely a consequence of imperialism—all those
ideas, attitudes, and beliefs that allow an empire to justify its rule
over a distant land (Said 1993:9). We must not lose sight of the idea
that archaeologists and anthropologists carry with them the bag-
gage of colonialism (Caufield 1974; Gough 1968). That archaeology
can be used to subvert history in the effort to create a past that
proves the "right" of colonialism is shown perhaps most dramatically by the ways the Nazis presented prehistory both at home and
in the lands they conquered (Arnold 1990; McCann 1990; Mikolajczyk 1990).

At its very base, colonialism is men and women from one place
confronting men and women in another place. These interactions
created wonder, fear, apprehension, misunderstanding, cooperation,

and a host of other emotions and reactions. Each contact was unique and transforming. Nonetheless, "with very few exceptions, Europeans felt powerfully superior to virtually all of the peoples they encountered, even those like the Aztecs who had technological and organizational skills that Europeans could recognize and greatly admire" (Greenblatt 1991:9). Why did this paradox exist? Why did these Europeans feel superior to people who were, in several ways, wiser about the world than the men and women who walked the dirty streets of Paris, Munich, or London? The answer begins with Eurocentrism.

EUROCENTRISM: FRIEND OR FOE?

Is historical archaeology Eurocentric? Definitions of the field suggest that it is indeed overwhelmingly fixated on things European. Historical archaeologists usually make it clear that their field is about Europeans in some fashion, starting with colonialism. For instance, Harrington (1952:336) linked historical archaeology with "people of European origin." Schuyler (1970) and Deetz (1977, 1991) said that historical archaeology focuses on the spread of Europeans into the non-European world. Even Fontana (1965:61), who categorized American historic sites on the basis of their association with Native Americans, defined the field as "archaeology carried out in sites which contain material evidence of non-Indian culture or concerning which there is contemporary non-Indian documentary record."

Based on these comments—and I could cite others with ease—we would have to conclude that historical archaeology is indeed Eurocentric. It seems that we cannot separate historical archaeology from Europe. But what does it really mean to say that historical archaeology is Eurocentric?

Eurocentrism pervades archaeological research in ways that are scarcely obvious. When I write, for example, that historical archaeology focuses on the world created "after A.D. 1415," I am being Eurocentric. I am making a Eurocentric association by choosing to calculate time in relation to Christ's birth. Though Christ was not European, we can agree that millions of Europeans have adopted the cause of Christianity. In a sense, Christ is a naturalized European. As Samir Amin (1989:90) wrote, Christianity is "the principal factor in the maintenance of European cultural unity." Instead of using

Christ's supposed birthdate as my temporal reference point, I could have conceivably used some other event from which to calculate time—Mohammed's flight from Mecca, the death of Buddha, or the fall of Troy (Russell 1994). I chose, however, to be conventional and to use Christ's birth, probably around 4 B.C., as my reference point. A universally approved, worldwide system of dating would solve my problem, but we would be called upon to answer several questions. Do we calculate years in relation to the cycle of the sun or of the moon? How do we decide when the world was created? If we cannot decide precisely when the earth began, where do we start Year 1? Who decides what point in time, which event, is most significant?

Many archaeologists have chosen to solve the problem by using the present as their reference point. Using this convention, I could say that historical archaeologists study the period that began 579 years ago, or "before present." Of course, I can only say this in 1994. In 1995, I would have to say "580 years before present"; in the year 2000, I would have to say "585 years before present," and so on. This system eases the problem of using Christianity as a reference point, but it relies on a 365-day year. Moreover, the "present" in "before present" is constantly moving. I could use the convention of radio-carbon dating and consider the "present" to be 1950. Since that is the date of my birth, however, it seems a bit presumptuous to reckon time in relation to it.

Locational associations also can be quietly Eurocentric (McGee 1991). When archaeologists record the longitude of a site, they give an unconscious nod to London. They recognize that the prime meridian (longitude zero) passes through the Royal Greenwich Observatory. In agreeing with this usage, they support the belief that the world begins in London. Maps of the world are usually drawn with the prime meridian running down the center, right where the eye falls first. All points outside first England and then Europe fall on the peripheries of our sight, at the edge of the world.

In placing Europe at the center, we have done more than simply created ways in which to compose maps and to reckon time. Our intention to perceive Europe at the center of things has even shaped our perception of the past. Eurocentrism has had many effects on archaeology. For example, in his survey of archaeological atlases, Chris Scarre (1990) found that authors and editors of the six English-language books he surveyed invariably gave prominence to European prehistory. Europe assumed the most important position in the texts, typically receiving about 30 percent of the total coverage. Non-European prehistory was given fewer, less prominent pages. North America received 14 percent of the pages, the Far East (again, a Eurocentric term) only 10 percent, and sub-Saharan Africa only a paltry 5 percent. Readers of these compendia would understandably reach the conclusion that much happened in prehistoric Europe that is worthy of attention, but that places like southern Africa or Asia were relatively quiet, unimportant, and therefore uninteresting.

The labors of Scarre and other archaeologists to discover the underlying Eurocentric assumptions of their field undoubtedly have their basis in current events and attitudes. Journalists and pundits of the popular media have recently discovered Eurocentrism. Their news stories and exposés often oppose Eurocentrism to multiculturalism. Eurocentrism and multiculturalism are usually portrayed as philosophical enemies in a cosmic struggle that is nothing short of a "war against Western culture" (Kimball 1990:xii). The battlegrounds in this war are often the public schools, where the armies of the right and the left fight for control of the curriculum (Bennett 1984; Bloom 1987; Gless and Smith 1992). Eurocentrist soldiers usually argue that the world has been built into a gloriously strong edifice largely through the hard work and rigid standards of the enlightened West. They believe that schoolchildren should be exposed to the works of authors and artists who have helped to create the West and who have shaped our perceptions of it. It is from these masters, many of whom are European-American males, that impressionable children will learn valuable lessons for life. Proponents in the United States say that universal knowledge of these great works will lead to a utopian, truly democratic future where all social classes and ethnic groups will share equally in the bounties of what they perceive as the greatness of America (Hirsch 1987: 11–12). Multiculturalists take a different view. They argue that the West was actually built by the sweat and toil of thousands of men and women, most of whom are today largely forgotten. In the multiculturalist view, works of vernacular art and literature have much to teach us (Hughes 1992:399–400). Often self-educated men and women living in the developing world or outside the upper echelons of Western society produced many of the classics. For multiculturalists, these are the masters to whom children should be exposed in the classroom. For some, the debate between Eurocentrism and multiculturalism is about academics and syllabi. For others, the curricular controversy is simply one aspect in the survival of the West (Erickson 1992:105).

Despite the often vociferous debate between Eurocentrists and multiculturalists, Eurocentrism is more than simply thinking about Europe as the center of the universe. The term carries a much deeper significance than what is implied by the haggling that has occurred—often for political reasons—over the public school curriculum or the continual prominence of the West. Eurocentrism has important meanings that relate to the beliefs and attitudes that shape the modern world (Gathercole and Lowenthal 1990; McGee 1991). The variety of meanings that exist within Eurocentrism shows that the concept is decidedly complex. Some experts see Eurocentrism as an ideological rationale that accompanies the expansion of capitalism into the noncapitalist world (Blaut 1970; Slater 1975). In this view, Eurocentrism provides the internal logic of an economic survival-of-the-fittest doctrine. Others see Eurocentrism as a belief in racial superiority, a kind of white man's burden that establishes an "us-and-them" mentality (Fanon 1968; Gathercole and Lowenthal 1990:7–8). For these thinkers, Eurocentrism makes it acceptable—and in fact even reasonable—to place "us" above "them." Whomever "they" are at the moment—Bantus, Ojibwas, Ibos, Tupinambás, Chinese—is largely irrelevant.

Regardless of which meaning we wish to scrutinize under the intense light of analysis, Eurocentrism is not a cogent doctrine or a single line of reasoning. It is not a unified belief system that contains a recipe for living. Instead, Eurocentrism is a distorted perspective that claims that the only way non-Western societies can survive is through imitating the West (Amin 1989:vii).

Called "Europeocentrism" by eighteenth-century French philosopher Jacques Bénigne de Bossuet (Gerbi 1973:43), the Eurocentric worldview first gained expression during the Renaissance. The clearest expression of Eurocentrism, however, rang out during the French Revolution when French patriots staunchly argued that every individual in the world "has an inalienable right to freedom and equality" (Boggs 1990:14). In this view, the acceptance of European faith, reason, and science would lead to total liberation and moral perfection. Eurocentrism became not just a belief in Europe, but "a pervasive condition of thought" to which many men and women around the world became party (Rabasa 1993:18). Eurocentrism became a universalist doctrine, not because it sought to situate all peoples along a single evolutionary track toward equality, but because it affected people everywhere in the world (Rabasa 1993:6).

Archaeologists have begun to cast light on the first and most obvious face of Eurocentrism, that which shows how Eurocentrism perverted archaeological research. Scarre's (1990) examination of archaeological atlases is a clear example of the affect of Eurocentrism on archaeology. We need not look too far to find more sinister examples of the ways in which people have used archaeological remains as a tool for promoting Europe at the expense of others. One striking example comes from Great Zimbabwe in southeast Africa.

Great Zimbabwe consists of a series of intricate, cut-stone ruins set in place without benefit of mortar. Though at least 12 buildings remain, perhaps the most impressive among them are the Hill Ruin, with its stone walls ingeniously interwoven with natural boulders; the Elliptical Building, a circular enclosure measuring about 61 by 92 m (200 by 300 ft); and the Conical Tower, a massive stone edifice measuring 5 m (18 ft) in diameter and 9 m (30 ft) tall. In one spot, the outer wall of the Elliptical Building is 5 m (17 ft) thick and 11 m (35 ft) high and decorated with stones placed in two rows of chevrons (Garlake 1978:88).

Sixteenth-century Portuguese explorers were the first Europeans to learn of Great Zimbabwe. Upon seeing the ruins, they immediately attributed them to either Prester John, the mysterious Christian king who was supposed to have lived in Ethiopia, or King Solomon. A German missionary first told the colonial British about the ruins in 1873. They followed the lead of the Portuguese and assumed that Africans could not have built the magnificent structures. When diamond king Cecil Rhodes outfitted the first archaeological expedition to Great Zimbabwe in 1891, his investigators assumed that the Phoenicians had built the settlement (Davidson 1966:60; Garlake 1978:34). Archaeologists now know that the Phoenicians, King Solomon, and Prester John had nothing to do with Great Zimbabwe. Excavations revealed that indigenous Africans built the settlement sometime around A.D. 1200 and that they maintained it as an important commercial center until the early 1600s.

Why are today's interpretations of Great Zimbabwe at such variance with those of the not-so-recent past? Can we simply chalk the difference up to the advances of archaeological science? Part of the answer is undeniably that archaeological thought has grown more sophisticated since Rhodes sent his explorers into the field in the late nineteenth century. More to the point, however, we must wonder what preconceived notions those excavators carried with them. Clearly, their Eurocentrism, undoubtedly tinged with racism, kept them from admitting that Great Zimbabwe was not a piece of European history in a foreign place, but an element of indigenous African history. Great Zimbabwe was built by Africans for Africans.

Eurocentrism translates to the way individuals treat others. But Eurocentrism was not an unstoppable force against which non-Europeans had no defense. In fact, many of the native resistance movements that occurred in modern history were in direct conflict with Eurocentrism. For example, historian Gregory Dowd (1992) masterfully documented the ways in which numerous Native American prophets in the central United States drew together their diverse peoples to resist the aggression of the newly formed American government. These spiritual men and women—Tenskwatawa, Tecumseh, the Wyoming Woman, and others—toiled to create a pan-Indian sense of "us" that could stand in marked opposition to the European "them." Their strength came not from anything the Europeans gave them but from their traditional, spiritual roots. In an important sense, though, their organization derived from Eurocentrism. Thus, we must learn to ask not only what is *included* in Eurocentrism, but also what is *excluded* and why (Said 1993:67). A Native American vision of spiritual rebirth and the return of traditional power was not part of a European worldview. Nonetheless, these elements of native resistance made Eurocentrism directly pertinent to the American settlers who sought to control Native American land. Without their Eurocentric attitudes, Europeans on the frontier may have had nothing to fear from the indigenous peoples who inhabited the dark forests that surrounded their tiny, wooden cabins and forts.

Eurocentrism and anti-Eurocentrism—sometimes called "nativism"—existed as an integral part of the interactions of real men and women in the world studied by historical archaeologists. This unshakable presence means that historical archaeologists must confront Eurocentrism to understand its force and power in the creation of modern times.

THE POWERFUL FACE OF CAPITALISM

In writing about colonialism and Eurocentrism, I have carefully avoided the word "capitalism." For many, my omission may seem odd, for if they have read widely, they will realize that historical archaeology and capitalism are intricately interwoven. In fact, I do not believe that the two can be separated. One need only survey recent statements of historical archaeologists to discover that this is so. Russell Handsman (1985:2), for example, wrote that "historical archaeology has always been about capitalism." Mark Leone and

Parker Potter (1988:19) stated in the introduction to their book *The Recovery of Meaning* that "whether or not historical archaeology is to be an archaeology of the emergence and development of capitalism has been settled in the affirmative." In her recent assessment of the field, Barbara Little (1994:16–23) devoted a long discussion to the archaeology of capitalism. In addition, I have repeatedly stated that capitalism is a proper focus for historical archaeology (Orser 1987:122, 1988b:315, 1992:23). These comments show that several historical archaeologists agree that their field concerns capitalism in some way (see also Leone 1995).

To understand the close relationship between historical archaeology and capitalism, we must understand capitalism itself. Unfortunately, this is not an easy task. In studying capitalism, we enter a world of dense jargon and often tortured reasoning. As if this were not enough, the very subject of capitalism is ideologically charged. It is difficult to write or to think about capitalism in a neutral way. All citizens of the United States, for instance, are expected to revere capitalism or to face the charge of being un-American. Members of emerging nations are supposed to look toward capitalism for their ultimate economic survival.

In addition to the effects of capitalism on the present, capitalism is difficult to understand fully in history. Capitalism was not static, for it wore many different faces in the past. Historical archaeologists must strive to understand these historical masks so that they may fully appreciate capitalism's impact.

We must first recognize that capitalism is foremost "an economic system in which those who provide the capital control the production of goods" (Curtin 1990:47). Though "capital" usually refers to money, the term also includes tools, machinery, fields, mills, factories, and everything else needed for production. These necessary things are owned by specific men and women—the "capitalists." One important hallmark of capitalism is that the men, women, and children who actually perform the work for the capitalists sell their labor as if it were a commodity. The capitalist does not need to coerce the people to work because the economic conditions are such that the men and women must sell their labor in order to survive.

Experts generally agree that capitalism had two major historical forms: a merchant phase and an industrial phase. The merchant phase, often termed "merchant capitalism," is the period typically thought to extend from about the fifteenth to the eighteenth century. It was during this phase that the agents of Europe's superpowers—

the Netherlands, Spain, Portugal, England, and France—spread out into the world, traveling great distances and often undergoing immense hardships to procure new capital. "Industrial capitalism" witnessed the Industrial Revolution, the creation of huge factories and industrial complexes, and the employment of men, women, and even children in often deplorable conditions (Desai 1983:65). This is the period that existed in the world until very recently. Today, a third phase of capitalism is unfolding. This phase is often described as "postindustrial" because much of today's production is not performed in factories or in mills. In fact, many people (like myself) do not "produce" anything but information. They toil not in steamy steel mills or lint-choked cotton factories but in air-conditioned offices at computer screens. Still, their production is a part of the economy in which they live.

The aspects of capitalism that were controversial in the past remain so today. Social scientists have not agreed on capitalism's precise historical periods, how different economic classes were formed, the role that class struggle plays in capitalist development, and the amount of influence the economy has over society. Scholars cannot even agree on exactly when capitalism started (Hilton 1976a:145–147).

Disagreements about capitalism often involve comparing the ideas of Adam Smith with those of Karl Marx. Smith's *An Inquiry into the Nature and Causes of the Wealth of Nations,* first published in 1776, stressed the power of the free market system and advised governments to keep their hands off business. Smith believed in the power of economies. When the economy works, the rest of a society generally runs smoothly as well. Conversely, Karl Marx said in *Das Kapital,* the first volume of which was published in 1867, that capitalism contained inherent injustices. He predicted that one day the huge mass of exploited laborers would rise up against their owners and create a society where the tools, factories, mills, and machinery would be owned by everyone. The ideas of Marx and Smith hover over today's economics, swirling in and out of vogue, endlessly debated and discussed in countless venues (Fry 1992; Roemer 1988).

A key characteristic of capitalism is the kinds of relations it establishes between people. As a serious student of capitalism, Marx provided perhaps the most insightful examination of these relationships. In his famous preface to *A Contribution to the Critique of Political Economy,* first published in 1859, Marx (1970:20–21) laid out the basic elements of production that helped to create and maintain an economy. Scholars have come to know these elements as a society's "infrastructure," or "the combination of the different material and social conditions which enable a society's members to produce and reproduce the material means of their social existence" (Godelier 1986:130). The infrastructure includes the environmental conditions in which people live, the "forces of production," and "the relations of production." The productive forces include the raw materials, tools, and techniques needed for production. They also include a people's mental and physical capacities to satisfy their wants and needs, because the tools are useless without the knowledge to use them. The relations of production are the social interactions people must cultivate to get things produced (Conway 1987:53–55; Rader 1979:12). The productive forces and the relations of production are distinct but never separate. They are always articulated, with the relations of production dominating (Godelier 1986:131). This domination occurs because the relations determine who works where and how the surplus production is divided.

The "mode of production" is the union between the forces and the relations of production. Though a formidable term, a mode of production is simply "a specific, historically occurring set of social relations [the relations of production] through which labor is deployed to wrest energy from nature by means of tools, skills, organization, and knowledge [the forces of production]" (Wolf 1982:75). Men and women work together to create relationships using what they have, what they know, who they know, and what they can make.

Like many of his contemporaries, Marx was a cultural evolutionist who believed that human societies progressed in a series of stages. Some cultural evolutionists based their ideas about human progress on improvements in technology. In their view, societies were better able to survive in the world—to progress—when they left their stone axes behind and learned to make axes from bronze. Their descendants replaced their bronze implements with iron tools, and so on until today. Marx founded his evolutionary stages on the more complex idea of production. He argued that human societies progressed through a number of modes of production, which he called "Asiatic, ancient, feudal, and modern bourgeois" (Marx 1970:21). Scholars of various economic and political stripes have spent years poring over Marx's writings in the attempt to learn what Marx really meant when he used these terms. Even during his lifetime, experts debated the meanings of his modes of production, and they still do so today. They have looked everywhere for tiny clues and bits and pieces of revelation in his copious and often confused writings. Some have even argued that his modes of production never existed (see, for example, Cohen 1978:134–174; Conway 1987:71–81; Elster 1985:303–305; Hindess and Hirst 1975; Honderich 1982; McMurtry 1978:188–239).

Academic debates over the truth of Marx's ideas are perhaps intellectually stimulating, but they hold little relevance here. It does not matter to me whether Marx was right or wrong about the individual modes of production. Twentieth-century anthropologists reject crude cultural evolutionism and there is no reason to accept Marx's antiquated view of it. Whether he understood the many nuances and subtle peculiarities of each historical phase he identified is also unimportant. The value of the mode of production concept lies not in its ability to create classifications but in its power to emphasize the importance of social relations in human production (Wolf 1982:76). We may easily envision the mode of production concept simply as "a way of thinking about relationships" (Wolf 1982:401), with the various modes simply being "a cluster of relations" (Ollman 1971:15). We also must be careful not to bind ourselves to the narrow view that production refers only to the creation of tangible "things." We may easily imagine that production also includes intangible things—ideas, attitudes, perceptions, and beliefs (Nowak 1983:137–152). These invisible products can forge powerful relations between individual men and women though they may have nothing whatsoever to do with the production of tangible objects. A priesthood striving to maintain its theocracy can be thought to *produce* obedience through the rituals and formal ceremonies that believers feel compelled for spiritual reasons to perform. We may even say that kinship constitutes a relation of production (Godelier 1975). Eurocentrism is clearly a relation.

The mode of production concept is a useful tool for studying societies that are described in ethnographic and historical sources. The use of the concept, however, is slightly more problematic in prehistoric archaeology. Archaeology was still in its infancy when Marx wrote most of his early works on political economy. In the late 1840s, when Marx was conducting his early research, Jacques Boucher de Crevêcoeur de Perthes had already published five volumes of his *De la Création: essai sur l'origine et la progression des êtres* (1838–1841). These volumes were coldly received (Daniel 1976:59) and no one knows whether Marx read them as he toiled in the British Museum. Marx (1967:180) made reference to correlating past "economic epochs" to tools made of stone, bronze, and iron, but he made no attempt to link his mode of production to prehistory. Perhaps he realized how little he actually knew about the new field of archaeology.

Australian-born archaeologist V. Gordon Childe (1946) introduced the mode of production to archaeologists in *Scotland before the Scots.* Childe used productive forces and relations of production as a framework to understand the ways the ancients had created prehistoric Scotland. He believed that archaeologists could learn a great deal by focusing on the "material forces of production—tools and machines—together with, of course, natural resources and the skills to operate them" (Childe 1947:72). Whether Childe was right that the mode of production concept can be used in prehistory is still a matter of considerable debate (McGuire 1992; Spriggs 1984). For us, it is enough that Marx used the mode of production concept to analyze the kinds of societies historical archaeologists study: literate, modern, capitalist ones.

Capitalism has at least two historical elements that have important relevance to historical archaeology. These concern the beginnings of capitalism and the ways in which the agents of capitalism spread their economic regime throughout the world.

The ways in which peoples across the globe came to capitalism is hotly debated. The capitalist mode of production grew out of an earlier mode called "feudalism" in Europe, or the so-called Asiatic mode of production in Asia. Wolf (1982:79–88) referred to each as a "tributary mode of production." In such a system, the people are dominated by a military, landowning aristocracy (Hilton 1976b:30). Experts do not agree on this definition because various forms of tributary societies can be found throughout the world. History is complex and individualized and there is no reason to imagine that what happened in one place should be mimicked in another. In any case, capitalism was not simply a more complex kind of feudalism. Capitalism was a "qualitatively new phenomenon" (Wolf 1982:85) that represented a "decisive break in world history" (Amin 1989:1); it was something new, innovative, and distinct.

The decisive break between capitalism and other economic systems is easy to imagine in the colonized world. When Quimby (1966) excavated copper kettles and brass gun parts at Native American sites in the western Great Lakes, the objects did more than simply signal the past presence of Europeans. They also served as visible

indicators of capitalism. They were tangible symbols that capitalism, in one of its many historical forms, was visited upon native men
and women who had never before imagined that such a system could
exist. When pioneer historical archaeologists met to discuss their
findings, they most certainly intended to compare one another's
gunflints, brass kettle parts, and blue and white glass beads. In
making these comparisons, however, they were really telling one
another that they had noticed something dramatic at their sites.
Capitalism had arrived. Soil layers at many sites revealed broken
glass bottles and fragments of glazed plates lying above unglazed
potsherds and chipped stone tools. What caused the difference between the layers was not simply the presence of Europeans. The
difference was caused by Europeans who were in the world to obtain
capital. They were the agents of capitalism.

The transition from precapitalism to capitalism is, of course,
much more difficult to see in Europe, and precisely when it occurred
has been debated (Hilton 1976c; Katz 1989). At the heart of the
controversy is the transition of men and women from feudal peasan-
try to agrarian capitalism. This transformation entails knotty issues
involving the rise of farming for profit and the development of class
relations. Historians on both sides of the Atlantic have considered
these questions at great length and in precise detail (Aston and
Philpin 1985; Hahn and Prude 1985; Kulikoff 1992). We can only
regret, perhaps, that they almost never mention the material side of
the transformations they observe in the written documents, though
Fernand Braudel (1973) has provided many clues.

British archaeologist Matthew Johnson (1993) has rectified the
historians' oversight by examining traditional architecture in Suffolk, England. Johnson focused on houses built between 1400 and
1700, the time during which the transformation from European feudalism to capitalism occurred.

In his survey of 79 houses from a huge collection of still-
standing buildings, Johnson discovered a fundamental change in
domestic architecture from 1400 to 1700. The builders of common
English houses changed the layout of rooms, their techniques of
construction, and even their forms of decoration. The ways in which
they altered house design is instructive. Medieval Suffolk builders
constructed houses with an open-hall design. In this style, one room
—usually a central hall—was open to the roof (Johnson 1993:44).
This open-hall tradition came to an end in the early sixteenth century, however, as builders began to construct houses that were more

closed. Builders also began to convert many standing open-hall houses into closed forms. By the late seventeenth century, Suffolk builders included parlors, separate bedrooms, and special-purpose rooms in their designs. Before long, these innovations became the standard. Such forms occur today throughout the Anglo-American world, and at least one researcher has studied it in two parishes in Warwickshire (Alcock 1993). For Johnson (1993:181), the alteration of housing design has implications for understanding the shift to a capitalist economy. He attributes the architectural change to modifications in the social structure. In rural England, gender and class relations were transformed with the rise of agrarian capitalism because the new mode of production engendered a new form of landlord–tenant relation. In his words, "such changes can be seen in terms of the origins of capitalism" (Johnson 1993:181–182). As the social and economic positions of landlords and tenants became more solidified with the progress of capitalism, the people's houses tended to reflect these new social stations. The transition from open to closed rooms can be viewed as a reflection of the increased segmentation of the workers' time, the creation of daily wages, and the segregation of people into discrete task-oriented jobs.

Historical records indicate that the amount of movable things in English houses, both in Warwickshire and in Suffolk, increased alongside the changes in building design. Common men and women began to experience an increased desire to own things. Historian Wally Seccombe (1992) observed this trend in his study of families in northwestern Europe during the transformation from feudalism to capitalism. He discovered that households gradually ceased to make the products they consumed and that neighborly exchange declined as men and women began to purchase mass-produced objects with the money they earned as laborers or craftspersons.

It will undoubtedly take years for archaeologists to interpret the precise ways in which the transition from feudalism to capitalism was materially manifested. Johnson in Suffolk, Alcock in Warwickshire, and Seccombe throughout northwestern Europe all saw aspects of this material transformation. The transformation in domestic architecture observed by Johnson may reflect changing attitudes about women's roles in the household and the growing social distance between masters and servants. But even Johnson (1993: 179) admitted that his analysis tended to oversimplify what was clearly a complicated process. We must not suppose that the process was or will be the same in all times and places just because capitalism was involved. Capitalism concerns men, women, and children standing in relation to others. Johnson's study shows quite clearly that the archaeological understanding of the transformation from feudalism to capitalism defies crude, monocausal interpretations. The capitalist world was, and is, complex.

The spread of the capitalist economy into the noncapitalist world is extremely important to historical archaeologists. Its significance is shown by its being implicit, perhaps even hidden, within those definitions of historical archaeology that stress the spread of European culture to non-Europeans.

Numerous experts from several disciplines have examined the spread of capitalism into the world. The list of researchers is long, but it includes historians (Abu-Lughod 1989; Braudel 1984; Chaunu 1979; Curtin 1984, 1990; Litvinoff 1991; Marcus 1980; Phillips 1988; Scammell 1981; Woodruff 1967, 1981), historical sociologists (Hopkins 1979; Wallerstein 1974, 1979, 1980), and economists (Cameron 1989; Frank 1978; Wallace 1990). Also included in the list are environmentalists (Sale 1990), geographers (Genovese and Hochberg 1989; Haggett 1990), urban sociologists (King 1989), and political economists (Goldfrank 1979; Martin 1990). All of these scholars (and many others whom I have undoubtedly overlooked) have studied how the capitalist economy reached into the noncapitalist world.

Many experts refer to capitalism as a "world-economy" because of its far-reaching tentacles. Unlike an empire, the capitalist world-economy has no overarching political organization to accompany it into the field (Wallerstein 1979:159). For example, when the Romans moved into Gaul and Britain to create their empire, they took their organizational genius with them. They created tidy little Romes throughout the world, politically tied to Rome itself. These little Romes were the political outposts of the empire. The capitalist world-economy is unlike ancient Rome because it is first and foremost an economy. It has a single division of labor that spreads throughout the world, creating a network of small subeconomies that make up the larger network of global capitalism. The many little non-Europes around the globe either adapt their economies to the world-economy or have them adapted through pressure.

How old is this world-economy? Several archaeologists have attempted to stretch the concept into prehistory. They have mainly focused on the large, complex states in Mesoamerica and Mesopotamia, but others have examined Europe and the American Southwest (Blanton and Feinman 1984; Champion 1989; Edens 1992; Kohl

1987a, 1987b; Mathien and McGuire 1986; Pailes and Whitecotton 1979; Rowlands et al. 1987; Schortman and Urban 1987).

The problem of projecting capitalism into prehistory can be demonstrated by the Aztec capital of Tenochtitlán, located under today's sprawling Mexico City. With its 150,000 or so citizens, the city hosted a daily market that attracted about 25,000 men and women. These shoppers bartered for goods and even exchanged several kinds of recognized currencies. The presence of watchful judges within the marketplace, situated to catch counterfeiters and to punish dishonest merchants, suggests some measure of profit motive among the Aztecs (Price and Feinman 1993:349). In addition, the presence of the pochteca (see Chapter 2), craft specialists, and a complex social hierarchy (Charlton and Nichols 1992) all seem to point the Aztecs toward capitalism. Even if we do grant that they had developed some form of indigenous capitalism, we would be hard-pressed to show that their economy had global significance. Within Mexico, the Aztecs undoubtedly held supreme economic power for a time, but their precise role outside their homeland is much debated (see Chapter 2).

Historian Janet Abu-Lughod (1989) convincingly argued that large, capitalistlike empires existed well before the European ascendancy. In her interpretation, Europe was not unique or special in developing capitalism. Between 1250 and 1350, Europe was only a tiny upstart among the regional networks that blanketed the known world. Each one of eight commercial subsystems, stretching from Genoa to Canton, developed a recognized, standardized currency, invented a system of credit, and created ways of pooling capital and sharing risk (Abu-Lughod 1989:15–18). Merchants became wealthy in each of the subsystems. These features would all later become the central elements of capitalism. The European subsystem was no different from the one created around the Arabian Sea or, for that matter, from the one centered on the Red Sea.

Abu-Lughod did concede, though, that Europe stood in front of the other subsystems by the sixteenth century. Europe had indeed become unique. Why? What had happened to make the European continent special? Abu-Lughod rejected all psychological or institutional explanations for Europe's eventual world domination. It did not excel because its men and women were smarter or more diligent than those who lived farther east. European monarchies were not better organized, nor did their kings and queens exert a tighter control than the royal governments of the other subsystems. What, then, accounted for Europe's ascendancy? Abu-Lughod (1989:18–20) found the answer not in Europe, but in the East. She discovered that the Black Death was less devastating in the West than in the East, that Arab and Indian shipbuilders could not keep pace with the innovations of Portuguese shipwrights, and that warring factions in the East disrupted the time-honored, highly successful trade routes that had originally built Eastern power. These factors pushed Europe to the forefront of world domination only as the other subsystems began to shrink into the background. If we think about Eurocentrism, we can see that one of its important functions was to make Europe seem better and smarter than all other places around the globe. The Europeans' natural superiority—as evidenced by all they had accomplished—could easily explain their growing world power and influence (see Chapter 8).

At this point, my exploration into the nature of capitalism leads directly to the modern world. It is no accident that the capitalist world-economy is often linked to the "modern world-system." Modernity, a subject of considerable controversy, has great significance to historical archaeology.

THE WORLD OF MODERNITY

What does it mean to say that something is "modern"? In Latin, the word *modo* means "just now" (Borgmann 1992:20). The *Oxford English Dictionary* followed the word back to 1500–1520 and said that it simply means something that exists "now." Samuel Johnson (1760), in his monumental *Dictionary of the English Language,* said that "modern" meant "late, recent, not ancient, not antique." In everyday speech, modern usually refers to something fashionable, fresh, courageous, and forward looking (Kolakowski 1990:6; Lukacs 1970). As Johnson (1760) said, "modernness" means "novelty." People have generally perceived modern art and architecture to be bold and different, irrespective of whether or not they liked it. Modern art broke from tradition, and was not, as Johnson would say, "ancient" or "antique." Bold colors, dramatic angles, and creative shapes suggested that something new, something modern, was upon the land.

If we think of modern as something that is current, something that exists "just now," how then do we know when to start talking about modernity. Is modernity simply "now?" Are we modern simply because we live now? Perhaps the attempt to find the beginning of modernity is a waste of time. An effort to fix the day or even the year that modernity began would be silly. Depending upon what measure we chose to use, we could expect to find modernity in many places and at many times. It would not really matter whether we decided that the modern age began in 1415, in 1492, or for that matter, in 1510.

Though I believe this to be true, historical archaeologists cannot run from "the modern." Some notion of modernity, however vague it may be, pervades historical archaeology. Modernity is important to the field because historical archaeology is often viewed as the archaeology of the modern age. In fact, this is precisely how I define the field. For me, this is what truly makes the field unique, important, and exciting. As a result, historical archaeology's inability to define what is modern, or its collective wish to treat it as given, weakens historical archaeology's appeal to other disciplines. It waters down what historical archaeologists have to say to their fellow moderns. Though the landscape of modernity is peppered with pitfalls, historical archaeologists must walk this ground, attempting to chart it as they go.

To obtain some initial notion of modernity, we may imagine that the world is divided into societies that we may designate modern or traditional. I use these terms with caution because they have been used as weapons in the past. They make it easy for us to trot around the globe pointing accusatory fingers at all those people we choose to call traditional or premodern. The designation implies that these people are not of the present; they are not "now." They have not modernized and they are not like us. Though this kind of judgment is dangerous, we must admit that some societies appear to be more modern than others. Why?

Singling out some peoples as nonmodern is simply a subtle facet of Eurocentrism. It is easy for us to imagine ourselves as better than everyone not like us. Nonetheless, men and women who make a living studying modernization typically describe it not as a condition—a way of being—but as a continuous process. As the process unfolds, people take advantage of key technological or scientific innovations or inventions that help them to progress, or to become modern (Antonelli et al. 1992; Black et al. 1991). The innovations and inventions are perceived as good for the people, and if they recognize this goodness they can become a "better" people by embracing the changes. The people whom we decide to call modern have accepted the innovations and inventions. Their acceptance makes them different from the people who have not accepted them, the people we choose to call traditional.

Ideas about how people are introduced to modernization's innovations and inventions in the first place, and whether they are in a position to take advantage of them, have sparked a fierce debate. Ideas about modernization generally fall into two categories. The so-called modernization theorists imagine that all the world's peoples can start on the road to modernity given the proper conditions. When faced with revolutionary inventions or dramatic innovations, the people must have the political, economic, and social ability to take advantage of the knowledge. They must be ready for the "modernization revolution." They must also have political leaders who are willing to accept the challenges that modernization brings (Black et al. 1991:18). Modernization theorists generally think in terms of discrete, identifiable nations, and they usually see the lack of economic development in these nations as related to a scarcity of capital. To rectify this shortage of capital—in other words, to encourage modernization—modernization theorists promote the generation of capital for domestic investment (Billet 1993:4). The building of roads and factories, the construction of dams, and the introduction of electricity can set a nation or a region within a nation on the road to modernization. Accepting modernization also often entails accepting an unfamiliar mode of production.

Dependency theorists disagree. They argue that modern nations exist only because they have exploited less technologically advanced peoples (Hopkins 1979:22). Modernization depends on the exploitation of traditional societies. Dependency theorists created the world-system perspective specifically in reaction to modernization theory (Bach 1982:165). The hallmark of the world-system perspective is that since the sixteenth century, a single capitalist world-economy has been the driving force behind the creation of the modern world. The modern world is characterized by a single economy that is colonial, international, and expanding. Within this world-system, multiple nations may have their own jurisdictions but they are all tied to other states through the single economy (Hopkins 1979:23–24). The premise of the modern world-system is that a "multi-level, complex system of social action" exists not in a "society" but across the entire world (Hopkins 1982; Hopkins et al. 1982).

In an intriguing essay, historian Enrique Dussel (1993) argued that the process of modernization is a purely European phenomenon. Europe is an "ideological construct" built around the concept of modernization (West and Brown 1993:148). For Dussel (1993:65), Eurocentrism and modernity are linked and inseparable: "Modernity appears when Europe affirms itself as the 'center' of a *World History* that it inaugurates; the 'periphery' that surrounds this center is consequently part of its self-definition" (italics in original). For Dussel, the idea of modernization is both rational and irrational. It contains a rational kind of emancipation, but at the same time it conceals an irrational justification of genocidal violence. At its roots, however, modernity is a myth.

Dussel (1993:75) explained the elements of the myth of modernity in a way that has great relevance to historical archaeology. Modernity began when Europe saw itself as the most developed, most superior place on earth. This attitude took hold even though, at the time, Europe was a hodge-podge of tiny, highly chauvinistic nation-states (Litvinoff 1991:1–20). In an important way, the Europeans' beliefs sprang from the perceived differences between themselves and the Islamic Middle East (see Chapter 8). In any case, their sense of superiority (Eurocentrism)—or their profound insecurity—obliged Europeans to "develop" or to "civilize" all those peoples whom they judged to be "primitive" or "undeveloped." The path that these barbarous peoples should travel to reach Europe's level of greatness should mimic that traversed by Europe itself as it struggled out of antiquity into the Middle Ages and from there to modernity. If the undeveloped peoples stand in the way of modernization—if they resent and resist the changes they must go through to become like Europe, or if they are not ready for modernization—then Europe can legitimately use violence against them. The victims of the violence are perceived to be ritual sacrifices for the greater good. For their part, the modernizing people tend to see the victims as guilty. In refusing to accept what was good for them, they got pushed to the ground. It was their own fault that their modernization was painful. The agents of modernization can imagine themselves to be innocent because they were simply doing what was "right." At the same time, though, they also can argue that modernization has the potential to absolve the traditional people of their guilt.

Because modernity has a redemptive character, the loss of the men and women in the violence was justified. The death and destruction were unfortunate, but necessary for modernization to bloom.

Dussel's perspective shows that modernization is a process that affected real people. A similar case is made, albeit in a different manner, by historian Ronald Dufour (1987) in his examination of the modernization of colonial Massachusetts. Dufour believed that both modernization theorists and dependency theorists fail to account for the psychological roots and consequences of modernization. He argued that the process of modernization does not occur to "societies" or to "cultures," but to individuals. The process of modernization is ultimately a deeply personal experience. This being the case, Dufour proposed that a truly complete modernization theory must examine the emotional and psychological transformations of individuals in addition to the larger political, economic, and social changes faced by the entire social group.

Dufour argued, for example, that the citizens of colonial Massachusetts underwent a severe psychological transformation when they cast aside Puritanism. Theirs was not a revolution in church doctrine alone. The transition in religious belief was a personal as well as a social transformation. The American Revolution was also part of the modernization process for the citizens of Massachusetts. As Dufour (1987:466) said, "In the transition away from a traditional society, group structures are battered, transformed, and even destroyed, leaving the individual to seek new means of security." Modernization was personal.

Though Dufour relied strongly on psychohistory, he did present a convincing argument. It is impossible to imagine the transition from traditional life to modern life in the absence of people. The stresses and strains of transformation were felt not by a society or culture that existed "somewhere." Men, women, and children simply going about the business of their daily lives directly experienced the pressures of change. Dufour's ideas are consistent with Carrithers' (1992) mutualist perspective. The American Revolution was not simply a change in political administration. Admittedly, the Revolution encompassed a transformation of attitudes, beliefs, and images, but it occurred only because men and women made it happen. And to make it successful, they had to stand in relation to one another. As Carrithers (1992:60) said, "we are not so much self-aware as self-and-other-aware."

PUTTING IT ALL TOGETHER
IN THE MODERN WORLD

Global colonialism, Eurocentrism, capitalism, and modernity obviously do not stand alone, although I have presented each in a separate section. I would have preferred to discuss them holistically, but I quickly realized that this would be impossible. My explanations would have been intermingled and confusing. Thus I have presented the four haunts individually in order to avoid confusion. Let me state unequivocally, however, that the four haunts of historical archaeology can never be truly separated. They work together in the modern world.

In this book, I make no explicit study of such important issues as gender, race, and class. This deficiency is not meant to diminish the significance of these elements of life. Instead, I subsume the relations enacted by men and women, ethnic Europeans, Native Americans, Africans, Asians, Arabs, workers, and laborers within the four haunts. My understanding of the importance of a feminist historical archaeology, for example, derives from the exemplary research of Elizabeth Scott (1994) and Suzanne Spencer-Wood (1991). Like these scholars, I believe that a feminist construction of historical archaeology will push the field to new interpretive heights. I also believe, though, that these heights cannot be reached without first acknowledging the four haunts. I believe that the haunts structured the way men and women interacted. In this book, I always refer to "men and women." I have not used these words simply to add women to the historical mix or to make this book seem politically correct. Rather, my usage is meant to suggest that men *and* women interacted, got things accomplished, and created the modern world. My plan in this book is to provide a framework for future study. I hope that other archaeologists will go from this starting point to delve into issues, such as gender, that I leave untouched for lack of space.

It now makes sense for me to state explicitly what I mean by the term "modern world." For me, it is the time when colonialism, Eurocentrism, capitalism, and modernity all come together. We may choose to begin the modern world with the Portuguese capture of Ceuta in 1415 (Litvinoff 1991:25) or with Columbus's first voyage in 1492 (Dussel 1993:66). We may even wish to consider the modern age to begin with the invention of the movable-type printing press around 1450 (Hodgen 1974:47), or with the printing of the first

English-language travel book about America in 1553 (Sale 1990: 253). The precise date does not much matter. Setting an arbitrary starting point says more about its creator and what he or she thinks about the past than about the past itself. What is important is that historical archaeologists accept that the modern age includes the four haunts. Global colonialism, Eurocentrism, capitalism, and modernity obviously incorporate numerous aspects that are ripe for archaeological study. Each has elements that are peculiar to a particular time and place. In this book, I use Palmares, Brazil, and Gorttoose, Ireland, as two times and places where the four haunts had an impact. I could just as easily have used other sites in other places. Colonialism, Eurocentrism, capitalism, and modernity were all put forth by men and women who chose their own ways of doing things, believed different things, and held unique jobs. Ultimately, they were caught up in their times just as we are today.

The four haunts exist in historical archaeology, affecting all sites throughout the modern world. They are an inexorable part of modern times. In many cases, the presence of each haunt may be difficult for an archaeologist to document. In some cases, one or more of them may seem irrelevant. As I said at the beginning of this chapter, at some sites the haunts may hide in the wings, apparently unconcerned with the events that took place there. For example, in Chapter 7, I explore the archaeology of Boott Mills, a site in Massachusetts associated with late nineteenth-century industrial capitalism. If we chose not to accept my global, mutualistic perspective, it would be difficult, indeed, to see how colonialism and Eurocentrism had any part to play at this industrial site. Our adoption of mutualism, however, makes us wonder who were the mill hands and how did they arrive in Massachusetts? Historical records show that many of the mill workers at the turn of the twentieth century included men and women of French Canadian, English, Scottish, Armenian, Italian, French, and Irish ancestry. Earlier in the nineteenth century, the few mill hands who were not born in New England were probably Irish (Bond 1987:36, 41). Thus, while it would be comforting to imagine that colonialism and Eurocentrism played no role at Boott Mill, careful consideration would reveal that these immigrants left their homelands for some reason. It may well be that colonial circumstances forced them to abandon the lands of their birth. Others may have fled injustice or prejudice. Still others were undoubtedly motivated strictly by economics. The point is not necessarily to identify each haunt at every site excavated. I believe that each haunt played some part in shaping the modern world, and that therefore each had some impact on every site. The point is to acknowledge the haunts and to understand that the relations forged in the name of each one helped to tie together the people of the modern world. Also, once haunts are acknowledged, they may be found in the most surprising places. To demonstrate the significance of the four haunts, I now turn to a brief consideration of Gorttoose. My comments are specific to its cultural and historical circumstances, but I hope that my exploration will encourage others to look for evidence of the weblike connections of the haunts at their sites.

The Haunts Confer
at Gorttoose

I first met Farrell O'Gara on June 13, 1994. An elderly farmer, Mr. O'Gara embodies rural Ireland. He is a quiet, deeply religious man. He is the sort of person from whom you can learn volumes in a few moments. He projects a quiet strength and a deep understanding of the Irish soil. I visited him at his neat farmhouse on the land that once contained Gorttoose, a late eighteenth- and early nineteenth-century village almost 5 km (3 mi) east of Strokestown in the north-central part of County Roscommon (Figure 4). His house was surrounded by a rich vegetable garden, a well-tended and colorful flower garden, and a yard of emerald green. Upon meeting Mr. O'Gara, I immediately felt that I had encountered Ireland itself. O'Gara's Ireland is not the playground of the tourist. It is not blarney stones and leprechauns, shamrocks and shillelaghs. It is the Ireland that is lived every day, the Ireland of actual history.

It would be easy for me to demonstrate the relevance of the four haunts of historical archaeology—colonialism, Eurocentrism, capitalism, and modernity—by leaving O'Gara and Gortoose behind and heading straight for exotic Palmares. After all, runaway slaves built the kingdom during what was clearly a colonial period, and Palmares was in many ways the logical antithesis of the Portuguese colonial endeavor. The African and Indian men and women who lived there were victimized by Eurocentric, even racist, attitudes and practices. The kingdom virtually embodied capitalism because without capitalist sugar production, Palmares would not have existed. And finally, the destruction of Palmares in 1694 was part of the Portuguese desire to progress to full-scale modernity, without the inconvenience of rebel slaves standing in their way. Clearly and without doubt, the four haunts can be seen hovering around Palmares.

The ease of demonstrating the significance of the four haunts at Palmares is seductive. By the same token, however, it is also a drawback. Palmares seems too special, too unique. Though hundreds of maroon communities sprang up throughout all slave-holding re-

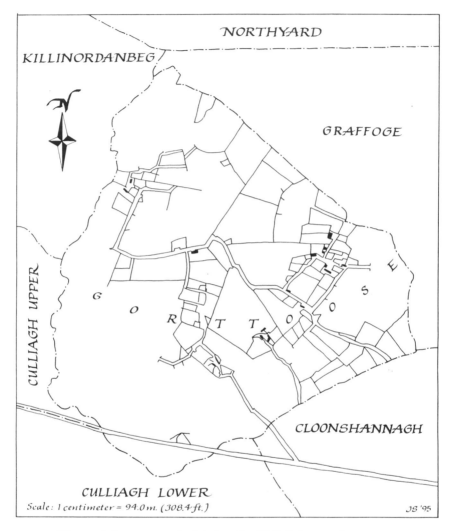

Figure 4. Gorttoose as depicted on the 1837 Ordnance Survey map.

gions of the world, they were never a major settlement form. Maroons, though deeply significant to history, were not one of its central features. Thus, any effort to explore the relevance of the haunts at Palmares may work against me, having the unintended effect of diluting my ideas. The relationship of the haunts to Palmares may appear given, expected, or pat.

Using Gorttoose as an example reinforces my view that the four haunts played a role in all the sites—houses, mills, factories, villages, and towns—of the modern world. At a place like Gorttoose we may easily see that capitalism and modernity played a role in shaping and structuring the social relations created and maintained there. The men and women who lived there were peasant farmers caught within a huge economy in which they were but cogs. But what about colonialism and Eurocentrism? Surely, these haunts had nothing to do with Gorttoose, a peasant village in the center of Ireland. Or did they? The purpose of this chapter is to identify the presence of all four haunts at Gorttoose by reference to historical information. The following chapters show one way archaeologists can study the haunts at sites of the modern era. Readers must remember that I use Gorttoose only as an example.

"IT IS A GRIEVOUS SITUATION THAT HAS BEFALLEN IRELAND" (DAÍBHI CUNDÚN, 1650s)

Irish men and women farmers settled on Gorttoose sometime in the late eighteenth century, perhaps around 1780 but maybe before. Gorttoose, sometimes spelled "Gurthuse" or "Gurtose," was one of several "townlands" associated with the sprawling Strokestown Park estate, in County Roscommon. After the individual family farm, the townland is the second most important geographic frame of reference in Ireland. The townland (*baile* in Irish) is the smallest administrative division in rural Ireland, and about 62,000 of them still exist, some reaching back to the days of the Celts (Cawley 1989:221). Researchers are certain in any case that most of the townlands can trace their ancestry to at least the beginning of the seventeenth century, many with almost no change (McErlean 1983:316). Historians have estimated that in the early nineteenth century three-quarters of the rural Irish population lived on the 62,205 townlands that blanketed the countryside (Scally 1995:13). Townlands typically range in size from 80 to 200 ha (198 to 494 acres), though they can be much smaller as well. No one lived at Gorttoose until the late eighteenth century because the land was boggy and of little interest. Strokestown estate records state that in 1727, the townland was "under woods." As the demand for land rose, however, even Gorttoose's inferior ground became an object of de-

sire. In order to obtain the land as tenants, four small farmers joined
in a partnership to make a bid. Bryan Murray, Daniel Maguire,
Walter Holmes, and James Carlos pooled their resources and became the head tenants of Gorttose. By the midnineteenth century,
Gorttoose was 102.4 ha (253 acres) in size (Griffith 1857:52). The
farmers of Gorttoose were surrounded by hundreds of men and
women much like themselves, who lived on townlands with the mu-
sical names of Graffoge, Culliagh Upper, Killinordan, Cloonshannagh, and Knocknabarnaboy.

Gorttoose's history is forever linked with colonialism. This
union, in fact, began long before anyone ever thought about creating
a townland named Gorttoose.

One could look at Irish history and name the island "The Land
of Invasions." Prehistorians have shown that Ireland had lasting
contacts with the larger island to the east. For example, the builders
of Passage Graves (piles of intricately interweaved stones with internal burial chambers) are thought to have arrived in Ireland
sometime around 2500 B.C. (Herity and Eogan 1977:57). Prehistoric
archaeologists have established other cultural links between Ireland and England and Scotland (Ryan 1991). Whether many of
these unions represent the willing adoption of cultural traits or
resulted from invasion is still largely unknown (Cooney 1993:634).
What is known, however, is that many outsiders invaded Ireland
during recorded history. The Celts were the first great conquerors to
arrive, coming in several waves beginning during the second half of
the first millennium B.C. (Ó Corráin 1989:1). The powerful Vikings
arrived in A.D. 795, the Normans—the descendants of the Viking
"Northmen"—invaded in 1169, and the Scots under Robert Bruce
attacked the north of Ireland beginning in 1315. In 1579, a combined force of Spaniards and Italians came ashore at Dingle Bay; a
year later, a papal force attacked the West; and the Spanish landed
a force in the south in 1601 (Edwards 1973:41–55).

For the land that would later be partitioned as Gorttoose, the
most relevant colonial invasion was that of the Elizabethans, who,
under direction of their queen, rigorously set about to Anglicize
Ireland. At the time of the Elizabethan conquest, Ireland was in the
hands of several ancient Gaelic families. The three most prominent
families in what would become County Roscommon were O'Conor
Don (in Irish Gaelic, *Donn* means "brown"), O'Conor Roe (*Ruadh*
means "red"), and McDermott (Canny 1976:112). Each was a powerful Gaelic family with long-standing roots in Roscommon. The fami-

lies were descended from the ancient kings of Connacht (Kelly 1939:79, 101; MacLysaght 1972:88–90, 114–115), one of four ancient provinces of Ireland (Dames 1992:17; Duffy 1993:15). Located on the west side of the island, Connacht includes today's counties of Galway, Leitrim, Mayo, Roscommon, and Sligo. Roscommon is on the far eastern edge of the province, alongside the picturesque and historically charged River Shannon, named for the goddess Sinnann (Condren 1989:27). In the midthirteenth century, the Anglo-Normans had designated the area of County Roscommon "The King's Cantreds." A cantred was an administrative unit based on a preexisting territorial unit. A few decades later, the Anglo-Normans would begin to use the designation "County of Roscommon" (Frame 1981:46, 122).

Today, people often speak of two Irelands. In saying this, they usually mean the division between the independent Republic of Ireland and Northern Ireland, which is, as of this writing, part of Great Britain. In describing Ireland of the past, however, the term "two Irelands" might be used to distinguish the far west from the rest of the island (Evans 1992:77). The west of Ireland has always been considered more wild naturally and more stubbornly Irish than the rest of Ireland. For example, most speakers of Irish still live in the west, in a region called "the Gaeltacht" (Edwards 1973:231). The English policy of "de-gaelicizing" Ireland may have deep historical roots, but it does not belong strictly to the past. Today's Irish nationalism contains a conscious plan to "re-gaelicize" Ireland (G. Adams 1994:125). But while the number of Irish speakers is steadily increasing (Heslinga 1971:88), full gaelicization may be more an aspiration than an expected certainty (Hindley 1990:37).

The separation between east and west was given additional weight by Cromwell's invasion of Ireland, beginning in August 1649. The Cormwellian assault on Ireland is well told and I need not paraphrase the historians (see, for example, Barnard 1975; Brady and Gillespie 1986; Canny 1976; Ellis 1988). I need only state that when Cromwell began his brutal repression of Ireland, he set aside for the Irish the county of Roscommon, as well as most of Mayo, Galway, and Clare (Ellis 1988:92). His policy of forcible removal of the Irish to the west spawned the famous saying that the Irish could go to "hell or Connacht." In other words, Gaelic Irish could either be driven to the west by Cromwell's forces or die in futile resistance. The population of the west swelled as a result of Cromwell's efforts (L. J. Taylor 1980:172).

In July 1635, the Crown confirmed its title to County Roscommon along with the lands of Sligo and Mayo (Foster 1989:599). In a complex process of negotiation, the Elizabethans dispossessed the Gaelic chiefdoms by convincing them that their best interests were served by swearing allegiance to the queen (Canny 1976:112). As part of the ongoing policy of colonialism, Captain Nicholas Mahon established himself in Strokestown by 1659. Mahon was one of Cromwell's "49 officers," a militia that hunted Irish rebels in the bogs and hills of central Ireland. Cromwell granted O'Conor Roe's lands to Mahon, including the Strokestown properties. The Mahons soon moved into O'Conor Roe's bawn, or fortified enclosure, eventually building a large Palladian mansion around the ancient structure (Chapter 6). With this act, the Mahons initiated a presence in Strokestown that continues to this day, and the roots of their presence there are colonialist to the core.

"MUSIC IS PROHIBITED, THE IRISH LANGUAGE IS IN CHAINS" (AINDRIAS MAC MARCAIS, 1570s)

The English and the Irish are not one people. In fact, the English viewed themselves as superior in every way to the Irish. In this respect, their attitude toward the Irish was no different than it was toward the many other peoples with whom the English came into contact during their colonial days, an attitude replayed by other colonial powers around the globe (Lebow 1976:103–112). The English viewed themselves as modern, progressive, and refined. They perceived the Irish as wild, bloodthirsty, and barbaric. Late sixteenth-century artists typically portrayed the Irish as unclean and unkept. For example, in a drawing completed around 1575, Lucas de Heers shows an Englishwoman in a long dress, wearing a cross around her neck, a neat, flat hat on her head, and a pair of unheeled shoes on her delicate feet. In contrast, the Irishman to her right is unshaven, barefoot, and wearing a long, loosely shaped cape over his head (Canny 1989:107). This image did more than simply to show how the English colonists and the Irish natives dressed. It reinforced a Eurocentric—in this case, Anglocentric—perception of the Irish. The distinction between the two individuals was obvious. Words were unnecessary; the message was successfully conveyed in the drawing.

For all their self-assured superiority, the English were confused by the Irish. The Irish had the same skin color as the English and they looked strangely English. Yet, the Irish and the English were not the same. The Irish were "wild" and decidedly un-English. In 1749, George Berkeley, Anglican bishop and renowned philosopher, wrote, "The negroes in our Plantations have a saying—'If negro was not negro, Irishman would be negro'" (Fraser 1871:439). This racist view was not restricted to colonial commentators. For example, in 1860, during a visit to County Sligo, in Connacht just northeast of Roscommon, English author and staunch anti-Catholic clergyman Charles Kingsley wrote:

> I was haunted by the human chimpanzees I saw along that hundred miles of horrible country. I don't believe they are our fault. I believe . . . that they are happier, better, more comfortably fed and lodged under our rule than they ever were. But to see white chimpanzees is dreadful; if they were black, one would not feel it so much, but their skins, except where tanned by exposure, are as white as ours. (quoted in Gibbons 1991:96)

Many other comparisons between the rural Irish and African slaves centered on similarities in their housing. For example, Sir George Campbell (1879:393), traveling through the American South in the late 1870s, observed that "some of the smaller [African-American] tenants live in places unfit for an Irishman" (for more on housing, see Chapter 6). During the 1840s, at the start of the Great Famine, African-American orator Frederick Douglass regularly had to remind his Irish audiences that Ireland's peasants were not just like America's slaves (Blassingame 1979:77–78). Though people could not resist comparing the two, slaves were property, not simply degraded men and women.

With their perceptions of the Irish firmly in their minds, the English became committed to Anglicizing them. History often reveals that the best way to make the "other" palatable to "us" is to transform them into "us." In regard to the Gaelic Irish, however, the English quickly discovered that their task would not be easy. For instance, in 1600, an English official was distressed to discover that his countrymen and women living in Dublin seemed to prefer speaking Irish to English (Ellis 1988:10). In fact, many of the English who had gone to Ireland in the preceding 300 years had eagerly adopted Gaelic as their tongue of choice. Between the midfourteenth and the midfifteenth centuries, Ireland experienced a Gaelic resurgence that threatened to overwhelm the culture and language of the invaders (Cosgrove 1995:168–169). In 1605, to speed the process of assimilation, the English found it necessary to proclaim that all Irish were subjects of the king rather than followers of a chieftain (O'Dowd 1986:144). Clearly, this measure would have been unnecessary if the Irish had flocked to the English as their new, rightful rulers. And many Irish stubbornly rejected the missionizing charity of the English. For these sturdy recalcitrants, the English deemed eviction to be the best option. The British sent some unacculturated Irish to the west of Ireland; they sent others far beyond the island. Around 50,000 Irish men and women were sent to Barbados or to other Caribbean Islands (Ellis 1988:154). On Montserrat—often called the Emerald Isle of the Caribbean—the Irish became a lasting cultural force (Messenger 1975, 1994). As an expression of both their prejudice against the Irish and the strength of their capitalist commitment, English plantation owners on the islands valued their African slaves more highly than their Irish indentured servants. Slaves were permanent possessions, whereas Irish men and women had only agreed to either five or seven years of indenture in return for passage to the New World (Ellis 1988:150). So, though the Irish were white and the Africans black, the Irish were more expendable to Caribbean plantation owners.

The men and women of Gorttoose, though a long way from their kinfolk in the tropics, undoubtedly felt the effects of Anglocentrism in many ways. We may expect that some of the changes they underwent were dramatic. Major transformations are readily identifiable in rural material culture, with changes in the landscape being a perfect example (Chapter 6). Some changes, however, had to be deeply felt and personal.

Farrell O'Gara's family history provides an illustration of the subtle effects of Eurocentrism on the Irish. Though the hierarchy of rural land tenure was as complex in Ireland as any place in the agrarian capitalist world, it can be boiled down to three basic levels: landlords, head tenants ("strong farmers"), and undertenants (subtenants). Subtenants were the laboring poor who felt the fullest effects of the periodic famines that swept through Ireland. Head tenants rented the land from landlords and then rerented it to undertenants, becoming landlords themselves (Donnelly 1975:9–10). Englishman Arthur Young (1780:14), after traveling through Ireland in the late 1770s, condemned head tenants as "the most oppressive species of tyrant that ever lent assistance to the destruction of the country." Because tenants made their farming arrangements directly with their landlord, the landlord (the estate owner) usually knew little about the subtenants, often not even knowing their names (Scally 1995:16). As a result, the peasants of Gorttoose and of a thousand other townlands are largely forgotten in historical records because the owners and their agents produced the estate's official documents. We can sometimes learn the names of the subtenants, but generally an estate's accounts pass a judgment of historical silence on its peasant farmers.

The names of head tenants are usually preserved in estate records. These silent lists carry subtle messages about the power of English colonialism and Eurocentrism. For example, in a published list of Gorttoose head tenants dated 1857 there appears a man named "Farrel O'Garra" (Griffith 1857:52). The frustratingly incomplete list tells us that O'Garra had a house, an office, and a garden on one rood of land rented from Henry S. P. Mahon (a rood is an ancient measure equalling about 0.1 ha or 0.25 acre). The assessor recorded the value of the land at 5 shillings, the same as O'Garra's buildings. A second list of head tenants, dating to the late nineteenth century, is still housed in the archives of the Strokestown Park House. Here is recorded a "Mary Gara, representative of Patrick Gara." She paid a rent of £4 5s for just over 4 ha (10.25 acres) of land.

Without a doubt, the Farrel O'Garra of 1857, the Mary Gara of the late nineteenth century, and the Farrell O'Gara of 1994 are members of the same family. Anyone who has done even a small amount of historical research will have no difficulty accepting the difference in spelling between "O'Garra" and "O'Gara." The loss of one r should not throw us off the trail; O'Garra and O'Gara name the same family. What is much more significant, though, is the loss of the prefix. The absence of the O is dramatic and meaningful.

Genealogists say that the Irish were among the first people in Europe to develop a system of hereditary surnames, with today's recognizable names coming into widespread use during the eleventh century (MacLysaght 1969:9). In the ancient system, the word Ua or Ó literally meant "descended from" or "grandson of" (Kelly 1939:2A; MacLysaght 1972:14). The Irish later added Mac, meaning "son," and Ní, an abbreviation of "daughter," as surnames for men and women, respectively (Kelly 1939:2A).

Many Irish families dropped the Gaelic prefixes of their names during the oppression of the seventeenth century (MacLysaght 1969:10). Irish genealogist Edward MacLysaght (1972:16) noted that the English did not pass laws against the use of Gaelic surnames, except perhaps in "the Pale," a politically unstable region including the counties of Dublin, Meath, Louth, and Kildare on the eastern side of the island (Aalen 1989:98–99). But they did make it advantageous for families to Anglicize their names. For example, the Irish chieftain O'Conor Roe wrote in 1637 that he would council the Gaelic leaders under his influence "to give up prefixes to their surnames" (MacLysaght 1972:16). O'Conor Roe only made this concession two years after Mahon gained control of his old Strokestown lands. Based on what Farrell O'Gara told me in 1994, it would seem that many Irish families dropped their prefixes as a survival mechanism and as a way to obtain some measure of social mobility within an anti-Irish, colonialist environment.

The creation in 1893 of the Gaelic League (*Conradh na Gaelige*), an organization dedicated to the resurrection and widespread use of the Irish language, probably had much to do with the increased use of the traditional prefixes. It was not an accident that Douglas Hyde, cofounder of the league and first president of Eire (elected in 1938), delivered a lecture in 1892 entitled "On the Necessity for De-Anglicizing the Irish People" (Foster 1989:447–448). For many people, the presence of Irish words on signposts, in names, and in literary works was an anticolonialist, nationalist act of cultural resistance. The action of the O'Gara family of first dropping the prefix and then rediscovering it represents the effort to regain some of the tradition they had lost to colonialism and Eurocentrism.

"MUCH LAND IS LET FOR GRASS POTATOES" (ARTHUR YOUNG, 1780)

The Great Irish Famine of 1845–1849 was a defining period for the men, women, and children of Gorttoose. It was this terrible event that placed them forever in the history books. The ravages of the Great Famine impelled their landlord, Nicholas Mahon's descendant Major Denis Mahon, to evict 185 of them along with thousands of others from the 27 townlands on the Strokestown estate. Thirty-three families from Gorttoose left their homes behind; at least 572 families from the other townlands did the same. A Justice of the Peace for County Roscommon, George J. P. Browne (1848) listed the following heads of families as having left Gorttoose:

John Murphy	Thomas M'Cormick	Pat M'Neal
James Dooly	Bryan Doyle	Michael M'Neal
Pat Murphy	Pat M'Guire	Pat Donohoe
Luke Murray	James M'Guire	Thomas Donohoe
Widow Murray	John Madden	Luke Farrell
Widow Brennan	James Murphy	Pat Kilkenny
James Long	James Madden	Cannon M'Guire
Thomas Murphy	Michael Murphy	Daniel M'Guire
Michael Colgan	Thady Kennedy	Widow M'Guire
Edward Holmes	Pat Cassidy	William M'Neal
Thomas Hanly	William Holmes	Peter Lyons

These now-lifeless names represent men, women, and children who either were forcibly removed from their homes or agreed to leave to escape a dire situation. Browne reported that the families ranged in size from two to eleven members. The number of evictees in all the evicted Strokestown townlands ranged from only 5 at Ballyhabert to 366 at Mahon's Yard, just north of Gorttoose. The average number of evictees from each townland was 107, and when the townlands are ranked on the basis of population, Gorttoose is 25th out of 28, the highest. Gortoose had the second highest rate of depopulation of the townlands immediately around it, nearing 80 percent (Table 1). Nonetheless, as individuals, we may assume that the men and women of Gortoose were not special or unique in any perceptible way when compared to the other families removed. Statistics reveal that during the height of the Great Famine (1846–1849), 37,286 evictions occurred and 16,400 houses were leveled (Vaughan 1994:230).

Major Mahon did not necessarily evict the peasant families because he hated them. His relationship with them was undoubtedly more economic than social. As one historian has written, "What most altered landlord-tenant relations after 1750 was that many proprietors abandoned paternalism for the lure of greater profits" (K. A. Miller 1985:44). In other words, landlords were willing to squeeze "their" people to increase their estates' profits. Mahon's unsuccessful attempt to attract Scottish protestants to his estate in 1848—in lieu of his Catholic renters—also suggests that he held the day's Protestant bias against popish peasants (Campbell 1994:42). But in his heart Mahon, and in fact all landlords throughout the world, expected his tenants, regardless of religion or personality, to pay their rent. Those who could not pay were simply a burden.

Table 1. Population Change at Gorttoose
and Surrounding Townlands, 1841–1851

Townland	Males	% Change	Females	% Change	Total	% Change
Gorttoose	139/33	−76.3	121/24	−80.2	260/57	−78.1
Graffoge	165/77	−53.3	203/88	−56.7	368/165	−55.2
Killiordanbeg	99/49	−50.5	94/44	−53.2	193/93	−51.8
Culliagh Upper	100/22	−78.0	100/19	−81.0	200/41	−79.5
Culliagh Lower	87/43	−50.6	79/34	−57.0	166/77	−53.6
Cloonshannagh	13/14	+7.7	14/10	−28.6	27/24	−11.1

Source: British Parliamentary Papers (1970:550).

Often, as at the Strokestown estate, they could be a substantial, draining burden. In the 1840s, John Ross Mahon, the Major's cousin and agent during the Great Famine, conducted a survey of eight townlands and discovered that 479 families, totalling 2,444 individuals, had paid no rent at all in two years (Campbell 1994:42). The rent in arrears totalled over £603. Documents in the Strokestown archives reveal that in 1842, the total rent owed by the four Gorttoose head tenants was £250, and that they had rent in arrears of £38. All subtenants who could not pay had to be removed; those who could not be removed would go into the workhouses or be kept alive by public works projects. Notes on file at Strokestown Park House, often scrawled by hands unpracticed in writing, beseech Mahon to help the peasants through the famine. The petition of James Smyth, made in 1846, is representative: "The Application of James Smyth of Ballyhabberd Respectfully begs your honour will cause him to get work at Cutting down Curraghroe hills. The Applicant is a poor Starving Man and has six in family." Smyth is not on the list of evictees. On the other hand, on January 11, 1848, John Ross Mahon received the following appeal from a literate agent: "A poor man named Edwd. Homes has Begged of me to write to you to Say he is prepared to pay a year's Rent for the quarter of land on which he now lives on in Gurthoose. If you can do anything for him I will be Most thankful." The Edward Holmes family, containing five members, was on the list of evictees. The Holmes family owed one-half of the rent in arrears in 1842.

Under the advice of his confidants and his chief land agent, John Ross Mahon, Major Mahon felt he could do little to help his starving, non-rent-paying subtenants. Perhaps thinking they would be better off in North America, or maybe only to spare himself further economic drain, he started to ship them out of Ireland on May 27, 1847 (Campbell 1990:19). When the story began to circulate that he had chartered "coffin ships" for the evictees and that one had actually sunk during the crossing, drowning all on board, the peasants vilified Mahon. Hatred for him must have festered in the emptying lands around his Strokestown mansion. On November 2, 1847, the anger came to a head as the lover of an evicted girl, who had supposedly drowned during the crossing but who was actually alive, shot and killed Mahon on the road to Roscommon town (Scally 1995:39; Woodham-Smith 1991:324–325).

Some may wish to see Mahon's murder as a simple act of passion. Such compelling interpretations are the stuff of romance writers. On a deeper level, though, we can situate his murder within a sphere of broader passions. We can envision his death as the playing out of a long-held hostility toward landlords, the perceived "enemies of the people" (Campbell 1994:49). During that winter, six other landlords were also murdered and one wounded (Scally 1995:38). Mahon was not killed because one girl was thought dead. He was executed in the name of hundreds, perhaps even thousands, of people, the majority of whom did not even live on his lands. His death was the symbolic murder of all the landlords who packed their starving tenants into overcrowded ships and sent them away to far-off lands.

The verdict is still out on whether Mahon was an evil landlord. Pat Browne, a farmer in Strokestown and the brother of the local bishop, said that Mahon was lenient with his tenants (Campbell 1990:27). Conversely, Father MacDermott, the local parish priest, was supposed to have cried from his pulpit (though he later denied it) that "Major Mahon is worse than Cromwell" (Woodham-Smith 1991:325). We cannot today be certain of Mahon's guilt as a robbing landlord. Undoubtedly, the final verdict will depend on what kind of evidence we marshal for or against him and how we interpret it (MacDonagh 1994:336–337). One thing that we can know for sure, however, is that Mahon was caught in the grip of the famine along with his tenants. In at least one sense, the impact of the famine was less severe on Mahon than on his tenants—he was not about to starve to death. We must not forget, however, that his reaction to the mass starvation raging through Ireland got him murdered. Surely, there can be no greater repercussion.

The Great Irish Famine has spawned an extensive literature

(see, for example, Daly 1986; Edwards and Williams 1957; Hill and Ó Gráda 1993; Kinealy 1995; Ó Gráda 1989; O'Rourke 1989; Woodham-Smith 1991), which will continue to expand. As I write, plans are being made to commemorate the 150th anniversary of the beginning of the blight in 1995. New books, conference, and papers will increase our understanding of the Great Famine as scholars attack the subject from several disciplinary directions. Many of today's experts disagree on how many people actually died as a result of the famine. Estimates range from one-half to one million men, women, and children (Daly 1986:98).

Scholars also cannot agree precisely why Ireland starved. Several possibilities exist. Was the human devastation caused solely by the arrival of the potato blight, *Phythophthora infestans,* on the shores of Ireland in 1845? Did Irish peasants starve as the result of oppressive policies enacted by the British government? Can the death and devastation be laid at the feet of the Irish themselves because they had too many children, lived in unsanitary conditions—often bedding their cattle in their houses—and had work habits unrelated to the Protestant work ethic? Or was the blight unavoidable? Was it a natural phenomenon designed to keep the world's population in balance?

Learned scholars will contest these important questions for years, and perhaps they will never reach a true consensus (Donnelly 1993; Mokyr 1983; Solow 1984). Most experts agree, however, that the Great Famine "is the great divide in modern Irish economic and social history" (Ó Gráda 1989:65) and that it "caused the permanent uprooting of the whole social system" of Ireland (O'Brien 1921:3). Regardless of what conclusions scholars finally reach about the actual causes of the Great Irish Famine, we can be certain that the relations of production created between landlords and tenants played some role. These relationships were a strong contributing factor to the human misery. As such, at least part of the cause of the Great Famine—and perhaps a large part—can be understood by adopting a mutualist perspective. After all, landlord-tenant arrangements are simply relations that tied together diverse people.

The connection between Irish agriculture and capitalism has a long-standing history in Ireland. At their most basic level, the links forged between landlords and tenants were capitalist in design. The earliest colonization of Ireland by the English was often portrayed as a struggle over the rights of economic speculation. The entire island was the prize if only the English could wrestle it away from the Irish (Ellis 1988:12). The ongoing battle between the English and the Irish would always involve the land to some degree. The British government recognized this and in 1843, on the eve of the Great Famine, established a royal commission "to inquire into the law and practice with regard to the occupation of land in Ireland" (Woodham-Smith 1991:21). The government selected the Earl of Devon to head what soon would be called the Devon Commission. During the course of their investigation, the commissioners questioned 1,100 witnesses and produced three tomes of evidence. The commission's central conclusion was simple and stunning: "the principle cause of Irish misery was the bad relations between landlord and tenant. Ireland was a conquered country, the Irish peasant a dispossessed man, his landlord an alien conqueror" (Woodham-Smith 1991:21).

The Devon Commission discovered four levels of subtenants. The first were unmarried farm servants who lived with their employers. Second were cottiers who held a cabin and a small plot of ground for a fixed rent; third were cottiers who held only a cabin and a garden. Small-holding farmers who worked their own land and passed pieces of it along to their descendants made up the fourth group (O'Brien 1921:9). The commission judged the unmarried servants to be the most fortunate. They had few expenses and could make limited economic progress in the agrarian system controlled by the landlords.

The small-holding farmers practiced an ancient system of agriculture called "rundale" (Evans 1992:59–60). Peasants were still using the rundale system in the nineteenth century, but by this time it had largely outlived its purpose (Evans 1957:23–24). Rundale plots were small and unfenced, and on the death of the farmer the coheirs each obtained a tiny plot of ground. The British found this system of inheritance and land division to be untidy and the cause of much confusion and violence. Lord George Hill reported in 1845, for example, that in County Donegal, north of County Roscommon, one farmer's ground might be contained in 30 or 40 tiny plots scattered across the countryside (Evans 1992:96).

The second and the third groups identified by the Devon Commission are called cottiers. The word *cottier* had many different, often regionally distinct, meanings (Beames 1975). The distinctions between different kinds of cottiers are important when attempting to understand the complexities of Irish agriculture in the late eighteenth and early nineteenth centuries. For my purposes here, I use

the term loosely to refer to poor farmers who could rent only the
tiniest plots of ground. Before the Great Famine, 80 percent of all
farms on the Irish landscape were smaller than 6 ha (15 acres)
(Evans 1957:20). Thus, when English social philosopher John Stuart
Mill (1979:30) wrote in October 1846 that "the grand economical evil
of Ireland is the cottier-tenant system," he referred to all impoverished, small farmers.

Tenant farmers generally received about 0.2 to 0.4 ha (0.5–1.0
acres) for potato ground (Donnelly 1975:19). Since the potato was
the staple for Irish peasants, being easy to grow, hardy, and high in
nutrients, potato ground meant food ground. Peasants usually
rented, on a year-by-year basis, less than 0.8 ha (2 acres) specifically
for the production of potatoes. This practice was called "conacre"
(Beames 1975:352–353). Taking conacre was a widespread practice
in Connacht before 1845 (O'Brien 1921:11). Most defenders of the
poor passionately condemned conacre. In a speech intended to be
delivered in 1867 but never read, Karl Marx observed that the conacre system led to the degradation of the peasant farmers and ultimately destroyed the fertility of the soil (Dixon 1972:122). James
Connolly (1922:162), the great Irish socialist executed for his role in
the Easter Rebellion of 1916, succinctly observed that "England
made the famine by a rigid application of the economic principles
that lie at the base of capitalist society." Conacre meant that peasant farmers would have to seek new agricultural contracts every
year. Potentially, they would have to relocate their families annually. In turn, they would have had no long-term commitment to a
particular plot of land. Though individual men and women may
have felt a special emotional bond with a specific place, they knew
that as long as they were on conacre their hold on that place was
exceedingly tenuous.

Conacre had a devastating impact on Irish peasants. Generally
it was true that only unmarried farm laborers could make any sort
of living from the system (Beames 1975:353). All others slid deeper
into poverty and despair until the Great Famine either swept them
away or cast them off to America, England, and Australia. Rent
books on file at the National Library in Dublin show that the poor
farmers on Mahon's Strokestown estate took conacre land. This system, along with the general conditions of peasant life, account for
the theft of Mahon's timber and wool in 1840 and 1841 (see Chapter
7). In a very real sense, capitalism and the other three haunts pitted

tenants against landlords in a constant struggle for power. The prize was life itself.

THE PRESENCE OF THE HAUNTS

My plan in this chapter has not been to present the history of Gorttoose or to probe the reasons for the Great Irish Famine. I have not attempted to explain in full the complexities of Irish agriculture or to argue that Major Mahon was an evil landlord. Each element of the complex story of Gorttoose demands a full exploration in another place. Instead, my goal in this chapter has been to demonstrate the interconnected place of the men and women of Gorttoose in the world around them. That they were members of complex webs cannot be debated. They were tied, not simply to their landlord, but to one another and to the past. They knew, as do the men and women of Strokestown today, that their ancient ancestors once held title to the Irish landscape. Today's O'Garas are well versed in the traditions of their ancient power, and only a brief glimpse of the massive gate at the entrance of the Strokestown Park House reminds them of their loss. Across the Irish countryside, the mysterious bogs, the rolling, green hills, and the craggy mountains were once free from colonialism, Eurocentrism, capitalism, and modernity. But these haunts from the modern age affected the emerald isle in multifaceted ways. The people of Gorttoose and throughout rural Ireland—and indeed across the rest of the colonized world, including at Palmares—interacted with one anther and had interactions forced upon them. These associations were often created and maintained by the haunts, which usually worked together in a historically unique fashion through agents and managers.

It would be unsatisfying to conclude that colonialism, Eurocentrism, capitalism, and modernity affected the people of Gorttoose, and the fugitive slaves of Palmares, and to let matters rest there. Historical archaeologists would be left to wonder how the haunts affect their research in tangible ways. My brief overview of Gorttoose, and my exploration of Palmares in Chapter 2, shows that the four haunts are important to historical archaeology. But what now? How can historical archaeologists use this information in their research when they are not working at either Gorttoose or Palmares?

Innovative archaeologists can undoubtedly create countless ways to study the impact of the four haunts on modern-age peoples. In the next three chapters, I use what I have set out thus far to comment on the analysis of three commonplace topics in historical archaeology: artifacts, physical spaces, and subservient groups. These explorations touch upon many issues of significance to today's historical archaeologists. At the root, each involves the four haunts and can be examined using a mutualist perspective.

The Entangled World of Artifacts | 5

"If History is bunk, then Archaeology is junk." So begins Paul Bahn's (1989:5) wickedly humorous book *Bluff Your Way in Archaeology*. Bahn, a freelance writer with a Ph.D. in archaeology from Cambridge University, goes on to say that archaeology is a "bizarre subject" that "entails seeking, retrieving, and studying the abandoned, lost, broken, and discarded traces left by human beings in the past." He concludes that archaeologists are just the opposite of janitors. Archaeologists collect and save trash, whereas janitors have the good sense to discard it.

Archaeology will be forever associated with artifacts. The larger-than-life, heroic archaeologists portrayed in film usually go in search of beautiful objects that can be sold to dealers or that are widely known to have mystical powers. A golden idol or some other mysterious object is typically the prize of the expedition.

The archaeology portrayed by such imaginary figures as Indiana Jones is not entirely fictitious. Though most archaeologists spend much of their time studying huge, immovable artifacts like temples, ruins, and even entire landscapes (Chapter 6), they spend perhaps even more time examining the small, seemingly insignificant portable things from the past. If truthful, all but the most cynical of professional archaeologists would probably admit that they would simply love to find a golden idol just once in their career. At least then they would have an answer for the question non-archaeologists most frequently ask of professional archaeologists: "Have you ever found anything important?"

Historical archaeologists focus much of their attention on the small things from the past, even though they also spend large amounts of time poring over faded manuscripts, struggling to decipher the handwriting of long-dead scribes. These tiny remnants from the past are the objects James Deetz (1977) immortalized as "small things forgotten." These small calling cards from history fascinate historical archaeologists as much as objects of greater antiquity captivate prehistorians. In many ways, artifacts are the bread and butter of archaeological research. Archaeologists have a strong commitment to interpreting the daily activities of the men and women who lived in past societies, but they never forget that their field is largely a science of things. Much of what archaeologists know about past society comes directly from the objects left behind.

A SCIENCE OF THINGS

For my purposes, I can easily accept a textbook definition of "artifact" as a portable object whose form has been "modified wholly or partially from human activity" (Sharer and Ashmore 1987:65). A more picturesque definition is "the bric-a-brac washed up on the shore of modern times and left there as the social currents within which [they were] created have drained away" (Giddens 1984:357). The first definition contains the idea that artifacts are produced by purposeful human activity. The second definition tells us that artifacts have a dual reality. Though they are actually from the past, they exist in the present. Artifacts have been washed up on the shores of our "todays" and, just like other flotsam, they can make us wonder about their points of origin.

One of the great challenges of archaeological research is to decide precisely what artifacts mean. Paul MacKendrick (1960) used one of the great archaeological titles of all time in his *The Mute Stones Speak*. MacKendrick tricks us into thinking that the stones on his laboratory table spoke to him. And Ian Hodder (1986:123) affirmed in an important book that "artifacts do speak (or perhaps faintly whisper)." Archaeological interpretation would be so much easier if the artifacts would just open up and tell us what they had seen and experienced. But MacKendrick's and Hodder's expressions are fanciful. The stones do not speak, and artifacts remain frustratingly silent and aloof. As a result, the archaeologist's main task is to interpret the past based on what he or she can discern from these silent objects. Artifacts must be given meaning. Here, then, is the rub of archaeological research, for how do archaeologists know what artifacts mean? And, more importantly, do the artifacts speak through us or do we speak through them?

This last question is an old one in archaeological circles and it has caused considerable debate. Its most famous airing was in the early 1950s when two prominent archaeologists disagreed about the secrets artifacts are capable of revealing. Albert Spaulding (1953) proposed that artifact types—visible characteristics that consistently appear together—are embedded in the artifacts and await discovery by clever archaeologists. Spaulding, renowned for his statistical dexterity, believed that carefully chosen statistical procedures could make the types spring to life before the archaeologist's eyes. For him, an archaeologist's primary task is to find or to invent the statistical tools needed to discover the types. The types were real; they only slept in the artifacts until being awakened. James Ford (1954) disagreed with Spaulding. He believed that archaeologists create types as a tool for helping them to understand foreign cultures. He argued that artifact designs, shapes, and materials of manufacture could be affected by several cultural and historical factors. But, because culture is complex and forever fluid, archaeological types only represent abstractions pulled from a particular point in time. For Ford, if the types slept in the artifacts, the sleep recognized by archaeologists was only that of a single night.

The question of whether artifact types exist or are created has, of course, interested historical archaeologists. In a vast number of cases, though, archaeologists have been able to use written documents to explain how historical objects were used and sometimes even to learn their names. For example, in a now classic article, George Miller (1980) argued that historical archaeologists should use the nineteenth-century potters' names for their English ceramics rather than to create broad chronological terms. Miller believed that the practice of inventing type names for European ceramics was a throwback to prehistoric archaeology, and the practice had no place in historical archaeology, unless where absolutely necessary. By a painstaking search of ceramic price lists, bills of lading, and account books on both sides of the Atlantic, Miller showed that the use of invented names was not required when analyzing nineteenth-century English ceramics. In fact, the artificial names tended to obscure the past. Another superb example derives from Robert Schuyler's (1968) use of Diderot's eighteenth-century *Encyclopédie* to discover the function and names of military objects found at Fortress Louisbourg, Nova Scotia. Schuyler easily correlated the excavated, rusted iron objects with those Diderot showed for use in firing cannons. His correlation had great power because the excavated objects and the *Encyclopédie* were contemporaneous.

The recourse to written documents helps historical archaeologists to interpret the artifacts they find in the ground. In fact, the connection between written records and artifacts is often so strong in historical archaeology that artifacts have actually assumed the status of historical documents. Pioneer historical archaeologist J. C. Harrington (1952:337) likened excavation to "the study of a new collection of documentary material." For him, a day at the site was like a trip to the archives. Archaeologists may get slightly dirtier collecting artifacts, but the outcome is the same. The idea that artifacts were historical documents easily took root in historical archaeology, and its practitioners regularly referred to artifacts as "three-dimensional" documents (C. P. Russell 1967:387), "three-dimensional additions to the pages of history" (Noël Hume 1972:5), and "sources of history" that can be read like texts (Glassie 1975:12).

The link between physical artifacts and written documents is strong. The idea that artifacts can be read like written texts suggests, perhaps, that artifacts are not so mute after all (Hodder 1986). Artifacts tell us about themselves from the locations in which archaeologists find them. As Hodder (1986:4) explained, "Artifacts are found in graves around the necks of the skeletons and are interpreted as necklaces." Hodder's logic is difficult to reject because it stems from a deeply held, accepted truth of archaeological research. We can imagine that the string of beads is saying the word "necklace" to us as we excavate it from the soil. But Hodder (1986:4–5) accepted that even with good archaeological context, such as is the case with this imaginary skeleton, archaeologists cannot claim that "objects tell us their cultural meaning." In other words, there are some things artifacts do not wish to reveal to us. Our imaginary necklace refuses to let us in on its deeper, more intimate secrets. Faced with this serious problem, how do archaeologists—and specifically historical archaeologists—prod artifacts into revealing their secrets? How do we impart meaning to the silent, often dull artifacts that rest on our laboratory tables? Much of the answer lies in the connections artifacts maintained with the people who made and owned them. Artifacts and humans are forever connected.

TECHNOCRACIES AND COMMODITIES

In *Technopoly,* Neil Postman (1993) provided a chilling account of the way in which today's men and women are surrendering themselves to technology. To illustrate his position about technology, Postman (1993:22) created a three-part cultural classification.

Tool-using cultures use technology to solve specific problems related to survival and to serve art, religion, myth, and politics. One hallmark of a tool-using culture is that the people do not allow their technology to attack the basic integrity of their culture. People create tools that do not nudge culture out of the way. Tool-using cultures can be complex, creating such monumental structures as Stonehenge, the Egyptian pyramids, and Strasbourg Cathedral, with its 142-m (466-ft) spire. Even these monuments, however, remain firmly rooted to the traditional culture, filling a well-defined and comforting niche.

Tools play a central role in technocracies, Postman's second cultural type. In these more technologically rooted cultures, the tools actually attack culture, seeking to replace tradition with technology. In a technocracy, the tools actually *become* the culture. According to Postman (1993:28–29), three inventions signalled Western Europe's transition from tool-using culture to technocracy. The mechanical clock changed the way people thought about time. The steady swaying of the pendulum segmented reality and made it seem that the clock's time was natural. People began to live around the dictates of the clock, allowing the created temporal segments to control them. The movable-type printing press attacked the time-honored tradition of storytelling. To obtain knowledge, men, women, and perhaps most importantly, children began to interact more with books than with their elders, the repositories of their culture's history and traditions. The invention of the telescope attacked the fundamental tenets of Christianity by showing that mortal men and women could actually probe the secrets of "the heavens." Inquisitive individuals supplemented and maybe even replaced their belief in what was "up there" with empirical knowledge of the stars and the planets.

The technopoly, the last category in Postman's classification, is a totalitarian technocracy. In technopolies, the people totally surrender themselves to their technology. Everything in society is redefined according to the requirements of technology. So far, only the United States is a technopoly, but Japan and several nations in Western Europe are moving in this direction (Postman 1993:48–49).

Postman's intent was to explain the dangers of technopoly. His ideas are interesting and often compelling, but what interests me here is the technocracy because this category neatly encompasses modern times. The technocracy, with its radical inventions, daring philosophies, and startling discoveries of "new worlds" and native peoples, is what historical archaeologists study. One of the technocracy's main features that has relevance to historical archaeology is the pervasiveness of commodities within it.

All human societies fashion artifacts as a way of insuring their survival in the world. In the course of human history, individuals and groups discovered that they were not completely satisfied with the things they could make or obtain in the environment around them. Individuals, probably through cultural interaction, realized that they wanted exotic things for which they did not possess the knowledge, the raw materials, or perhaps even the skills to make themselves. To obtain the foreign things they desired, people learned that they would have to obtain the objects either through warfare or by establishing friendly relations with those who had the desired things.

Social scientists have long recognized the importance of trade to human societies (see, for example, Befu 1977; R. M. Emerson 1976). In fact, famed French historian Fernand Braudel (1977:15) has even gone so far as to state that "without exchange there is no society." Exchange is so important that societies can be classified according to how they conduct exchange, what they think exchange means, and the cultural importance they attach to it (Kopytoff 1986:68).

The presence of trade in a society means, of course, that people must make items available for exchange. Objects intended for trade are called "commodities." Commodities can take many forms, including portable artifacts, services, narratives, recipes, and even whole landscapes. Most bizarre is the idea that even people can become commodities, and examples are easy to find. In late medieval Ireland, for instance, women were exchangeable commodities for prominent men who strove to increase their power (Condren 1989:158). The capture and enslavement of Africans, and the marketing of today's movie stars and sports figures, are well known examples of human commoditization.

However we precisely choose to identify a commodity, the importance of commodities grew throughout the course of world history. Commodities were obviously important at places like Tenochtitlán (Chapter 3), but the significance of commodities exploded during the modern age with the rise of European, capitalistic technocracies. European commodities exerted their influence at home and abroad. In tool-using, medieval Europe, only the nobility had access to truly scarce, exotic objects. But with the rise of capitalism and the push for modernity, commoners gained access to exotic things from far away. Eager merchants flooded the streets and alleys of the Old World hawking strange items produced by people of different languages and strange customs. With the rise of capitalism and the appearance of wages, men and women suddenly had access to exotic objects, and could bring them into their homes for the first time. People not in royal bloodlines no longer had to wait for an inheritance to acquire precious material objects (McCracken 1988: 14–21; McKendrick 1982:9–13). Outside Europe, commodities were the tangible agents of colonialism, Eurocentrism, capitalism, and modernity. The trade goods found by Quimby (1966) at Native American villages in the Western Great Lakes are not-so-subtle reminders of the rise of commodities in the global marketplace.

For all their apparent simplicity, commodities are deceptive. The commodity is, as Marx (1967:72) said, "a very queer thing." Commodities are mysterious and troubling. What philosopher of technology Lewis Mumford (1967:23) said about all objects is especially true of commodities: they "may stubbornly defy time, but what they tell about man's history is a good deal less than the truth, the whole truth, and nothing but the truth."

One hidden truth of commodities is that they are the physical embodiment of human relationships. Commodities are not simply things; they are things that link individuals. At a bare minimum, a commodity involves two individuals: one willing to dispose of the commodity and one willing to obtain it. If the person who trades the object is not its manufacturer, then the commodity links three people. If the person who acquires the object is working as someone else's agent, then four individuals are joined together through the one, seemingly inanimate commodity. Thus, we can easily see that commodities are social things. They are mutualist to the core.

The concept of value is buried within the exchange process. For an object to be a commodity, someone must want to possess it. Someone somewhere must impart value to the thing. Ideas about "value" extend back to Aristotle, and many of his intellectual descendants have devoted great time and energy to thinking about this concept. Though "value" is an extremely broad term, three values can be said to exist: exchange value, use value, and esteem value.

Exchange value is the number of objects or services that a particular object can command in trade. For example, on December 12, 1804, French Canadian fur trader François-Antoine Larocque found the exchange value of a horse among the Native Americans of the Upper Missouri River to be 1 red Hudson's Bay shroud, 1 chief's coat, 1 large ax, 100 balls and powder, 2 knives, 2 dozen rings, a few beads, and a lump of vermillion. Several days later, on January 6, 1805, Larocque found the exchange value of a horse to be 1 blanket, 1 pair of leggings, 1 hoe, 1 calumet pipe, 1 lance, 1 dagger, 100 balls and powder, 1 knife, and a few beads (Wood and Thiessen 1985:142, 147). In instances such as these, we can equate exchange value with "price." Strictly speaking, though, price is not value. Price is really just an exchange value expressed in a standard medium, like money or, in Larocque's case, horses.

That Larocque encountered different exchange values only days apart is significant. The reason for the variation probably relates to use value. Use value is the ability of an object to satisfy a human want. In Larocque's case, the two individuals with whom he traded probably set different use values on horses, as well as on the trade goods they were to receive in exchange. In other words, Larocque and his Native American exchange partners, and the two Native American traders themselves, probably did not agree on the ability of the objects or the horses to be useful. Larocque needed the horses, so for him they had great use value. The same perhaps may be said for the trade items the natives received in exchange for the horses, but we cannot know for certain. We can surmise, though, that they wanted the items or they would not have traded their horses for them.

Esteem value (Walsh 1901:1), or aesthetic value (Simmel 1978:73–74), is perhaps the most mysterious of the three values because it originates in an individual's perception of an object. Esteem values arise from a feeling—typically pleasure—an object evokes. We may say, perhaps, that esteem value is a special kind of use value because the esteemed objects are "useful" for causing pleasure. In Chapter 2, I mentioned that archaeologists in the Ozarks found a badge from the Columbia Exposition, and that in South Carolina my research team discovered a medal from the St. Paul Ice Carnival. We may assume that these objects had little exchange value. They were probably inexpensive and, at the time, they probably could not command much in the way of exchange. They may have had some use value, perhaps to symbolize the owner's knowledge of the events or to show familiarity with the outside world. They may even have shown that the final owner of the souvenirs was respected and remembered by someone who had traveled far. Regardless, we may well suppose that the objects had high esteem value to their owners. The medals' owners may have cherished them because they came from a world far removed from the work-a-day world of the Ozarks or the fields of rural South Carolina. They may have valued the tiny objects because they were freely given by a friend or an admirer who had thought of them during an exciting holiday. Of course, we will never know the precise esteem value these objects held for their past owners. Archaeology is ill-equipped to provide such information, and the written documents from the sites associated with the medals are silent on their behalf. As a result, we are left to wonder about the exact meaning of these exotic medallions. Of course, today we may well imagine that the two objects command great exchange value to collectors of old medals. This ability to assume different values over time is precisely my point. Value, however perceived, is fluid and rooted to the situation in which an object finds itself.

Use values and esteem values have existed throughout human history. We may suppose that the first person to fashion a stone scraper readily recognized its use value. The producer probably invented the scraper to perform a specific task. We may also suppose that our prehistoric craftsperson—or his or her compatriots—attached esteem value to the object because of its unique character or the beauty of its form. The scraper may have been an inspirational artifact, establishing awe in all who beheld it.

It is an anthropological truism in the 1990s to say that all artifacts are recognized to carry social meanings (Douglas and Isherwood 1979:59). Anthropologists and other scholars of material culture now agree that artifacts are not inert. They were not created to remain dead. Instead, material objects are "actually involved in the social world" (Shanks and Tilley 1988:117). Artifacts carry meanings, convey messages, and mediate between individuals and groups in complicated ways. Much of this activity has nothing whatsoever to do with physical survival as such. Many objects control our minds and cause us to reevaluate the situations and events in which we find ourselves. Objects "affect what a person can do, either by expanding or restricting the scope of that person's actions and thoughts" (Csikszentmihalyi and Rochberg-Halton 1981:53). Thus, we may conclude that objects are not "a superficial or optional feature of life," but are "a definitional component of human existence" (Jhally 1987:1). People find artifacts to be indispensable.

Historical archaeologists have generally accepted that the artifacts they find on archaeological sites had active lives while they were in the world. During their long sleep in the ground, artifacts were dormant pieces of the human experience, simply waiting to be awakened. Studies of garden landscapes (Leone 1984), eighteenth-

century pewter objects (A. S. Martin 1989), toothbrushes and nap-
kins (Shackel 1993), and nineteenth-century proprietary medicine
bottles (Orser 1994a) reinforce the idea that artifacts led active,
social lives while they were in the care of their living owners.

The idea that artifacts lead social lives suggests that what is
important about artifacts is not necessarily "what they were made
to be, but what they have become" (Thomas 1991:4). Artifacts, and
especially commodities, were constantly being "recontextualized"
throughout their lives. The meaning of an artifact changed with
each new social situation within which it was located. This almost
constant transformation, what cultural anthropologist Nicholas
Thomas (1991:27) terms "the promiscuity of objects," is particularly
apparent for commodities. The souvenir medallions found in the
Ozarks and in South Carolina help to explain recontextualization.
First, someone made the medals for a merchant who planned to sell
them as mementos. When the manufacturer turned them over to the
merchant, the medals were recontextualized. The act of transferring
them from one person to another transformed them from manufactured products to merchandise capable of being sold. The objects
were again recontextualized when hawkers at the fair sold them to
fair-goers. This time, the medals were transformed from merchandise to souvenirs. If the buyer of the medals gave them to someone
else, then the objects were again recontextualized, this time from
souvenirs to gifts. When the medals were lost or discarded, they
were again recontextualized, changing from gifts to either lost mementos or unwanted refuse. Finally, when archaeologists unearthed
the medals, they transformed them again from lost souvenirs to
archaeological specimens. The medals could be transformed again
into museum pieces. In a cruel twist of fate, the medals could even
be recontextualized back into sellable commodities if our archaeologist sold them to antique collectors. The collectors might impart
great esteem value to the medals while being cognizant of their
exchange value. Our hapless archaeologist would assume that the
medals had great use value as he or she used the ill-gotten funds to
buy food for his or her starving family.

My imaginary biography of the festival medals (after Kopytoff
1986) is purposefully sketchy because I do not know how the medals
actually spent their lives in the world. What this life history shows,
however, is that the medals—and by extension all objects, and especially commodities—are entangled in the world around them
(Thomas 1991:3). The entanglements tie them to people, and it is

from these interlaced individuals that the objects obtain their values. Without people artifacts would have no value at all. And furthermore, without the networks within which the individuals moved, the values would have no cultural meaning. Thus, we cannot ever hope to understand artifacts—especially the commodities made and used in modern times—outside their entanglements. Artifacts and people work together in the world for many purposes. They can accomplish good, they can entrap one another, they can subjugate whole cultures.

People and artifacts have been entangled throughout human history, and they will be forever engaged in complex networks of meaning. Archaeologists in the present become entangled within these ancient networks as they impart meanings to artifacts and as they recontextualize them in our understanding of the past. The tangible objects, their makers and users of long ago, and the present-day scholars who study them become members of the same extended network. The entangled association of modern-day researchers with objects made and used in the past can be remarkably subtle. More interesting, the relationships can change as we learn more about specific artifacts and as we decide what they meant in the past. The changes in interpretation that can result from a lifetime of study are usually portrayed as advances in knowledge. This characterization is often accurate. Sometimes, however, advances in knowledge are merely recontextualizations of artifacts by creative archaeologists. Archaeologists learn more about a certain kind of artifact or develop an innovative interpretation, and then simply place the artifact within the new interpretive environment. They have recontextualized the artifact in the past through the change in their knowledge in the present. This process may sound mysterious, but it only shows how archaeologists and their artifacts are intertwined. I could find several examples to illustrate my point, but one particularly useful case comes from the history of Colono Ware.

THE STRANGE CAREER OF
COLONO WARE POTTERY

Archaeologists working in the American South have become entangled with a coarsely made, unglazed pottery they principally find along the coasts of South Carolina and Virginia. This pottery, also found in the Caribbean, appears at slave plantations occupied in the late seventeenth century and throughout the eighteenth century. The ware was largely gone from the plantations by the early nineteenth century, replaced by glazed European and American ceramics.

Historical archaeologists have taught themselves many lessons with Colono Ware pottery. The ones I wish to focus on relate to how archaeologists entered into various relationships with this ware since the 1960s. In the 30 years that archaeologists have examined Colono Ware, they have recontextualized it many times, changing its meaning along the way. They have taken Colono Ware from the archaeological shadows of obscurity to the spotlight of academic research and cultural appreciation.

The story of Colono Ware pottery begins in the early 1960s with Ivor Noël Hume, then chief archaeologist at Colonial Williamsburg. While excavating the earliest sites associated with the English colonization of Virginia, Noël Hume and his excavators found bag loads of coarse, unglazed pottery. They quickly discovered that the potters of this ware had fashioned it into shapes reminiscent of European skillets and other vessels commonly used far across the Atlantic. Generally, though, the ware was decidedly non-European. Faced with the odd mixture of European and non-European cultural traits in the same pottery tradition, Noël Hume (1962) decided to call the pottery "Colono-Indian Ware." Both his vast knowledge of the artifacts of English colonialism and his solid understanding of the Native American archaeology of the area convinced him that the term was valid. The ware dated to the colonial era and it looked like the Native American pottery commonly found by archaeologists throughout the eastern United States.

But all was not well. One important loose end hung from the interpretation. What was troubling about this pottery was that archaeologists usually found it at sites never inhabited by Native Americans. In fact, archaeologists usually found it at sites associated with African-American slaves. Noël Hume was not bothered by this apparent contradiction and he simply devised a creative interpretation to explain it. He figured that inventive Native American potters had made the vessels to appeal to slaves, who eagerly bought it with meager funds or bartered for it. His interpretation of Colono Ware as a commodity was brilliant. The sale of the pottery to slaves elegantly explained how Native American potters could have made the ware and how African-American slaves could have used it. The pottery was recontextualized by a relationship forged between Native Americans and enslaved Africans living in the New World.

Whether Noël Hume's interpretation was correct is largely insignificant. The importance of his idea lies in what it said about the power of Colono-Indian pottery to link together people who were culturally and historically distinct. From the very beginning scholars admitted that Colono Ware was a strongly mutualist artifact.

Following in the footsteps of Noël Hume, several other archaeologists showed an interest in Colono Ware and many studied it with enthusiasm. A full decade after Noël Hume expressed his views on the pottery, archaeologist Steven Baker (1972) linked the pottery with the Catawba, a Native American group living in South Carolina. With Baker's interpretation, archaeologists could associate the pottery not just with "Indians" but with a particular people. Baker effectively contextualized the pottery not only in time but also in cultural space. The pottery "belonged" to the Catawba. They invented pieces as commodities and used them to help ensure their survival in the rapidly changing economic world of the American South. Baker (1972:16) suggested, however, that Noël Hume had been too conservative in stating that Native Americans sold their wares only to slaves. Instead, Baker said that the market for these coarse though highly functional wares also attracted other Native American peoples and even many Europeans. Baker argued, then, that Colono Ware was even more mutualist than Noël Hume had suggested.

The interpretation that Native American potters made Colono Ware held firm until the 1970s. It was at that time, largely because of the awakening caused by the Civil Rights movement, that archaeologists in South Carolina began to wonder if Noël Hume and Baker were correct (Ferguson 1992:xxxv–xxxvi). Could it be that enslaved African Americans were not the recipients of the native-made pottery but the actual producers of the ware? According to Leland Ferguson (1978:69), once this realization was made "the lid was cracked on a box of ideas that has sat covered with dust in the darkest corner of North American historic sites archaeology—the contribution of Afro-Americans to the pottery we call 'Colono-Indian.'" Ferguson (1978:79) soon led the charge to demonstrate the African character of this ware, concluding in his first major study that "I believe it a reasonable hypothesis that Afro-American slaves made much if not most of the Colono-Ware we see in the archaeological record."

Though looking mostly toward enslaved women potters of African descent, Ferguson also said that Native American potters should not be overlooked. Clearly, they had probably made some Colono Ware pottery. The important thing, though, was that Native Americans were not the ware's major producers.

Even with the door left open to Native American craftpersons, the interpretive focus of the pottery shifted to African Americans. This shift was not insignificant. The identification of Colono Ware with Native Americans implied that native potters learned the craft of pottery manufacture in their home region. Pottery manufacture was a traditional technology, rooted in North American time and place. Prehistorians in the American Southeast had already shown the antiquity of aboriginal pottery in the region. In fact, fiber-tempered pottery, which shows that native potters had used plant material to hold the clay together and to absorb unwanted moisture, represents the earliest pottery in North America, dating to around 2500 B.C. (Skibo et al. 1989; Stoltman 1966). As an Indian ware, Colono Ware represented the technology of a tool-using culture. The pottery had a firm and recognizable place within a traditional culture. The interpretation was quite different, however, if archaeologists viewed the pottery as a commodity, or in other words, as an inherently and undeniably mutualist artifact. The association of Colono Ware with African Americans meant that enslaved potters brought the concept of pottery manufacture with them across the Atlantic Ocean. With this new interpretation, archaeologists created a new network of association. Colono Ware tangibly tied together two continents rather than simply introducing colonists and slaves to an existing aboriginal tradition. With the African connection made explicit, archaeologists successfully recontextualized Colono Ware and it accordingly assumed an entirely new meaning.

The recontextualization of Colono Ware opened new interpretive doors to archaeologists. With Africa in the picture, archaeologists could argue that Colono Ware had more than a functional significance. Colono Ware pots were not just pots, they were charged with political meaning. The pottery, in effect, allowed slaves to "struggle with pots" (Ferguson 1991). Its apparent use value, as a pot, had become an important esteem value, as a political and cultural statement. Colono Ware sherds screamed to the outside world that they were part of a cultural tradition that was decidedly non-European.

The tangible link between the slave South and the African homeland of millions of slaves, via Colono Ware, empowered historical archaeology. Historical archaeologists could finally prove their contribution to knowledge. Their long hours at plantation sites in the hot sun and oppressive heat had paid off at last. They could demonstrate something colonial observers had chosen to ignore. Information about Colono Ware pottery and its importance to the New World's slave communities were not available to historians. When plantation masters and estate managers sat in their offices gazing out over their cultivated fields, they refused to see the pottery sherds scattered around their slave quarters. Archaeologists had unearthed these tiny fragments and, though it had taken a while, had finally accorded them their rightful place in history. But Colono Ware sherds were not just historical documents. They were revolutionary broadsides tacked to the walls of plantation big houses.

The excitement over the tangible link between Africa and the American South through Colono Ware was profound and important. The enthusiasm, however, was somewhat tempered by insights provided by Matthew Hill (1987). An archaeologist with considerable experience in Africa, Hill examined Colono Ware pottery with puzzled fascination. Try as he might, he could see nothing particularly African about it. Hill looked for Ferguson's "Afro" and simply did not see it. Significantly, Hill did not belittle Ferguson's interpretation that Colono Ware could have been made by African slaves. He simply said that the pottery appeared to resemble not just African pottery but a "basic, non-wheel, unglazed, clamp-fired pottery" found throughout the world (Hill 1987:136). Hill stressed, however, that what was most noteworthy about Colono Ware pottery was not that it had African characteristics but that it was distinctively non-European. Colono Ware indeed allowed enslaved men and women to struggle with pots, but as non-Europeans rather than strictly as Africans. Technically speaking, both Native Americans and African-American slaves could have easily made Colono Ware. Both peoples struggled against the forces of colonialism and Eurocentrism in the New World.

Hill's ideas pointed toward a new conceptualization. Instead of the sherds representing a throwback to Africa—a retention of cultural traits from the Old World—they connoted a system of resistance and cultural diversity that strove to set itself apart from the dominant, European culture. These two interpretations are really quite different. Instead of African women simply remembering how to make pottery as their mothers or grandmothers had taught them in their homelands, the sherds implied that non-European potters sought to celebrate their difference in their pottery. Africa was clearly important, but equally or perhaps even more important was the process of "creolization," the making of a new culture from many diverse strands. As Martin Hall (1992:385) argued, archaeologists have no reason to expect that enslaved men and women would choose to signify their struggle against oppression simply with artifacts that reminded them of Africa. Enslaved peoples all over the world sought several strategies in their ongoing battles with their oppressors. Some of these strategies concerned imparting meaning to material things; others involved outright conflict. Ferguson (1992) realized this and situated Colono Ware within the process of North American creolization, in which Africans, Native Americans, and Europeans blended elements of their diverse cultures.

The evolving picture of Colono Ware is that it was not a cultural marker. Rather, the pottery represents a process of interaction. Colono Ware is a truly mutualist artifact. African, Native American, and European men and women could make and use Colono Ware to "create new worlds" (Mouer 1993:152). That seventeenth-century Apalachee Indians in the Florida panhandle made Colono Ware vessels for Spanish soldiers shows how embedded the pottery tradition was in the social networks of the past (Vernon 1988; Vernon and Cordell 1993). Because Colono Ware is a mutualist artifact, it is unimportant whether the Colono Ware of the Apalachee resembles the Colono Ware of South Carolina's slaves, or whether it looks like the pottery made by the Catawba. These differences are fodder for archaeologists bent on creating classifications of Colono Ware. Further sophistication in the analysis of the pottery itself will come with time, just as it did with undocumented prehistoric wares.

The great majority of artifacts made and used during the modern era were mutualist commodities. That even a handmade, cottage-craft artifact like Colono Ware could assume important mutualist dimensions, however, is highly significant. Its importance demonstrates the power of the four haunts in modern times. Colono Ware would have been impossible without the widespread capitalist use of slavery for profit, and without the related, condescending view that Europeans were superior to all non-Europeans. Also required, however, was the impulse of European nation-states to colonize the world in their haste toward modernity. If the four haunts can be so easily related to a coarse, unglazed pottery, what does this say about their relationship to the tons of other material objects associated with European markets and factories? The glazed ceramics shipped from Staffordshire, England, and the mass-produced trade goods dumped on aboriginal villages immediately spring to mind, but other, more obscure artifacts also figure prominently in the picture.

THE MYSTICAL PIPES OF PALMARES

Strangely enough, the Colono Ware pottery found in the American South is relevant to Palmares. In Chapter 2, I explored how fugitive African slaves, Portuguese settlers, and Tupinambá Indians all worked together to create the kingdom of Palmares. We may suppose that several of the artifacts that await discovery on the Serra da Barriga, the site of Palmares' capital city, will permit a better understanding of the cultural processes at work in the kingdom. Given the cultural connections of the rebel settlements, we may reasonably conclude that many, perhaps even most, of the artifacts used by the Palmaristas were inherently mutualist. We may also suppose that much of the pottery we have collected from the surface of the Serra da Barriga may be correctly classified as Colono Ware. The pieces are coarse, unglazed, and usually unadorned with surface decoration. Unfortunately, I cannot now make definitive statements about the pottery because the archaeological work at Palmares is only beginning and because the prehistoric archaeology of the state of Alagoas is now so poorly understood. Rather than to focus on the pottery, I wish to take a different tack and explore an artifact that oddly seems to accompany Colono Ware wherever it is found. This artifact is the decorated clay tobacco pipe.

The archaeological history of decorated clay tobacco pipes strangely mimics that of Colono Ware. The first archaeologists to unearth these pipes charted the same course for them as they had for Colono Ware, largely assuming that Native Americans had made them. The pipes were not made of brilliant white clay in the common, long-stem tradition known in Europe and throughout the colonies, so it was easy to assume that they were part of another manufacturing tradition. Though some archaeologists thought that European colonists may have made the pipes when they could not obtain the white clay variety from Europe, most ascribed them to

Native Americans. Archaeologists called these pipes "aboriginal," "Virginia made," and "locally made" and wondered about their aboriginal producers (Henry 1979; Mouer 1993:124–125). Oddly enough, one interpretation used by archaeologists to explain the appearance of these pipes was one they sometimes used to account for the production of Colono Ware: economics (Henry 1979:15–18; Vernon 1988:80). Their reasoning was that European colonists accepted Colono Ware and locally made smoking pipes only when embargoes and economic depressions necessitated such sacrifices. This explanation implied that the smoking pipes, and also the Colono Ware pottery, were objects of last resort, symbolizing nothing more than a scarcity of the objects the European colonists found desirable, and perhaps even more comforting.

Research by Jerome Handler (1983; Handler and Lange 1978: 130–131) and by Matthew Emerson (1988, 1994), however, soon recontextualized the pipes, situating them squarely within the African community. In his pioneering research, Matthew Emerson (1988) showed that the pipes found at seventeenth-century sites in the Chesapeake region were the product of Native American, European, and African traditions. Most of the almost 700 pipes Emerson examined from 15 different archaeological collections reflected an intriguing mixture of European forms and West African surface decorations. Clearly, the smoking pipes of the Chesapeake region are important artifacts.

Within the past few years, visitors to the Serra da Barriga turned over four decorated clay smoking pipes to the museum in União dos Palmares, the small town at the base of the hill. The Serra da Barriga was the site of Macaco, the capital city of Palmares. The pipes were brought to my attention in 1993 by José Alberto Gonçalves, the museum's chief administrator. Unfortunately, we must completely contextualize the pipes since they were not found during controlled archaeological excavation, but instead are the product of unsystematic surface collection. Our surveys in 1992 and 1993 failed to recover similar pipes among the artifact scatters on the 14 sites we discovered (Orser 1993), but we believe Gonçalves when he says that the pipes came from the Serra da Barriga. The pipes have a totally unique appearance in the region, being completely unlike the simple clay pipes regularly ascribed to prehistoric native groups.

Two things about the four pipes are immediately striking. The first is their form. The pipes have short stems attached to rounded bowls, suggesting that they were smoked by inserting a reed or hollow piece of wood into the stem (Figure 5). This form alone is not particularly noteworthy since archaeologists commonly find this pipe style throughout the world. What is most compelling about the style, however, comes from comparing them with two archaeological sites located far to the northwest of Palmares. One site is the slave cemetery at Newton Plantation in southern Barbados, and the other is a suspected maroon settlement in the extreme eastern end of Santo Domingo. At Newton Plantation, Barbados, Jerome Handler and Frederick Lange (1978:130) found a pipe similar in form to the Palmares pipes. They found the pipe in the undisturbed grave of an old man who was buried with an elaborate necklace containing a large reddish orange carnelian bead, seven cowrie shells, 21 drilled dog canines, and five drilled vertebrae from a large bony fish (Handler et al. 1979). These artifacts led Handler and Lange (1978:131–132) to conclude that the man had been a revered folk doctor and "probably of African birth." The man had been buried in the late 1600s or early 1700s, a time roughly contemporaneous with Palmares' final years.

After painstaking research, Handler was able to associate the short-stemmed clay pipe from Newton Plantation with an African tradition. He quoted late eighteenth-century English observers who witnessed Barbadian slaves using this kind of pipe, often burning their noses in the process because they did not attach a reed to the stem (Handler 1983:24). When Handler (1983:250) asked Africanist archaeologist Merrick Posnansky about the pipe from Newton Plantation, he learned that it "could quite easily be dropped into a late seventeenth century collection from Ghana and would be quite at home." Thus, it seems clear that the Newton Plantation clay pipe linked Africa and Barbados in an unambiguous way.

Archaeologists in Santo Domingo discovered four short-stemmed pipes, similar in form to the one from Barbados, at a probable maroon settlement on the far eastern part of their island (García Arévalo 1986:50). Like the four pipes from Palmares, the four pipes from Santo Domingo came from the seventeenth century. Also like the pipes from both Palmares and Barbados, these pipes have short stems. Manuel García Arévalo (1986:50) reported that a researcher in Cuba found a similar pipe at a cave associated with maroons on that island. Thus, it appears that a short-stemmed pipe tradition is somehow associated with maroons.

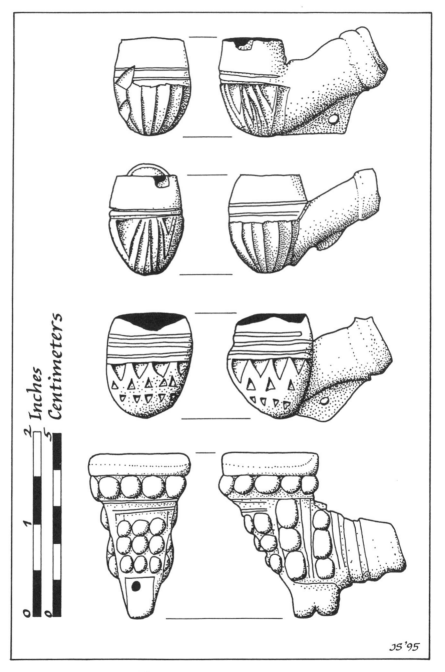

Figure 5. The pipes of Palmares.

The Barbados pipe contains a small connecting piece situated across the angle between the stem and the bowl. In the center of this piece is a small, drilled hole (Handler and Lange 1978:130; Handler 1983:248). Two of the Palmares pipes contain a similar feature, and it appears to be broken off a third Palmares pipe. Though the makers of the Palmares pipes placed this piece on the bottom of the stem, the drilled hole is there nonetheless. Though obviously not a major feature of the pipes, this tiny element connects the pipes from Palmares to the one from Barbados.

The bowl decorations also forge connections between the pipes. The makers of the Palmares pipes decorated all four specimens by cutting unique designs into each. As was true of Handler's find (1983:249), I also cannot say whether the Palmares pipes were molded before firing or whether an artist carved the designs into the pipes after they had hardened. It would be instructive to know more about the manufacturing process used in making the pipes, but the decorations themselves are significant. One Palmares pipe has triangular patterns on the bowl and three bands encircling the bowl near the rim. The decorator of a second pipe placed rows of raised, circular rosettes throughout the bowl's surface. Both decorations are purposeful ornamentations that undoubtedly had some meaning to their designers. The pipes may even have carried messages to others. Archaeologists someday may be able to interpret these apparently expressionless decorations. For now, they remain a mystery. It is intriguing that the maroon pipes from Santo Domingo and from Cuba also have triangular patterns scratched into their bowls (García Arévalo 1986:50, 64, 65). These pipes seem to connect Caribbean and Cuban maroons with the men and women of Palmares, even though there is almost no possibility that the maroons could have ever met one another.

The two remaining pipes from Palmares are slightly different from the others. Whoever fashioned these two pipes decorated them with a design that can be perceived to represent palm trees. On both pipes, the fronds reach up from the base of the bowl, appearing to cradle it. If these stylized decorations were indeed meant to represent palm trees—and for now I am comfortable with this interpretation—then we are confronted with two significant artifacts from Palmares. These pipes suggest that the men and women of Palmares were, to paraphrase Ferguson (1991), "struggling with pipes." In decorating the pipes with stylized palm trees, the artists proclaimed the power of Palmares to the world. The pipes announced the continued existence of Palmares in terms its colonial enemies could not ignore and would well understand. Readers will remember from Chapter 2 that the residents of Palmares called their kingdom Angola Janga, though the Portuguese and the Dutch knew the kingdom as "the place of palm trees." The representation of palm trees on smoking pipes—those seemingly insignificant but tangible pieces of daily life—was not a neutral decoration. The pipes proclaimed that the rebel kingdom existed, and as such was a constant reminder that colonialism was not all pervasive. The men and women of this upstart, fugitive slave kingdom could produce their own symbolically charged artifacts. The pipes were the messengers of resistance and rebellion. They showed the cracks in the slave regime and loudly announced its fragility.

During their "lives," the pipes of Palmares commanded almost constant recontextualization. They could have been used at Palmares as smoking pipes, or they could have been traded to Portuguese settlers as evocative commodities. The pipes also could have been sent to the coast as symbolic reminders of Palmares, or they could have been carried back to the coast by marauding Portuguese or Dutch mercenaries as trophies of war. The pipes could have had use value, exchange value, or esteem value at any point in their complex recontextualizations. In any case, the pipes linked the renegade interior of northeastern Brazil with the settled, "modern" European coast. The pipes mediated between cultures and linked South America with Africa and Europe. They also linked Africans enslaved throughout the New World. Surprising to many, perhaps, the pipes also link displaced seventeenth-century Angolan slaves in the New World with twentieth-century Angolans engaged in the struggle with the same Portuguese colonial masters. Angolan artists have always fashioned artifacts as symbols of cultural and political resistance (Hersey 1974).

The pipes of Palmares are mysterious partly because I do not know much about them. I cannot relate many of the "facts" that would intrigue most traditional historical archaeologists. I do not know the source of their clays, the precise ways they were made, or how the artists produced the designs of their bowls. An understanding of the physical properties of the pipes will come with time. At this writing, these mundane facts are less important than the realization that the pipes are mutualist. They allow us to situate Palmares in the middle of a world that connected men and women from diverse cultural traditions. That the pipes resemble African and

Caribbean pipes is exciting. That the pipes allow us to glimpse the cultural connections created by diverse peoples in the frontier of northeastern Brazil at the height of European colonialism is equally exciting.

The pipes of Palmares, Colono Ware pottery from South Carolina and Virginia, and smoking pipes from Barbados, Santo Domingo, and Cuba collaborate to tell the story of the four haunts of historical archaeology. These objects from long ago also demonstrate the interpretive power that results from a mutualist perspective when investigating the modern world. Artifacts are obviously central to any archaeologist's interpretations of the historical past. Portable material things, though important, do not tell the whole story. Artifacts, like the people who made and used them, did not float around like weightless astronauts. Human beings and artifacts were firmly anchored on the ground. They were surrounded by landscapes and environments of their own creation. They had, in fact, invented space within which to locate themselves.

Invented Place, Created Space

On the first page of *The Return of the Native,* Thomas Hardy (1959) introduced an unusual, nonhuman character—Egdon Heath. The heath, a wide-open, barren plain, was not a typical actor. By all reckoning, the heath should have been a silent, natural spectator, a desolate and foreboding stage upon which the passions of Clym Yeobright and Eustacia Vye could be played out. But for Hardy, as for millions of readers since the novel first appeared in 1878, Egdon Heath was neither a mere backdrop nor a disinterested eavesdropper. Hardy infused the heath with an emotive and passionate character, and pressed its weighty presence down upon the story's characters. Egdon Heath became "almost one of the leading characters in the novel" (Hutchings 1968:65).

Hardy's high regard as a storyteller and poet is well symbolized by the burial of his ashes in the floor of the Poet's Corner, Westminster Abbey. I will let his adorning fans and zealous critics debate the literary merits of his tearful, fatalistic tales. Hardy was not greatly concerned with archaeology, though occasionally he infused a poem with a romantic notion of antiquity. Still, archaeologists can learn from his use of Egdon Heath. Hardy saw something important in the brooding countryside. In his personal sketch of the area, Hardy depicted the heath as connected to a network of narrow roads, including one phenomenally straight highway built by the Romans. In the center of the heath, Hardy drew three prehistoric earthen mounds, called Rainbarrow (Pinion 1968:313). Tradition says that the English signalled the arrival of Napoleon's invading army from the summit of these earthen promontories.

Within Hardy's world, we may easily suppose Egdon Heath to have been situated within two networks, one topographic, and other human. The heath was part of the unfeeling natural environment, but at the same time it participated in the human actions that unfolded around it. Hardy used the heath as an unchanging, powerful device that could serve, by its very timelessness, as a counter-

point to the human emotions and passions of his invented characters. The simmering power of the heath derived not from the length
of its grass or the height of its barrows but from the way in which it
was an invented place. Egdon Heath was a creation, not just of
Hardy's imagination, but of all the human actors who moved upon
it. The heath was alive and powerful; it could imprison some and
liberate others. At its roots, though, the power of the heath came not
from nature but from the network of men and women who empowered it. They invented the heath as actors in Hardy's novel, and
the heath is reinvented every time a new reader picks up *The Return
of the Native.*

ARCHAEOLOGISTS AND INVENTED SPACE

Archaeologists are not novelists and only a tiny percentage of us
will ever be able to write with the passion and depth of Thomas
Hardy. As a result, the lesson of Egdon Heath should not be lost on
us. Archaeologists have always been interested in where settlements are located and what they meant to the men and women who
built them, toiled in their fields, and died in their houses. Much of
what archaeologists wish to know about past settlements has something to do with networks and mutualist relations. Oddly, though, it
was only with the research of Gordon Willey (1953) in the late 1940s
that archaeologists began to think about ancient settlements as being situated within networks of interaction and association.

Willey performed a pioneering survey in the Virú Valley in
northern Peru as part of a combined anthropological and geographic
study of the region. With the publication of his findings in 1953,
the concept of settlement networks entered the archaeological consciousness. Though Willey did not overtly mention networks as
such, they nonetheless pervaded his research. For example, in explaining the settlement of the Puerto Moorin period (A.D. 0–300), he
mentioned an interconnected "constellation of dwelling-site-politico-
religious" centers (Willey 1953:377–378). Similarly, the spatial arrangement of Late Gallinazo period sites (dating roughly to A.D.
600–700) suggested to Willey that "a strong centralized government
or a tightly knit and amazingly smooth-running confederacy" had
once tied them together (Willey 1953:396). So, without actually saying it, Willey incorporated into his interpretations the idea that
networks of settlement had once stretched throughout the prehistoric Virú Valley.

Willey's research forever changed the face of settlement archaeology (Trigger 1989:284). No longer was it enough simply to locate the most representative site in a region and excavate it. Willey told archaeologists that they had to consider a site's wider settlement environment and to appreciate how individual sites had been stretched into complex, interacting networks.

Since the publication of Willey's Virú Valley study, several prehistorians have followed his lead and have shown how individual sites existed within large networks. In fact, many archaeologists have adapted and even created sophisticated analytical procedures to study ancient, human settlements (see, for example, Fish and Kowalewski 1990; Hodder 1977; Hodder and Orton 1976; Zimmerman 1977).

Understanding the linking aspects of past settlement networks can help archaeologists to explain the distribution of artifacts. For example, Peter Danks (1977) showed how late eighteenth-century Lowestoft porcelain moved through eastern England when merchants traveled a network of roads to take bowls, saucers, and cups to regional markets and fairs. Though he did not make it explicit, Danks' perspective derived from "directed network" models. Directed networks indicate how commodities, such as natural gas, oil, telephone messages, and even porcelain, flow through complex webs in an orderly and purposeful manner (Mandl 1979:1). The roads of eighteenth-century England sending porcelain to market can be likened to pipelines feeding petroleum to a metropolis.

The archaeological study of spatial distribution is often inspired by geographers, and a close association often exists between archaeology and geography (Allen et al. 1990; Earle and Preucel 1987; Wagstaff 1987). Some archaeologists have taken their inspiration from geographers with an explicit interest in network analysis (Haggett 1965; Haggett and Chorley 1969). Archaeologists have even advocated the direct application of geographical network theory to their research (Clarke 1968:463–490; Hodder and Orton 1976:66–71; Trombold 1991).

Archaeologists are intrigued by their ability to represent schematically the links between networked ancient sites. They can plot the sites they find on hills and in floodplains, and they can connect them by reference to roads, paths, canals, rivers, and highways. This process of connecting discrete, individual sites shows what it took for peoples in the past to interact with one another. We can see that they crossed streams, forded rivers, and skirted mountains just like we do today. Traveling to interact is, in fact, a time-honored activity. As historian Eric Leed (1991:18) observed, travel is "a central rather than a peripheral force in historical transformations." Much of this traveling occurred over routes that have a lasting archaeological presence. Peter Danks (1977) demonstrated the importance of roads in eastern England in the eighteenth century; David Wilson (1990:142) did the same in coastal Peru just south of Willey's Virú Valley for the early Middle Horizon Black-White-Red culture (A.D. 650–1150); and Jason Dowdle (1987) discovered that the Romans in France, rather than building their own roads, simply upgraded and expanded the earlier routes laid down by the Gauls. Roads, rivers, paths, and highways have been important for generations. That archaeologists can locate and map these connecting routes is a significant contribution to knowledge.

In accordance with their general urge to classify things, archaeologists have invented a typology of the connectors, expressing them as microlevel (within buildings), semi-microlevel (within sites), and macrolevel (between sites) (Clarke 1977:11–12). Of course, in conjunction with the connecting elements, archaeologists have shown great interest in the sites themselves. Confronted with a considerable variety of sites and possible settlement designs, archaeologists have devised typologies of settlement. These classifications generally have extended from individual buildings to regional patterns (see, for example, Trigger 1968:55–70).

At about the time that many archaeologists were beginning to comprehend the importance of large-scale settlement networks in antiquity, anthropologist Edward T. Hall (1963a, 1963b, 1969) was inventing a new way to think about the use of space. Hall was not so interested in where things were situated but, in a twist of archaeological logic, in the distance *between* things. Thus, Hall was interested in where things were not. He named his study "proxemics," and defined it as "the interrelated observations and theories of man's use of space as a specialized elaboration of culture" (Hall 1969:1). The subject matter of proxemics is "the distance between men in the conduct of daily transactions, the organization of space in his houses and buildings, and ultimately the layout of his towns" (Hall 1963a:1003). Hall (1969) argued that the perception of space is tied to the senses, so that visual, auditory, olfactory, and tactile space all exist. In addition, Hall (1969:103–112) created his own typology of space. Fixed-feature space includes all those things that are not movable: houses, wells, icehouses, and basements. Movable items, such as tables, chairs, dividing screens, and beds are examples of semifixed-feature space. Dynamic, or informal, space refers to the spatial use of humans as they communicate and interact.

Though Hall accorded a large role to culture, his real intellectual inspiration sprang from ethology, the study of animal behavior. In writing about social distance, for example, Hall (1969:13–14) observed that both humans and social animals prefer to stay in touch with one another. When a dangerous situation arises, animals of the same species will move closer together. A frightened baby gorilla will slide toward its mother in the same way that a young child may reach for her father's hand on an overcrowded sidewalk. Birds sitting on a wall will space themselves in a way that is remarkably similar to the way urban commuters situate themselves while they wait for a bus.

Hall's major contribution to spatial thought stems from his demonstration that place (where something is) and space (where something is not) are interrelated. He showed that the space between things is meaningful. Using his ideas, we can say that in situating their settlements, past men and women perceived both place and space. They knew where they were, and they knew where they were not.

Archaeologists have not been drawn to proxemics in large numbers. The reasons are not immediately clear, but one reason for their lack of interest may stem from the strong psychological element Hall attached to human spatial usage. Some of Hall's ideas about the human use of space lack the materiality that many archaeologists cherish. Still, some archaeologists have been comfortable with Hall's perspective. For example, in his overtly proxemic analysis of sixteenth- and seventeenth-century Iroquois settlement, Bruce Wright (1979) examined the classic proxemic subjects of territoriality, overcrowding, and stress. Though Wright's study bears the influence of Hall's use of psychology, his analysis betrays the underlying mutualism of proxemics. As Wright (1979:43) observed, his investigation was about how "people relate to space in terms of their homes, their towns, and *their interaction with other people*" (emphasis added). He implies that at its core, proxemics is mutualist. Elsewhere, I coined the term "social proxemics" to downplay the ethological and psychological elements of classic proxemics (Orser 1988a:83). My addition of the word "social" is meant to suggest the strong association between proxemics and a mutualist perspective.

Social proxemics proclaims the importance of considering not only where things are but also where things are not. When archaeologists conduct spatial analyses to show where sites are located, they also show (perhaps often quite unwittingly) where the sites are not located. In measuring where a site is situated, an archaeologist also assesses its "betweenness" or "nearbyness" with other things (Wynn 1989:10). Fixing this space becomes as important as the site location itself because a significant characteristic of a site is where it ends in space.

Though most archaeologists' perception of spatial significance has become much more sophisticated since 1953, we must distinguish between space and spatiality. In its broadest sense, "space" refers to the physical reality of where things are not located. Space is irrefutably linked to place, the spot in which something is located. Spatial awareness has influenced philosophical and scientific thought for generations, whether the subject was the movement of the heavens or the settlement patterns of ancient peoples. All archaeologists are interested in space and place in some way. "Spatiality," by contrast, refers to the conscious creation of space. Spatiality is a "constituted objectivity, a 'lived' reality and not a natural given" (Feenberg 1980:112). Thinking about spatiality in this way promotes the view that space is a social product, that space is intrinsically social and that society is intrinsically spatial (Hillier and Hanson 1984:26; Soja 1989:79).

French sociologist Henri Lefebvre (1979) advanced this view of spatiality when he argued that space cannot be explained by reference to the environment, to human nature, to the internal psychology of species, or even to culture. Rather, he said that even though the use of space has limits imposed upon it by climate and topography, every mode of production known to human history has produced a particular kind of space. The ordering of space—spatiality—"is really about the ordering of relations between people" (Hillier and Hanson 1984:2).

Capitalism, as a distinct mode of production, therefore, had a distinct though changeable spatial character. According to Lefebvre (1979:287–288), capitalist space has at least three important functions. First, it is a means of production. The "network of exchanges and the flow of raw materials" and "the spatial arrangement of a city, a region, a nation, or a continent" exist as part of the capitalist productive process. In other words, in capitalism "one uses space just as one uses a machine" (Lefebvre 1979:288). Second, space is an object of consumption. People consume space when they go to the beach, hike in the mountains, or expand their settlements. Finally, space is a controllable political instrument. Space can be converted into an active political tool for repression, genocide, and resistance. An important characteristic of capitalist space is its global pervasiveness. As Lefebvre (1979:288–289) observed, "History emerges on a world level and . . . produces a space at this level: the formation of a world market, an international generalization of the state and its problems, new relations between society and space. World space is the *field* in which our epoch is created" (emphasis in original). When viewed from this perspective, it is difficult to separate capitalism from its global usage of space and place.

LOCAL IDENTITIES AND WORLD SPACE

Lefebvre's (1979) ideas about space are instructive. He made it clear that the "cultural process by which people construct their understandings of the world is an inherently geographic concern" (Anderson and Gale 1992:4). Lefebvre showed that place is concrete. It refers to the precise location of factories, workers' quarters, mills, banks, houses, roads, and parks. Space, though measurable, can be an abstraction tied to an invisible net. As such, spatiality has a dual character that embodies both physical and mental elements. The spatiality of capitalism, for example, combines banks, savings and loan houses, factories, sweatshops, and the houses of laborers, owners, and shopkeepers with interest rates, mortgages, and rates of inflation. That these last elements of space are symbolized with money only indicates the materiality of capitalism.

Ideas about the duality of space are not new to archaeologists (see, for example, S. Kent 1990). Archaeologists realize that spatiality gains expression within finely crafted landscapes. This acknowledgement, however, does not necessarily translate into an understanding of mutualism. In fact, historical archaeologists often explore landscapes without using any concept of mutuality. For example, William Kelso (1990) perceived the landscape of Jefferson's Monticello to be a simple physical feature that could be reconstructed through the efforts of careful archaeologists. The landscape of the mansion's gardens, for instance, was merely an expression of what Jefferson wanted it to be, "a subconscious submission to the way things should be" (Kelso 1990:20). James Deetz (1990:2) took a more anthropological tack and differentiated between a landscape—"the total terrestrial context in which archaeological study is pursued"—and a cultural landscape—"that part of the terrain which is modified according to a set of cultural plans." In this framework, the gardens of Monticello are a cultural landscape. Like all cultural landscapes, they compose a human statement about what a garden ought to be. In the light of this understanding, we should not be surprised when Deetz (1990:1) said, "At the southern tip of the African continent, one finds a little piece of England." English colonists in South Africa settled in what was for them a new environment and created a cultural landscape that evoked their faraway homeland. They modified the South African land to suit their cultural biases and expectations; they re-created a piece of Old England in new South Africa.

Deetz's perspective is seductive because historical archaeologists encounter cultural landscapes around the world. They recognize, for example, that eighteenth-century European forts look much the same wherever they are found. The broad, global distribution of Monsieur Vauban's four-bastioned fortress seems to provide clear and irrefutable proof of Deetz's wisdom. The seventeenth-century Fort Orange in New York was nearly identical to its contemporary, Forte Orange, or Forteleza de Santa Cruz de Itamaracá, in Pernambuco, Brazil, located not far from Palmares (Huey 1991:46; Menezes and Rodrigues 1986:110). The Dutch built both fortresses, apparently in compliance with the requirements of their culture.

So, it seems that Deetz is correct. Cultural landscapes exist and are indicative of a people's understanding of how a terrain should be transformed and shaped. The global nature of Deetz's concept makes it compelling. Unfortunately, his concept of a cultural landscape is not mutualistic. If anything, his understanding is specifically antimutualist because it gives supreme preeminence to culture. Culture appears as a mysterious thing that hovered over the English settlers in South Africa, causing them to construct houses that were unmistakably British. Culture also floated above the Dutch like a cloud when they built their two Fort Oranges.

Contrary to Deetz's culturalist view, we may envision a landscape in mutualist terms as a spatial arena within which relations are enacted. The relations encompass both human–human and human–nature associations (Godelier 1986; Marquardt and Crumley 1987). Landscapes thus incorporate both physical and sociohistorical structures (see Chapter 8). The physical structure is composed of elements that lie outside human control: climate, topography, subsurface geology, hydrology, and other naturally occurring conditions. The interactions between the people coexisting in the physical landscape compose the sociohistorical structure.

A concept of "landscape" invariability includes a concept of "boundary" because landscapes must end somewhere in space. When a landscape is thought to be composed of both physical and sociohistorical structures, though, it is easy to imagine that the boundaries are flexible and difficult to characterize. Depending on one's perspective, the center, or core, of one landscape can be the edge, or periphery, of another. Cores can be peripheries, and the peripheries, cores depending upon one's scale of analysis (Soja 1989:111) (see Chapter 8).

Archaeologists often conceptualize landscapes as occurring within regions. We may suppose, for example, that the Tomaval sites studied by Willey (1953) constitute one landscape within the Virú Valley region. Though this conclusion seems entirely sensible, some archaeologists have begun to rethink the idea of "region." For example, Jeffrey Parsons (1990:10–11) noted that archaeologists can perceive a region as having any size. In fact, a region need not be permanently fixed as a specific territory. Just because it is tangible on the ground does not make a region more "real" than a time segment. Regarding his own area of expertise, Parsons concluded that some day the "Valley-of-Mexico-centric view" will be replaced with a regional concept rooted in "ethnographic and ethnohistorical information." For him, this perspective will be more open-minded in its understanding of how far the Valley of Mexico was actually thought to extend at certain points in the past. At present, archaeologists are usually content with defining a region by its topographic characteristics. Thus, Willey (1953:15) bounded the region of the Virú Valley by a series of hills that separated it from other coastal valleys. We can easily imagine the Virú Valley to be a physical region composed of several landscapes, each one of which reflects a set of cultural norms. Again, this perspective is seductive. As mutualists, however, we may conversely envision the individual sociohistorical expressions in the Virú Valley—Tomaval, Gallinazo, Puerto Moorin, and others—to represent particular sets of relations between individual ancient humans, and between ancient humans and their natural environments.

We can define a region in a mutualist manner as a spatial expression of relations "that exhibit recognizable areal distribution" (Marquardt and Crumley 1987:3). In this view, even different continents may be considered to be within the same region. For example, when the English first went to Jamestown in the early seventeenth century they left one landscape in Europe—one that had taken centuries and numerous ethnic groups to construct—travelled across the ocean, and encountered a new landscape in the New World. The Atlantic Ocean was a "boundary" in a way, but it was both core and periphery. It was peripheral to all those colonists who crossed it to settle on its shores. The ocean was also a core element of the slave trade that linked the Old and the New Worlds, and it was an integral player in the rise of the transatlantic plantation complex (Curtin 1990; Gilroy 1993; Solow 1991). It may be comforting to imagine Europe and America as two cultural landscapes connected by a shared culture. I prefer instead to see the two landscapes as parts of the same region. What tied these landscape together, and what made them part of the same region, was not a commonality of culture but an intricate web of relationships that stretched across the Atlantic. All peoples were changed by contact and interaction (see Chapter 3), and it is much too simplistic to downplay the intricacies of human association in the name of culture. Thus, we can think of the connections between continents as "transpatial relations" (Hillier and Hanson 1984:40–41).

The human agents of historical archaeology's four haunts created and re-created transpatial relations around the globe. The presence of two Fort Oranges, one in New York, the other in Brazil, is testimony to the far-reaching landscape of colonialism. From a purely topographic or geographic perspective, we would be reluctant to envision New York State and northeast Brazil as being within the same region. Also, from Deetz's (1990) perspective we may be reluctant to see the forts as related in any real way but culturally, since the Dutch built both of them. From a mutualist viewpoint, however, the landscapes of New York's Fort Orange and of Pernambuco's Forte Orange are within the same region of interactive colonialism. By the same token, Eurocentrism, capitalism, and modernity all played some part in forging a link between the two.

If we can forget our inclination to think only geographically, we can easily imagine that a four-haunt web linked New York and Brazil into a single, Dutch region. In her overtly global analysis of Oudepost I, a seventeenth-century Dutch post on the southern tip of Africa, Carmel Schrire (1991) took care to demonstrate the far-flung connections maintained by those who lived at the remote outpost. In the worldwide region of the Dutch modern era, we have no need to separate Oudepost I from the rest of its colonial network, including the two Fort Oranges. Nonetheless, we would oversimplify history if we imagined Oudepost I, Fort Orange, and Forte Orange to be identical. Each Dutch fort was unique because its inhabitants created local identities. This act of creation is inherently mutualist.

INCLUSION AND EXCLUSION
IN THE SPATIAL WORLD

Most historical archaeologists readily accord to indigenous peoples a significant role in helping to shape past landscapes. It would be the grossest kind of scholarly oversight, for example, to ignore the Khoikhoi while considering the actions of the Dutch at Oudepost I. I could easily cite several case studies that have focused on the impact of indigenous peoples on European settlements. One brief example, however, will suffice. The seventeenth-century Spaniards at San Luis de Talimali in the Florida panhandle laid out a town that was essentially European in design. It incorporated a four-bastioned fort and a church. Every indication is that the town's builders conformed to the explicit instructions set forth in the "Royal Ordinances Concerning the Laying out of New Towns." Nonetheless, the town's planners also included several Native American elements in their final design. A traditional council house capable of accommodating as many as 3,000 people, and a large, flat, open plaza were reminiscent of local aboriginal towns (Shapiro and Miller 1990:98–100).

Without belaboring this point with additional examples, it seems clear that the relations between colonizer and colonized, capitalist and noncapitalist, modernist and traditionalist are never simply social. People interacting in the world also create spatial relations. In many cases, these relations are not equally conceived or created, and the invented spatiality reflects the spatial views of the dominant elite (see Chapter 7). This means that power relations necessarily play a role in settlement design (see Chapter 8). In the words of geographer Allan Pred (1990:9): "the scope of human agency is enabled and constrained both by already existing power relations and their associated social logics, rules of behavior, and modes of regulation (social structures) and by the full array and relative location of features humanly built into given geographical areas, by spatial patterns of transformed nature (spatial structures)." As French philosopher Michel Foucault said, "space is fundamental in any exercise of power" (Rabinow 1984:252). This exercise of power and the response of others inevitably lead to ideology.

Ideology is one of those difficult terms that has multiple, highly contested meanings. Rather than to reinvent the concept here, I wish to draw upon Randall McGuire's (1988) use of the term and specifically to relate the term to spatiality.

Most analysts today agree that ideology works to hide and even to misrepresent the social relations that exist between men and women. Many archaeologists who have studied ideology have adopted a unidirectional, or "instrumentalist," model: they imagined that the leaders of a society used ideology as a tool of domination (McGuire 1988:437). Instead of accepting this viewpoint, McGuire used the term in a more complex way and linked it to a historically created and constantly re-created tool that is expressed in the negotiation of social relations. A society's dominant members can use ideology to maintain their hold over their subordinates. Leaders can use ideology to mystify their power and to make their control seem natural and usual, timeless and perpetual. But, for their part, subordinate members of a society can either accept the ideology of the elites or transform it into an ideology of resistance. Dominant ideologies can mystify a society's social relations either by covering up social inequality, by claiming that the inequalities are caused by some flaw in the subordinates, or by maintaining that the social differences are ordained from the heavens (see Chapter 7).

Power relations and the struggles they engender always have spatiality; they occur in some place and at some time (Pred 1990:12). Significantly, though, spatiality can be obscured by ideology. As Lefebvre argued, the survival of capitalism itself was constructed upon an ever-expanding foundation of spatiality that was hidden from critical view by ideology (Soja 1989:50). The act of creating the illusion of space has many functions, but at a minimum it gives the appearance of including some and excluding others from landscapes.

In his brilliant analysis of the naming of streets in Stockholm, Sweden, in the 1880s, Allen Pred (1990:201–206) showed how the dominant elements of Swedish society created an ideology of space. Troubled by increased labor tensions and the demands for expanded voting rights, the Stockholm City Council, composed of the urban, economic elite, decided to rename many streets in the city center. They called for the renaming of 109 streets, and the naming of 70 previously undesignated streets and squares. The names they chose were not selected at random. In fact, in 1884 and 1885 those in charge of naming the streets drew from only five categories: patriotic and historical names, Nordic mythology, famous places near the city, the southern provinces, and the northern provinces. Later, the City Council expanded the "patriotic and historical names" category to include famous Swedish authors and prominent men in technology and engineering. According to Pred (1990:204), the names chosen "were heavily laden with the ideology shared by elements of the financially powerful and the well-to-do middle classes."

The ideological domination of nonelites by the Stockholm City Council—as represented by something as tangible as the naming of streets—would seem to be total. Street names are written in personal addresses, they appear in shop advertisements, and they are reported in newspapers. Even the streets themselves proclaim their own names. Surprisingly though, the domination of the street namers was not total. On the contrary, nonelites in Stockholm used folk humor in the form of "comic irreverence and lewdness" to rename the streets, alleys, and squares they walked every day (Pred 1990:196–201). They also renamed many prominent, local landmarks. With clever plays on words they thumbed their collective noses at the city's power structure. For example, in referring to an obelisk near the Royal Palace as the "king's toothpick," the people of Stockholm showed their disrespect for the Crown in a bawdy and unmistakable manner. In speaking of a wealthy avenue as "the snob gutter" they unveiled their true opinion of the elite. The people's folk re-creation of Stockholm street names suggests that the landscapes built by elites are only a representation of dominance, a conceptual or ideological landscape that may never completely control the populace (Hillier and Hanson 1984:260).

The association of ideology with constructed landscapes is not new in historical archaeology. Following the lead of Mark Leone's (1984) now-classic interpretation of William Paca's garden in Annapolis, Maryland (see Chapter 7), several historical archaeologists have pursued the tangible evidence for ideology at numerous sites (Johnson 1992, 1993; Kryder-Reid 1994; Leone 1987, 1994; Monks 1992; Mrozowski 1991). In fact, I could cite so many studies that one may easily conclude that the search for ideology is now the historical archaeologist's main pursuit.

A mutalist perspective helps archaeologists to understand past landscapes and regions and to conceptualize where spatially expressed ideology originates. A prominent element of the mutualist point of view is that "we are not so much self-aware as self-and-other-aware" (Carrithers 1992:60). Humans have a capacity for narrative thought that exists as part of their self-and-other awareness. In Carrithers's (1992:82) terms, narrative thought embodies the ability "to cognize not merely immediate relations between oneself and another, but many-sided human interactions carried out over a considerable period." People understand both the minute realities of their own daily lives and the larger abstractions of their social situation. To accomplish this constant thought process, Carrithers (1992:84) said that men and women must understand both the "inner landscape of thought" and the "outer landscape of events." The two landscapes are inseparable because a change in thought can entail a change in action. Changes in thought can affect social relations because "people do things because of what others feel, think, and plan" (Carrithers 1992:84).

Carrithers (1992:82) made it clear that his perception of the narrative thought process occurs in "social rather than physical space." I see no need, however, to withhold the process from the physical landscape. In fact, we may imagine that much of the spatial rearrangement that occurs in the modern age is in direct response to someone else. Spatiality is the physical side of self-and-other awareness. The renaming of Stockholm's streets occurred as part of a complex web of activities that included an increase in disaffection among the urban majority. Both the elite City Council and the non-elite men and women of the city understood the social landscape, though each understood it in a slightly different way. I do not intend to suggest that all builders of landscapes were reactionaries, simply responding to the challenges they confronted. What I do mean to say is that the construction of modern landscapes is motivated by the network of relations that exist between people and between people and the natural environment around them. In creating landscapes, men and women are self-and-other aware. Their relations exist in webs that can stretch across vast distances, pulling parts of different continents into the same region. Gorttoose presents an excellent place to demonstrate my point.

THE CREATED WORLDS OF GORTTOOSE

On entering Strokestown today, modern visitors are immediately struck by several spatial worlds that exist side by side.

Though the physical landscape has changed since the nineteenth century, the place is nonetheless remarkably timeless. Neat, gray, dry-stone walls bisect lush green fields, and here and there ancient, circular ringforts spring forth from the meadows. Dark green hedge rows, thick with brambles, run past crumbling, medieval ruins, and grazing sheep dot the fields in moving splashes of white. Green, the very color of Ireland, washes the landscape with its many hues. In the distance, the faraway mountains appear blue and magical.

The visual contrast between the blue of the distant mountains and the green of the nearby fields symbolizes the historical landscape of Gorttoose. The greens and the blues, though distinct and significant in their own right, work together to create the landscape. Mountain and field could exist alone, but they stubbornly coexist. The same can be said for the human geography of Gorttoose. Numerous webs came together at the townland to create myriad landscapes that coexisted and re-created one another. At least three separate physical landscapes coexisted on the lands surrounding Gorttoose during the late eighteenth and the early nineteenth centuries. Together these three landscapes—Strokestown, the Strokestown Park House, and the townlands that contained and cradled Gorttoose—created a single landscape. Each landscape, though it existed on its own, also helped to create and sustain the other two. Also, each was connected to other landscapes geographically far removed from Strokestown.

Strokestown's wide main street and the grand demesne of the Strokestown Park House, upon which the street terminates, have attracted the attention of visitors for years. In 1837, Samuel Lewis drew attention to the street and the demesne when he observed that Strokestown "consists of two streets intersecting each other at right angles; one is 49 yards wide, and the other 21. . . . The main street is terminated by the grand entrance to Lord Hartland's noble demesne, a new church being at the other end, on the highest ground in the town" (Lewis 1970:581). One hundred and thirty-three years later, Sean Jennett (1970:210) said of Strokestown:

> [It] is one of the most handsome of Irish small towns, and made so mainly by the ample width of its main street. . . . At the upper end of the gently sloping street the spire of the Protestant church forms a vertical just where it is needed, and at the lower end is the ivy-grown gateway to the demesne of Strokestown House.

The Fodor's guide for 1993 offered the following comment: "Like many villages near a 'big house,' Strokestown was designed to com-

plement the house. The widest main street in Ireland—laid out to
rival the Ringstrasse in Vienna—leads to a Gothic arch, the entrance to the house grounds" (Collins 1992:178). These observations,
separated by 156 years, indicate that the main street of Strokestown
has been appreciated largely as a kind of visual space. The street is
broad, magnificent, and straight. But there is more to the visuality
of the street than just its physical characteristics. Also important is
where the street goes. At one end sits the town's small but proud
Protestant church. At the other end stands the massive main gate of
the Strokestown demesne. Both of these elements of the physical
landscape carry a potent ideological meaning. They do nothing less
than to link the secular and the sacred power of the landed aristocracy in rural Ireland.

By all accounts, the Strokestown Park House is a fine mansion.
As I noted in Chapter 4, Captain Nicholas Mahon, upon taking
control of the area in the name of England, established residence in
the fortified enclosure, or bawn, that once belonged to the Gaelic
leader O'Conor Roe. By the first decades of the eighteenth century,
the Mahons were so well established in Strokestown that they felt
comfortable expanding their home beyond the bawn. They built a
large, unfortified mansion as a symbol of their dominance and power. The mansion's architects carefully followed the rules laid down
by then-popular, sixteenth-century Italian architect Andrea Palla-
dio. Around 1830, a little-known amateur artist, Sir John Thomas
Selwin Ibbetson, painted a watercolor of the house. The watercolor
shows a blocky house with a stark, almost unforgiving symmetry
(Figure 6). The large building to the right of the central core of the
mansion still contains the spectacular vaulted-ceiling stable, and
the low building on the far left contains the remnants of an inventive indoor privy. The O'Conor Roe bawn appears on the far right of
the complex, incorporated neatly into the mansion. The blending of
the bawn with the fabric of the mansion was an ideological way to
obscure the former prominence of the Gaels in Ireland. The visual,
fixed-feature space of the bawn was collapsed into and engulfed by
the visuality of the Palladian mansion. The transformation was not
simply architectural; it carried a potent message to people throughout both Ireland and the world. In an ironic twist of fate, however,
the centrality of the bawn has been recaptured. Today, it houses the
internationally renowned Famine Museum.

The mansion appears within a building tradition associated
with the Protestant Ascendancy. The term "Protestant Ascendancy"

Figure 6. Watercolor of Mahon's Strokestown Park House mansion as painted by Sir John Thomas Selwin Ibbetson around 1830. Used by permission of Desmond FitzGerald, Knight of Glin.

has an intricate history, but it was probably first used in 1782 as part of a Parliamentary debate on Catholic relief (Hill 1989; Mc-Cormick 1987). The term is still used today to describe the attitudes of unionists in the six counties of Northern Ireland (G. Adams 1994:25). Though the term has important, time-worn political and social significance, historian Roy Foster (1989:186) said that "the most lasting creation of the Ascendancy" was the magnificence of its built landscape. In making this claim, Foster specifically referred to the buildings and parks of Georgian Dublin, but he was quick to point out that the much-heralded premier of Handel's *Messiah* in Dublin on April 13, 1742, was part of the Ascendancy's geography (Foster 1989:185). Clearly, the Ascendancy had myriad social and physical elements that allowed it at least to fill visual and auditory spaces. Architects began designing cut-stone Ascendancy mansions sometime around 1740, and the Mahons had their Strokestown Park House erected as part of this trend. According to an explanatory panel in The Famine Museum, "The new house was constructed in the fashionable Palladian style, which perfectly expressed the confidence of the newly emergent ruling-class to which the Mahons belonged." The architects and residents of the house imbued it with an ideological and physical strength that situated it in a visual space extending far beyond Strokestown.

The landscape complex formed by Strokestown's main street as it extended from the Protestant church to the arched gate of the Strokestown Park House, and from there to the winding path that leads to the mansion, presents an impressive and powerful image. It is a visual space that may be rarely exceeded. Still, for all its power, the mansion and the neat town are only a partial landscape. Inseparable from the house, and perhaps even dwarfing it, is the surrounding demesne.

The demesne has a venerable history in Ireland. In the last half of the sixteenth century, Queen Elizabeth I began her efforts to wrestle the province of Munster, in southern Ireland, away from the Norman earl of Desmond. After a long struggle, the queen's forces were victorious and the earl was murdered in 1583. With the earl out of the picture, the queen was free to dispose of some 121,450 ha (some 30,000 acres) of his land. But, worried that the Spanish would attempt to enter Catholic Ireland from the south, the queen decided to settle Protestants on the land to serve as a human shield. This settlement was the famed "Munster plantation" (Power 1991). The queen's agents divided the lands of the Desmond estate into 35 separate seignories. As planned in 1586, the Munster seignory included over 29,600 ha (12,000 acres). The estate's designers established small plots for cottages and reserved a spot in the center for a church and a mill. On the northwestern edge of the planned settlement, they set aside land for a "gentleman's demesne," containing 2,470 ha (1,000 acres) (Foster 1989:68). Many of Ireland's demesnes have not disappeared from today's countryside. According to geographer Frederick Aalen (1989:107), "The old demesnes, which were the cores of the estates, remain, even in their decay, some of the most distinctive and picturesque elements of the landscape."

Usually set off from the rest of the landscape by a high wall, demesnes typically contained ornamental trees, formal gardens, deer parks, lakes, and ornate fountains (Malins and The Knight of Glin 1976). The demesne is thus a neatly differentiated and carefully controlled visual space. The Strokestown demesne was no different. When he traveled through Ireland in the late 1770s, Arthur Young (1780:184) was much impressed by Mahon's demesne, particularly by the way in which Mahon had planted it:

> Mr. Mahon's woods are all of his own planting, and having besides 100 acres, a vast number of hedge-rows well planted round many inclosures, which join those woods, they all take the appearance of uniting into one great range of plantations, spreading on each side [of] the house. It is one of the strongest instances of a fine shade being speedily formed in the midst of a bleak country that I have anywhere met with, being a perfect contrast to all the neighborhood. He began 35 years ago with ash, which trees are now 70 to 80 feet high.
>
> But the generality of the plantations are from 17 to 30 years old, and are for that age, I think, the finest woods I ever saw; they consist of ash, oak, [E]nglish and [F]rench elm, beech, maple, spruce, scotch and silver fir, larch, etc.

Young's admiration of Mahon's willingness to plant was not misplaced. A bill dated October 23, 1841, records that the major purchased the following trees that day: "600 larch, 300 silver fir, 300 spruce, 200 scotch, 300 oak, 300 ash, 20 variegated holly, 20 copper beech, 20 Portugal laurel, 20 arbutus, 20 evergreen oak" (Pakenham-Mahon Papers). This purchase was grandiose by any standards.

Mahon's demesne is still an impressive visual space. In the nineteenth century, it contained over 384 ha (948 acres) and was segmented into 48 separate, special-use fields (Figure 7). On the west, closest to Strokestown, was the mansion complex. This group of elite structures included the mansion house, a walled, formal garden with ornamental plantings, an expansive front lawn, and an orchard. In front of the house were the ruins of an ancient chapel; behind the house, and visible from the ballroom, were the crumbling walls of a medieval priory, or monastic house. These picturesque remains were not-so-subtle reminders that, while the Mahons may not have been the first residents of the land, they were certainly the most powerful. Included within the demesne walls were several pastures, a goat park, a deer park, and numerous special plantings.

The presence of the encircling wall, the neat appearance of the fields and parks, and the massive residence all made it clear that the demesne was the property of a wealthy landowner. The interlocking pieces of the landscape tied the estate to Strokestown to be sure, but they accomplished much more as well. The mansion and the demesne proclaimed to the world that the Mahons were members of the Protestant Ascendancy. Their massive buildings and expansive fields linked them to a world that existed far beyond the hills of central Ireland. The property was part of a network that had extensions throughout Ireland, into England, and across the Atlan-

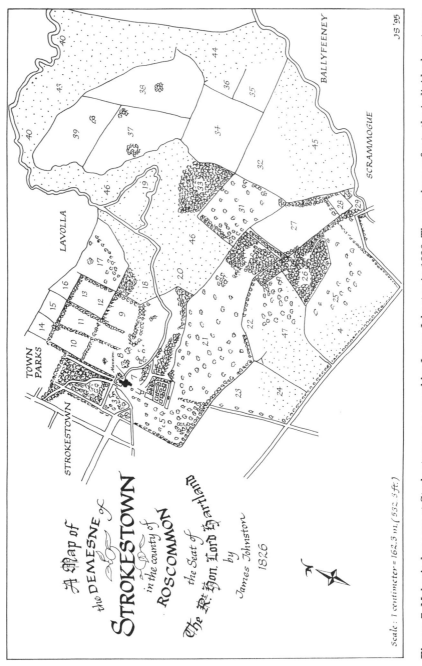

Figure 7. Mahon's demesne at Strokestown as mapped by James Johnston in 1826. The numbers refer to the individual pastures, lots, and fields for Mahon's records.

tic to America. But the demesne, for all its grandeur and power, could not stand alone. In fact, the lord of the manor was surrounded by a landscape that was decidedly alien even though he owned it. Gorttoose was an integral part of this landscape.

As the crow flies, only about 4.8 km (3 mi) separates Gorttoose from the southeast corner of the formal garden in Mahon's demesne. The 1837 Ordnance Survey reveals, however, that this space is deceptive. Actually, the distance between the garden and Gorttoose was much greater. For example, if John Ross Mahon—the major's agent during the Great Famine—wished to travel by road from the garden to Gorttoose, he would have to make the following journey. First, he would have to go from the front of the mansion and turn left and follow the path to the arched gateway. Passing through the gate, he would proceed straight to the Strokestown crossroad and turn left. Following the road out of town, Mahon would go through the townland of Farnberg, passing along the way a brewery, schoolhouse, and several dwellings. After going about 0.8 km (0.5 mi) Mahon would turn left on the road to Newtown. He would then follow the road through the townlands of Newtown, Bumlin, Treanacreeve, and Scramoge for about 2.4 km (1.5 mi) until the road forked. Mahon, by now not far in straight-line distance from the formal garden but surrounded by a foreign landscape of Catholic, peasant farmers, would follow the fork to the left and proceed through the townland of Scramoge. Five roads came together at a small enclave in Scramoge, and Mahon would go straight, winding through Gortlustia and entering Culliagh Upper. He would see the clustered village of Culliagh Upper on the right, and proceeding straight into Culliagh Lower, he would see the police station also on the right. This post may have offered Mahon some comfort because it was a symbol of Protestant power and dominance and part of the landlord's spatial network. After the station, Mahon would finally enter the townland of Gorttoose (Figure 8).

During the course of Mahon's journey to Gorttoose, he would have passed through the peasant's world. Though the land itself was owned by his kinsman, the landscape was not familiar; it was not truly controlled. Arthur Young's (1780:184) comments about the peasants on Mahon's lands are directly relevant here:

> The people are on the increase, but not much; they are better fed than 20 years ago, and better cloathed, but not more industrious, or better housed. They live on potatoes, milk, and butter. Scarce any but what keeps a cow or two; they are not allowed to keep pigs in general, but

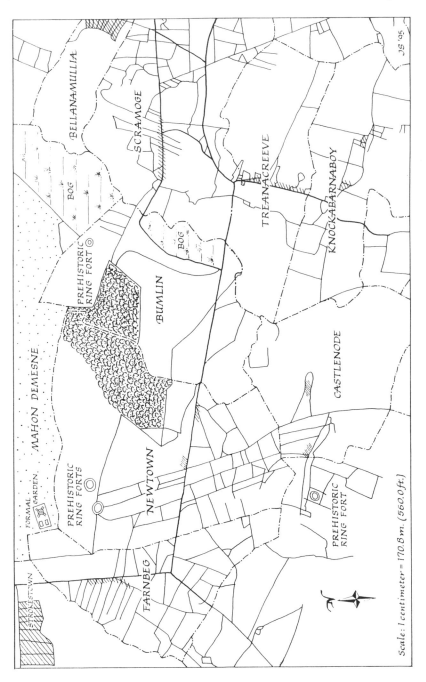

Scale: 1 centimeter = 170.8 m. (560.0 ft.)

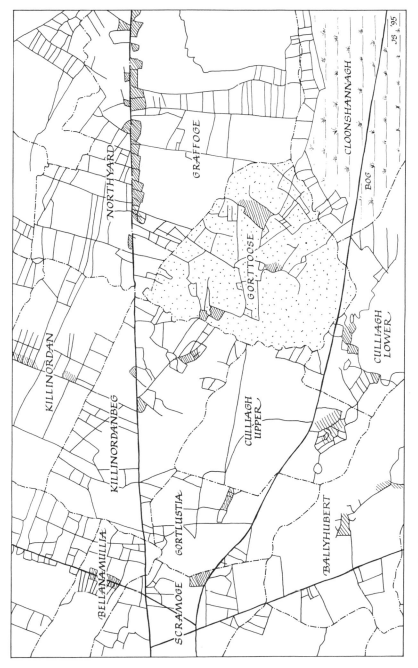

Figure 8. The townlands surrounding Gorttoose as they appear on the 1837 Ordnance Survey map. The hatched lines show areas of settlement.

many will a tolerable quantity of poultry. The rent of 1 acre and a house
is 20 s., the grass of a cow, 1£ 2 s. The men dig turf and plant potatoes,
and work for their landlord, and the women pay the rent by spinning.
Great rise in prices, butter one-third, beef one-fourth, poultry one-
half. . . . A mud cabbin 5£ 5s, ditto stone and slate 15£.

Clearly, the peasants' homes formed a major part of the native
landscape that Mahon would have encountered during his travel to
Gorttoose. The housing of common Irish farmers attracted the attention of most visitors to rural Ireland. In 1835, the famed French
nobleman and commentator Alexis de Tocqueville visited Ireland,
and in fact passed through Strokestown. Though sadly he did not
mention the village, he did give a shorthand but terse description of
the housing he saw in eastern Ireland: "Most of the dwellings of the
country very poor looking. A very large number of them wretched to
the last degree. Walls of mud, roofs of thatch, one room. No chimney,
smoke goes out the door" (Larkin 1990:39). Young (1780:25–26), who
was more verbose than Tocqueville, gave a typically thorough description of peasant housing:

> The cottages of the [I]rish, which are all called cabbins, are the most
> miserable looking hovels that can well be conceived: they generally con-
> sist of only one room: mud kneaded with straw is the common material
> of the walls; these are rarely about seven feet high, and not always
> above five or six; they are about two feet thick, and have only a door,
> which lets in light instead of a window, and should let the smoak out
> instead of a chimney, but they had rather keep it in: these two conve-
> niences they hold so cheap that I have seen them both stopped up in
> stone cottages, built by improving landlords; the smoak warms them,
> but certainly is as injurious to their eyes as it is to the complexions of the
> women, which in general in the cabbins of Ireland has a near resem-
> blance to that of a smoaked ham. The number of blind poor I think
> greater here than in England, which is probably owing to this cause.
>   The roofs of the cabbins are rafters, raised from the tops of the mud
> walls, and the covering varies; some are thatched with straw, potatoe
> stalks, or with heath, others only covered with sods of turf cut from a
> grass field; and I have seen several that were partly composed of all
> three; the bad repair these roofs are kept in, a hole in the thatch being
> often mended with turf, and weeds sprouting from every part, gives
> them the appearance of a weedy dunghill. . . . The furniture of the cab-
> bins is as bad as the architecture.

Young did admit that not every "cabbin" in Ireland was as bad as
those he described, but in general he and Tocqueville agreed that
the key word was "wretched" or "miserable." Maria Edgeworth
(1992:186), famed novelist and daughter of a wealthy landlord who
lived near Strokestown in adjacent County Longford, used the term

"wretched" in describing a peasant's cabin in her novel *Ennui,* first published in 1809. By all accounts, peasant housing was inadequate and unhealthy (Scally 1995:9–10).

The contrast between the mansions of the landlords and the peasants' "hovels" is striking. Given the nature of the relations between landlords and tenants, we can conclude with justification that much of the fault for the condition of the peasants' houses can be laid at the landlords' feet. Improving landlords, like Major Mahon, were probably offended by the visual, auditory, and olfactory spaces created by their tenants. As a result, landlords built high walls, not only to delimit their personal spaces, but to "protect" their families and their guests from the spaces of the peasant villages. For their part, the tenants had little incentive to maintain or to upgrade the conditions of their homes. The evictions during the Great Famine provided the tangible and irrefutable reason why: peasants could be ousted from their homes at any time. Their cottages, situated as they were on someone else's land, were often ripped down when the families were forced out on the road (see Litton 1994:94–99). Historical records suggest that evictions were relatively rare, except under the extreme pressures of the Great Famine (Daly 1986:112). Nonetheless, in the normal course of things, peasants undoubtedly understood their tenuous existence on the land.

Only the most unimpressed reporter could fail to see the differences between the elegant mansions of the landlords and the rough cabins of the tenant farmers. The extensive, manicured demesnes stood in stark contrast to the simple potato patch, or lazybed of the common Irish peasant (Evans 1957:140–150). These features, though highly indicative of the social distinctions present in the Irish countryside, were not all there was to the landscape. The 1837 Ordnance Survey reveals another significant difference. This distinction contrasts the straight, perpendicular streets of Strokestown with the nucleated clusters present in the townlands. Though Mahon was clearly an improving landlord, he may have had little impact on the prefamine settlement strategy of the townlands. As revealed on the 1837 plat, the little settlement clusters John Ross Mahon would have encountered when venturing beyond the high walls of the Strokestown demesne resembled rundale villages.

The rundale village was a small settlement of between 10 and 20 houses associated with the rundale system of agriculture (see Chapter 4). These settlements were not true villages because they did not incorporate any of the shops and churches of a town. Instead, they were inhabited by farming families who tilled the surrounding, unenclosed farm fields (Mitchell 1976:209). Renowned Irish geographer E. Estyn Evans (1992) argued that the nineteenth-century rundale village, which he called the "clachan," was a heroic survivor from an earlier Celtic past. To his thinking, clachans had once blanketed Ireland, but by the nineteenth century they could only be found in the wild, less-Anglicized western counties. Recent research by cultural geographer Kevin Whelan (1994:64), however, shows that the rundale villages were not remnants of a communal past but "a functioning feature of the aggressive spread of settlement into adverse environmental territory." Rundale villages were clever adaptations to the wet climate, high winds, rocky soil, and poor drainage of western Ireland.

Some improving landlords broke up the rundale villages, resettling their inhabitants in a line along a road (Evans 1992:60; Mac Aodha 1965:24–25). Mahon may have accomplished this kind of settlement reorganization because a linear settlement appears on the 1837 Ordnance Survey map, stretched along the road separating the Northyard townland from Graffoge. Graffoge was the townland immediately east of Gorttoose. By and large, however, the townlands within which Gorttoose was nestled contained nucleated, rundale settlements. Many geographers consider these settlements to hold the key to understanding the prefamine, rural Irish landscape.

Rundale villages were never fixed entities, because the number of residents could expand or contract depending upon numerous factors (Evans 1992:60). Around Strokestown, as around many other stately mansions, the Great Famine occasioned major changes in the landscape and affected the rundale villages. I mentioned the severe population decline suffered by Gorttoose and adjacent townlands in Chapter 4. The devastating depopulation entailed a decrease in the number of houses on the landscape. The 1851 census reveals that Gorttoose declined from 46 inhabited houses in 1841 to only 8 in 1851, a decline of 82.6 percent. Housing declined in the immediately adjacent townlands in a similar way: Graffoge, from 74 to 20 (−73.0%); Killinordanbeg, from 38 to 18 (−52.6%); Culliagh Upper, from 36 to 6 (−83.3%); Culliagh Lower, from 32 to 10 (−68.8%); and Cloonshannagh, from 5 to 4 (−20.0%) (British Parliamentary Papers 1970:550). This decline in the number of houses shockingly reveals the clearance of the countryside in the late 1840s. In the decade between 1841 and 1851, the landscape of Gorttoose dramatically changed. The tragic plunge in population expanded the nets of Gorttoose, as the townland's inhabitants were forced out of Ireland and into the world. At the same time, the visual space of the peasants' landscape was denuded as both people and houses were removed.

The effects of the removal are unmistakable today. In 1994, the Strokestown Park House was still standing and open to tour groups. The demesne wall is largely intact, and sheep still graze the fields. The countryside is dotted with neat bungalows arranged along narrow roads. All physical evidence for Gorttoose is gone, and today the townland is an empty field. Soon, a new national road will run across the land, destroying a major portion of Gorttoose forever. The land around Gorttoose still reflects much of the landscape Mahon created. The three or four houses now at Gorttoose sit on the plots of land divided among the head tenants after the terror of the Great Famine had largely passed.

I have proposed in this chapter that a mutualist perspective has value for unravelling the complexities of past settlement. In Chapter 5, I made the same claim for artifacts. In this chapter, I show how men and women created landscapes through the give and take, the self-and-other awareness of mutualism. Clearly, Mahon built his mansion not simply to house his family, for a cabin would have done just as well. He build the demesne wall, not just to demarcate his personal gardens and pastures, but to close off the peasants, to create space between them. Mahon created spatiality across the Irish countryside. For their part, the peasant farmers also created space. They most certainly controlled personal, semifixed-feature space inside their cabins and they built and maintained rundale villages. Still, the very invisibility of the townlands today, except on maps and in postal addresses, speaks to the staying power of the Irish landlords. As geographer T. Jones Hughes (1965:79) argued, the landlord "effected and controlled some of the most significant modifications" in the landscape. Remnants of folk landscapes do exist throughout Ireland. But at the rural townlands themselves, such as at Gorttoose, it is the landlord's improving hand that is most obvious. The net that landlords threw over the land was powerful and permanent. It was made of brick walls, massive mansions, and granite archways. The peasants, with their single-room mud cabins and their lazybed fields were erasable. That prefamine cabins and remnants of lazybeds can still be found in rural Ireland indicate that the landlords, whether or not they were improvers, were not completely able to clear the landscape of its poor.

The poor and often-invisible men and women of the past, like those at Gorttoose, are frequent subjects of historical archaeological research. So important is the archaeology of these men and women to the cause of global historical archaeology that I turn fully to them in the next chapter.

Can the Subaltern Speak? | 7

Just about twenty years ago I bought a book entitled *Who Speaks for Appalachia?* (Haddix 1975). The main point of the book is to show that Appalachia, for all its oppressive poverty and frequent bad press, is inhabited by men and women whose life stories deserve respect. Transcriptions of folk songs and texts penned by several prominent Appalachian-born writers—Thomas Wolfe, O. Henry, Robert Penn Warren, Caroline Gordon, Elizabeth Madox Roberts—implore readers to see the men and women of Appalachia as significant. Thinking about this book today, I am impelled to ask myself why I bought it. I have never been particularly drawn to Appalachia as a research subject, though my research on southern farm tenancy and slavery suggests that I have an abiding interest in poor and disenfranchised American southerners. Looking back on this book, though, I believe it attracted me for two reasons. First were the people themselves, the men and women of the mountains who, though desperately poor in economic terms, lived in dignity and projected an aura of strength and deeply felt tradition. The title of the book also drew me toward it. I was intrigued by the notion that speaking for Appalachia could be a contested issue. As the editor noted, however, the people of this remote, mountainous country have usually had others speaking for them, as if they were somehow incapable of self-expression. Screenwriters and movie directors have used them as the subject of ridicule and humor, rural sociologists have pitied them for their poverty, and anthropologists have analytically dissected their daily lives and traditions (Haddix 1975:x–xi). The people of the mountains were seldom heard on their own terms in much of this scholarship. To rectify this situation, the editor of *Who Speaks for Appalachia?* believed that she could use the power of her contributing authors' words to express the grandeur and strength of the Appalachian people. As an aspiring historical archaeologist, I was fascinated by the prospect of listening to men and women seldom heard in the annals of the past. Hearing the heretofore silent men and women of the past seemed to open new vistas of history and, for me, this realization made historical archaeology a deeply relevant subject.

In *Historical Archaeology,* Brian Fagan and I said that one of the greatest strengths of historical archaeology is its ability to shed light on the lives of people who are poorly represented in historical records (Orser and Fagan 1995:202–204). This aspect of historical archaeology has a global significance. Our position was not startling or even surprising. Most historical archaeologists accept and, in fact, cherish this capability of their field. What is in doubt, however, is precisely how historical archaeologists can ever hope to let the disenfranchised people of the past speak for themselves. Archaeologists are not members of the groups to which they wish to listen, and anyway, most of what is heard is filtered through the words and concepts of modern archaeology. Admittedly, historical archaeologists have more in common with their subjects than do prehistorians. Historical archaeologists and their subjects live together in the modern world. Nonetheless, historical archaeologists are not truly members of the same cultures as the people they study, even though much about the historic past has a familiar ring to people alive today. Faced with this truth, can historical archaeologists ever really expect to make the subaltern speak?

LISTENING TO THE SILENT MEN AND WOMEN OF THE MODERN PAST

The archaeology of the silent men and women of the modern past got a large boost in the late 1960s with Charles Fairbanks's pioneering excavations in Florida. Others had sporadically investigated the remains of obscure peoples (see, for example, Bullen and Bullen 1945), but Fairbanks's ground-breaking research was purposeful and sustained. Focused specifically on African-Americans, Fairbanks started at a maroon community and then moved on to plantation slave cabins (Fairbanks 1974, 1983:22–23). His first excavation of this sort was at Kingsley Plantation, where he initially planned to provide information for the eventual reconstruction of a slave cabin (Fairbanks 1983:23, 1984:1). His attention soon shifted, however, from the bland details of architecture to the exciting and heretofore largely mysterious world of the daily lives of slaves (Ascher and Fairbanks 1971; Fairbanks and Mullins-Moore 1980).

The burgeoning archaeological urge to examine the daily lives of African-American slaves fits within the general trend in scholarship at the time. Beginning in the late 1960s, historians began to call for the study of "bottom-rail people" (Davidson and Lytle 1982:172). In accordance with this trend, historical archaeologists turned to the inarticulate peoples of the past (Ascher 1974:11). The fuel that powered their research was the simple truth that up until then most scholars had concentrated solely on the homes, properties, and documents of the elites. Historical archaeologists had shown, for instance, that they could excavate an antebellum plantation and completely ignore the slaves who had lived, toiled, and died there (see Watkins 1968). A focus on the bottom-rail people allowed historical archaeologists to look at past society from the bottom up, to turn the tables on the archaeological convention of excavating only a site's largest, most well-preserved, and most spectacular remains. Looking back today, we can clearly see that research on bottom-rail men and women has been a rich scholastic mine, and both historians and archaeologists have constructed full-scale interpretations of that part of the hidden past. Bottom-rail research has proven to be centrally important to the maturation of historical archaeology (Orser 1990:122–129).

Within recent years, however, the bottom-rail perspective has come under attack. Perhaps the most serious challenge was assembled by Mary Beaudry, Lauren Cook, and Stephen Mrozowski (1991). The basis of their assault was not that the men and women of the bottom rail were insignificant. On the contrary, they argued in clear and unambiguous terms that the disenfranchised were inarticulate only if archaeologists chose to think of them as such. For them, all historical archaeologists could devise creative ways to discern the voices of the disenfranchised in the hubbub of history. They asserted, however, that it is inadequate to examine the "inarticulate" masses from the bottom up. Instead, they said that the people of the bottom rail must be studied "from the inside out" (Beaudry et al. 1991:163). The medium of communication would not be songs or written texts because these peoples seldom wrote about themselves. The texts would be the artifacts these silent men, women, and children had left behind. If archaeologists chose to listen, the voices of the inarticulate could be heard among the broken dishes and the shattered bottles resting on the laboratory tables.

In principle, I could not agree more with Beaudry, Cook, and Mrozowski's intent. They pursued the noblest of causes in archaeological research: They sought to drop the veil of silence and to reveal lives quieted for far too long by an unconcerned present. But what I found troublesome in their analysis was the way they chose to remove the curtain of historical secrecy. In seeking to provide an inside-out perspective, Beaudry et al. underestimated the power, strength, and accomplishments of the very people they set out to humanize.

Beaudry et al. took their inspiration directly from Henry Glassie's (1982) account of Ballymenone, a community in the north of Ireland. In his rich and often moving study, Glassie (1982:86) asserted that

> even scholars who strive to be democratic sometimes accept the ugly metaphor and propose to study things from the bottom up. Society is not peaked like a pyramid or layered like a cake. It is composed of communities simultaneously occupying space and time at the same human level. Some are composed of upper-class fox-hunters, some of middle-class scholars, some of poor farmers. All seem reasonable from within, strange from without, silent at a distance. The way to study people is not from the top down or the bottom up, but from the inside out, from the place where people are articulate to the place where they are not, from the place where they are in control of their destinies to the place where they are not.

Beaudry et al. (1991:163–164) quoted this passage to support their inside-out perspective. Paradoxically, though, they also occasionally argued as well for a bottom-rail view, which they took from E. P. Thompson (1978) (Beaudry et al. 1991:156). Their main point, though a bit muddled, was that many historical archaeologists have examined society only from the top down, using the records left by the articulate members of society. To correct this methodological perspective, they advocated Glassie's inside-out perspective, which, as shown in the above quote, is clearly opposed to studies from the bottom up.

In many ways, Glassie's (1982) book is as eloquent, powerful, and stunning as Beaudry et al. (1991:163) believed. His work in folklore, architecture, and material culture is respected by other historical archaeologists (see Deetz 1983:29), and he is widely regarded as a committed, thorough, and deeply humanistic scholar. In his intimately human picture of Ballymenone, Glassie repeatedly made it clear that he cherished and respected the men and women who allowed him to live among them as he measured the dimensions of their homes, sketched their old furniture, and recorded their time-honored songs. Glassie danced, drank, and toiled as a regular member of the community in the best sense of participant observation, and he even bequeathed the resulting book's royalties to the people of Ballymenone. In many cases, Glassie lovingly transcribed the residents' stories as poems. This heartfelt "landscape of the page" (Pred 1990:9) aptly symbolized Glassie's emotional attachment to the accepting men and women of Ballymenone.

Glassie's research was impressive, and it really does seem that he studied the community from the inside out. He situated himself among the men and women of Ballymenone, he let them speak, and he listened to them. But while reading his book, I was nagged by one relentless question: How did Glassie become an insider in this tiny corner of rural Ireland? I must confess to feeling a bit self-conscious and slightly embarrassed in even thinking this way because the query, just in its very formulation, seems to impugn Glassie's integrity. This is not my intention at all, but I cannot help asking the question nonetheless. The success of the inside-out perspective advocated by Beaudry et al. (1991) hinges on our acceptance that Glassie was indeed on the inside.

In the beginning of the book, Glassie (1982:xix) made it clear that he was "not Irish, or even Irish-American," though he came to realize that his father's mother's family had lived near Ballymenone sometime in the eighteenth century. He took great pains to show his gradual acceptance by the community, visiting it in 1972, 1974, 1976, 1977, and 1979. He developed lasting friends in Ballymenone and people there certainly know his name and his face is familiar. But was he ever really an insider?

My doubts about his status increased when I read Rosemary Mahoney's (1994) account of her experiences in western Ireland. An American raised in Boston, Mahoney built lasting friendships in Ireland; she sat in the pubs and walked the narrow lanes with the townspeople, she listened intently to their tales, and she became involved in their lives. Throughout the experience, though, Mahoney made it clear that she was never regarded exactly as an insider. No matter what she did, she was usually referred to as "the American," even though, unlike Glassie, she held Irish citizenship through her grandfather. Her grandmother was so passionately Irish that she had a framed copy of the Irish Republican Proclamation of 1916 proudly hanging on her wall. Her grandmother had harbored Liam Mellows, the proclamation's editor, and it was he who planted the shrubbery in her front yard (Mahoney 1994:xiii). Mahoney herself had spent part of her high school years in Ireland, and she had more than a working knowledge of Irish Gaelic, sometimes knowing more than her hosts. She was welcomed into the Irish community and she could have stayed among her new-found friends forever. But she was clear to state that she was never really on the inside. Our acceptance of her Irish account stems from her skilled powers of observation and interpretation, not from our belief that she was an insider (Keough 1995:24). A comment from one of her Irish friends summed up how she was perceived in the community, "I couldn't really see why a person like yourself would come to a village like this" (Mahoney 1994:302). This comment showed that Mahoney was viewed as someone who did not belong, someone who had experience and knowledge that extended far beyond the people's little corner of Ireland. Mahoney was special simply because she was not an insider.

Without question, the situations faced by Glassie and by Mahoney were not identical. As independent individuals, each met different people and had unique experiences. Glassie is a folklorist, Mahoney a writer. Still, Mahoney's feeling of being an outsider—accepted but outside nonetheless—is striking when compared to Glassie's experience. Perhaps Glassie really was an insider. As a highly skilled folklorist he undoubtedly knows how to situate himself within a community and to take notes quietly and unobtrusively. Still, I cannot but wonder at the way Mahoney felt like an outsider even though she had a strong, intensely personal Irish background.

The trick of gaining acceptance in a strange community is an old issue in anthropology and folklore, and I will leave its resolution to trained specialists. For my part, though, the disparity between Glassie's and Mahoney's experiences leads me to ask how an archaeologist can ever even think about acquiring an insider's view of the past. Archaeologists cannot transcribe folk songs or listen to tales told over peat fires and glasses of Irish stout. They cannot watch the scythes make their steady, gentle arcs to the hum of discussion and muted laughter. This simple realization makes me wonder if archaeologists can ever make the subaltern speak from the inside, and leads me back to Beaudry, Cook, and Mrozowski (1991).

SPEECHES OF THE HIGH AND THE LOW

In order to make their case for an inside-out perspective stronger, Beaudry, Cook, and Mrozowski (1991) argued against the "dominant ideology thesis" they saw many of their colleagues in historical archaeology using to explore the lives of the inarticulate. They took their analysis of this thesis from two sources: the sociological critique of Nicholas Abercrombie, Steven Hill, and Bryan Turner (1980), and from Martin Hall's (1992) and Ian Hodder's (1986) assessments of how Mark Leone (1984, 1988) had used the thesis in his studies of Annapolis, Maryland.

The dominant ideology thesis has caused considerable intellectual excitement. Surprisingly, though, its source comes from a single sentence in Marx and Engels's *The German Ideology* (1970:64): "The ideas of the ruling class are in every epoch the ruling ideas, i.e. the class which is the ruling *material* force of society, is at the same time its ruling *intellectual* force" (emphasis in original). Many scholars have used this sentence to argue the dominant ideology thesis, or, that those who control the money, the factories, and the political and legal power in a society also control its ideas and intellectual life. After thoroughly examining the entire passage in which this sentence occurs, Abercrombie, Hill, and Turner (1980:7–8) proposed two possible meanings. In the weak version, they said that Marx and Engels may have meant that only the ideas of the ruling class are visible in a society because the ruling class controls all the intellectual institutions. Subordinates are present and active, but they do not have the public institutions that permit their ideas to be heard. In the stronger reading, Abercrombie et al. suggested that Marx and Engels may have meant that because of the total power of the elites, the subordinates are completely compromised. Only one culture exists—that of the elites—and all the members of the society share it regardless of their social standing. The subalterns completely adopt the ideas of their rulers and as a result become inarticulate.

Modern readers have long had difficulty understanding precisely what Marx and Engels meant in their writings, and many interpretations of their works are possible. Their sentence defining the dominant ideology thesis is no exception. I suppose that this constant reinterpretation is what inspires many Marxist scholars to keep working. And given the convoluted nature of many of Marx's writings, we must not be surprised that Abercrombie et al. (1980:8) found both the weak and the strong versions of the dominant ideology thesis in *The German Ideology*. After a careful analysis of several other works by Marx and Engels, however, Abercrombie et al. concluded that Marx and Engels probably meant the softer interpretation in their now-famous sentence. The reason for this conclusion derived from the important thread of class struggle that runs through most of Marx and Engels's tracts. In fact, if modern readers know nothing else about Marx and Engels, they usually know that they analyzed class struggle. To be convinced, the curious reader need only recall the opening line of the *Communist Manifesto;* "The history of all hitherto existing society is the history of class struggles" (Marx 1954:13). Marx and Engels never strayed far from class struggle, writing explicitly about controversies over the length of the workday, unfair labor practices, child labor laws, and several other issues in dispute between different groups of people.

Given the prominence of class struggle in classic Marxian thought, why did the stronger version of Marx and Engels's sentence become the basis of the dominant ideology thesis? According to Abercrombie et al. (1980:9), it was because twentieth-century activists, to rationalize the lack of radical class consciousness among workers, laid the blame for disorganization at the feet of the overpowering ideology of the ruling class. The workers of the world are not cohesive radical bodies, said modern-day revolutionaries, because of the all-encompassing intellectual power of the ruling elites. To be made powerless, workers must perceive the ideas of the ruling class to be everyone's ideas. Saying that the subordinates are duped by the intellectual domination of the elites is a powerful message for someone looking to change a complex, modern society in a revolutionary way.

Archaeologists Martin Hall (1992) and Ian Hodder (1986) saw Mark Leone's interpretation of William Paca's eighteenth-century formal garden in Annapolis, Maryland, as an acceptance of the stronger version of Marx and Engels's sentence. In his classic and important study of Paca's garden, Leone implied that all members of Annapolian society tended to perceive the garden as Paca wished it to be seen. Thus, "In the Paca garden we can see that space was manipulated to create a perspective" (Leone 1984:33). For Leone, the perspective was both visual and social; it projected both an image of the garden itself and of society as well. When Leone (1984:26) said that ideas, "when accepted uncritically, serve to reproduce the social order," his critics took this to be support for the strong reading of the dominant ideology thesis. According to Hodder (1986:65), "There is no indication anywhere [in Leone's analysis] that the same material culture may have different meanings and different ideological effects for different social groups." Another way of saying this is: Why must we assume that all people in Annapolis accepted Paca's perception of his garden? Can we not suppose that nonelite men and women created their own, quite different meanings for the garden? At its root, Hodder is basically asking: Where are the subalterns at Paca's garden?

This is an intriguing question. Why would we imagine that William Paca—wealthy attorney, signer of the Declaration of Independence, governor of Maryland, slave owner—would permit the subaltern members of Annapolis to affect his living space in any significant way? Leone (1984) made it clear that the garden was a tangible statement uttered by Paca. Part of the statement was a negation of the subordinate, for clearly Paca was, in the words of mutualism, self-and-other aware. As part of his awareness, the construction of the garden was a conscious attempt to show his prominence in the social hierarchy. Paca had a fancy, well-manicured garden and his social inferiors did not. He signed the Declaration of Independence; he spoke for all those men who were created equal; he taught the fine points of English law.

In a later statement about the criticisms of those archaeologists who disagreed with his perspective, Leone (1994:223) said that Hodder (1986) and Beaudry, Cook, and Mrozowski (1991) were correct to wonder where the "protest and resistance" were at Paca's garden. Rather than to wonder about the personal presence of the subaltern, I would argue that protest and resistance were planted in the garden and were abundantly visible. Part of what Leone saw in the garden was Paca's protest and resistance to becoming part of the subordinate. This is a clear statement of self-and-other awareness. The only way that subalterns can ever be said to speak at Paca's garden is through the voice of Paca himself, in his visual attempt to negate them. He had to make them invisible through his visibility.

Beaudry et al. (1991) agreed with Hodder's assessment of Leone's handling of Paca's garden. As they put it, "The problem seems to be that Leone's analyses have examined only Paca and his activities and motivations, ignoring those of the 'ruled'" (Beaudry et al. 1991:157). In exploring Paca's use of the garden, Leone clearly failed to mention the subaltern. To illustrate further the theoretical problems with Leone's approach, Beaudry et al. (1991:158–159) relied on the idea of "cultural hegemony" developed by Italian Communist Antonio Gramsci (1971). To Gramsci, who died in 1937, ideology was not simply the all-powerful iron fist of the ruling elite. Instead, all social classes maintained their own ideologies based on their self-perceived interests. Because the ideologies compete, the "class relationships consist of the negotiation of these ideologies in the cultural arena" (Beaudry et al. 1991:159). Ideology does not simply reflect the economic position of a class but also the group's everyday experiences. In Gramsci's view, subaltern men and women can enact their own positions, roles, and cultures without relying on the elites to do it for them. This idea is significant for archaeology because the conscious actions are symbolized in everyday material culture.

The cultural hegemonic model allowed Beaudry et al. (1991) to see the past as composed of a series of "discourses" between the different groups in a society. Focusing on the Boott Cotton Mills in Lowell, Massachusetts, they showed how they could observe the give-and-take of the discourses in the excavated artifacts, specifically smoking pipes, liquor bottles, and household ceramics. Beaudry et al. (1991) argued their case well, and their article promises to have an impact on historical archaeology. Their cultural hegemony perspective is gaining favor among many historical archaeologists because it appeals to an anthropological sense of cultural development and integrity. It makes great sense to anthropologists to argue that people have free will to create their own ways of life and to be true to their own traditions. Having said that, however, I also believe that their argument is seriously flawed. Their wish to provide an inside-out perspective, and their avowed intent to discredit Leone's perspective in his Paca garden study, make their approach incompatible with mutualism as I understand it. I can illustrate the defects in the article by Beaudry et al. by examining their interpretations of alcohol bottles and household ceramics, two of the kinds of items that evoke cultural hegemony.

Historical records indicate that the owners of Boott Mills vigorously frowned on the consumption of alcohol by their work force (Bond 1989a:29). In a tangible contradiction, however, excavators in the workers' quarters unearthed 84 medicine bottles and 72 alcohol bottles (Bond 1989b:121). For Beaudry et al. these empty bottles offered mute testimony to the subtle, nonverbal negotiation between workers and owners in regard to alcohol consumption. Subordinate men and women actively resisted the demands of the mill owners and drank in their company homes. The bottles found by archaeologists provide irrefutable proof of this defiance. The bottles provide evidence that the workers constantly established their own leisure behavior "in small acts of everyday resistance" (Beaudry et al. 1991:169). In the process, the workers constructed a unique subculture. As Beaudry et al. (1991:169) phrased it, "It was in leisure behavior and off-work time, as well as personal dress and comportment, that individual workers expressed themselves and signaled the affiliations of ethnicity, subculture, and class." The workers of Boott Mills used liquor and patent medicines containing large amounts of alcohol to create identity and self-awareness.

The interpretation of Beaudry et al. is important because they forcefully argued that the Boott Mills hands were not automatons. Though they worked all day in the oppressive mills, during their off-work hours they were free to express themselves. Part of this self-expression was realized through imbibing alcohol. Their interpretation empowers the workers and makes them active participants in the life of the mill. This is an appealing picture. But at the same time, their interpretation also makes it appear that the workers were able to negotiate with the mill's owners concerning the creation of their subculture. In other words, Beaudry et al. give the impression that the owners controlled the day, while the workers controlled the evening and the nights. Each group controlled part of the 24-hour day.

This perspective, though intriguing, stands at odds with Beaudry's (1987) statements in the original Boott Mills excavation report. In this study, Beaudry (1987:9–11) convincingly argued that the owners of Boott Mills maintained a 24-hour control over their work force. Terming this control "corporate paternalism," she said that the goal of the owners was to eliminate "the possibly of labor unrest that might arise in a stable workforce" (Beaudry 1987:9). She further argued that the mill owners created an artificial community in the Boott Mills tenements by separating the work force by sex, nationality, and perceived status (Beaudry 1987:11). In the same report, Edward Bell (1987:58) said that "through the policy of corporate paternalism, the social lives of workers were regulated and their physical environment controlled." And in the introduction to the third volume of the Boott Mills study, Beaudry (1989:1) explicitly said that the focus of the study rested on two themes: "the boardinghouse system and its effects, direct or otherwise, on workers' lives; and workers' response to the conditions engendered by the system." This statement made it clear that the emphasis, at least of the report filed with the National Park Service, was principally on the owners, with the mill hands acting in counterpoint as reactionaries. The negotiation, if one actually existed, was not one of equals, but of rulers and ruled.

The statements about "corporate paternalism" suggested rather concretely that the men and women of the Boott Mills work force lived in a fabricated community created, as Beaudry (1987:9) observed, "for the manufacture of cotton and woolen goods." In fact, by her account alone, we may justifiably conclude that the haunt of capitalism reigned supreme at Boott Mills, but the specter of corporate paternalism raises intriguing and important questions. Did the owners of the mill know about the drinking of their workers and permit it? And if the owners did not know about it, would they have allowed it to continue if they had discovered it? These are not trivial questions, because they go to the heart of whether drinking in the tenements was part of a negotiated cultural hegemony. If the drinking truly was clandestine, then it suggests that the owners of the mill really did have overpowering, 24-hour influence over their work force, particularly if drinking in the tenements meant dismissal from the factory. A worker could choose to drink openly and risk loss of job, or drink secretly and keep his or her position in the mill. Is this a negotiated relation, and does secret drinking help to build a subculture?

Beaudry, Cook, and Mrozowski's (1991:169–174) examination of household ceramics is equally fascinating. When they studied the ceramics from two backlots at Boott Mills—one from a boardinghouse and the other from a tenement—they discovered that the assemblages were similar. This led them to conclude that the men and women in the buildings had similar ceramic-buying habits (Beaudry et al. 1991:170). This reasonable interpretation is tempered, however, by evidence that the boardinghouse operator "probably purchased goods and furnishings at wholesale prices" from establishments specifically geared to supplying boardinghouses (Bond 1987:37–40). Accordingly, the residents of the boardinghouse "did not participate in discourse through ceramic selection and use" (Beaudry et al. 1991;174).

In any case, the distribution of ceramics at the two sites led Beaudry et al. (1991:170) to a startling conclusion that "the tenement residents sought to emulate middle-class dining habits by including more vessels in a table setting per person even though these were unspecialized in function." Further, "the tenement household emulated mainstream middle-class dining rituals by adapting its limited ceramic assemblage to reproduce as closely as possible a middle-class table service" (Beaudry et al. 1991:171). This interpretation is surprising. Why would the working class decide to emulate the middle class? It almost seems as if Beaudry et al. are asking

us to believe that the mill workers, in their efforts to "express themselves," decided to mimic a superordinate class. Did the workers re-
create themselves in the image of the superordinate middle class?
Beaudry et al. (1991:171–172) said that "ceramic assemblages from
late in the second quarter of the nineteenth century tend to reflect *a
set of ideals* that developed more or less as a response to changing
social conditions brought about by industrialization and the emergence of the middle class" (emphasis added). Their conclusion seems
amazingly like the weaker reading of the dominant ideology thesis.
The set of ideals the mill workers tried to emulate was part of an
ideology impressed from above. Perhaps another way to phrase
Beaudry, Cook, and Mrozowski's conclusion is to say that the middle
class was so successful in impressing its ideals on the working class
that the working class decided to copy them. Hall (1992:383) observed that the urge to copy middle-class ideals may only signal the
"increasing success of market manipulation by manufacturers and
merchants" rather than "an ideological confidence trick." True
enough, but if this is the case, we must ask: Precisely who are the
manufacturers and merchants if not part of the elite and what does
market manipulation entail?

The way out of this troubling conundrum is to argue that the
middle class is not a society's elite. The middle class is socially
situated precisely where its name implies: between the elites and
the lower class. Thus, because it is not dominant in a society, it
cannot have a dominant ideology. But, the point Leone (1988:242)
made in his study of Georgian Order in Annapolis is that the middle
class, "even though they were being impoverished, fiddled and star-
gazed along with the rich." Hall (1992:382) took this to be a clear
indication that Leone accepted the dominant ideology thesis because he said that the middle class accepted "the set of ideals" put
forth by the upper class. Following the refutation of the dominant
ideology thesis by Beaudry et al. (1991) and by Hall (1992), we
should reject Leone's assertion. But because Beaudry et al. rejected
the dominant ideology thesis, should we accept their interpretation
that the working class at Boott Mills accepted the set of ideals of the
middle class?

Beaudry, Cook, and Mrozowski's conclusion oddly rests on the
"trickle-down theory," a perspective they openly rejected because it
"tends to deny the very existence of working-class culture" (Beaudry
et al. 1991:157). Sociologist Georg Simmel invented the trickle-down
theory in 1904 as a way to account for changes in fashion. The

theory fell into disuse in the 1960s and 1970s, but material culture specialist Grant McCracken (1988) revised and reintroduced it. In essence, Simmel's view was that two principles work to spur fashion change: imitation and differentiation. His idea was that in a hierarchically arranged society, the subordinate social groups try to establish increased social positions by adopting the clothing styles of the superordinates. For their part, the superordinates work to stay ahead of the subordinates by constantly changing their fashions. In a sense, the fashions of the superordinates "trickled down" to the subordinates. In his reinvention of the theory, McCracken (1988:94) pointed out two important problems with Simmel's proposal. First, he said that Simmel had misnamed it. The engine that drives fashion is not a trickle-down effect, but an upward "chase and flight" pattern. The subordinates are the ones who influence fashion by their constant imitation. Second, McCracken believed that Simmel failed to say that two social classes exist that do *not* conduct both imitation and differentiation. The true elites in a society do not engage in imitation because they have no one to imitate; the true subalterns do not engage in differentiation because they have no one from which to set themselves apart. In the light of these ideas, we might expect that the William Pacas of the world engage solely in ostentatious displays of wealth as markers of their high positions and little else. For the subalterns, Paca's garden can have a "displaced meaning." Displaced meaning is an esteem value placed on something by someone who does not possess it, but aspires to do so (McCracken 1988:106). Perhaps some subalterns in Annapolis thought, "If I just had a garden like Paca, then I would be happy." In this way, the garden would indeed have had a different meaning for the subalterns than it had for Paca, as Hodder (1986:65) would have it. Or would it? Perhaps Paca's construction of the garden was meant specifically for this purpose. Perhaps the garden was intended to evoke envy and wonder among those who could only dream of owning such a garden. In addition, we must also keep in mind that we have no reason to expect that the garden's displaced meaning would be symbolized in the subaltern's material culture or that Paca would insert the subaltern into his garden except as he chose to symbolize their very invisibility. As McCracken (1988:69) made clear, material culture cannot express everything. Artifacts are not language and attempts to make them appear to operate like language are doomed to fail (see, for example, the attempt made by

Deetz 1967:83–94). Clearly, if a discourse exists, one party is usually talking much louder than the other.

A central problem with the cultural hegemony perspective advanced by Beaudry et al. is purely practical. Their perspective was that men and women of whatever station in life have the ability to create an identity through their actions, attitudes, and material culture. In other words, they argued that the subordinates in a society, and everyone else for that matter, are free to choose precisely how they will symbolize their identities. Individual men and women will accept and reject aspects of their group identity as they see fit. In principle, I agree with them, remembering, of course, the propositions of imitation and differentiation. I would add one important point. In the modern world, the subaltern men and women are never completely free to choose. The four haunts act against social equality. I agree that "people transform the meaning of goods through their actions" (Beaudry et al. 1991:177), but I would also argue that men and women in the modern world do not have an unbounded universe of material goods from which to symbolize their identities. The vast majority of artifacts they have available are commodities not of their making. This situation was certainly true of the workers at Boott Mills. Only people who manufacture their own material things have complete freedom of expression. (This is one reason why Colono Ware is so exciting; see Chapter 5.) But at Boott Mills, the men and women who purchased material objects were constrained by two important factors: the range of commodities available, and what they could afford to buy using their mill wages. In neither case are the subordinates in control. Neither are they merchants nor did they set their own wages. Mill-working consumers confronted a prescribed range of objects they could purchase. Within this range they could select the objects they felt symbolized them either as individuals or as member of social groups. But in giving the workers this freedom of limited choice, we must remember that the manufacturers and merchants decided which items would be produced and in what quantities, and they decided the strategies that would be used to make the goods available and desirable. I can freely admit that the alcohol-drinking Boott Mills workers could have consciously selected patent medicines they knew to have a high-alcohol content, if in fact they had this information. Clearly, though, when Samuel Hopkins Adams (1912:17–18) wrote his famous series of exposés on the frauds of the patent medicine industry, not everyone knew which medicines contained alcohol or in what amounts. This lack of knowledge was dramatically apparent in Adams's (1912:17) account of the lady from the Women's Christian Temperance Union who came to dinner fully intoxicated from her kidney and liver medicine! By contrast, many people apparently did know which medicines contained the greatest amounts of alcohol, and we must assume that the Boott Mills workers were among this knowledgeable group.

One significant problem with Beaudry, Cook, and Mrozowski's (1991) analysis is that they skirted the issue of social power. They said that "belonging—group identity, group membership—is inevitably linked to relations of power and to social differentiation," and they mentioned social power in two endnotes (Beaudry et al. 1991:156, 177, 178). Even though so much of their interpretation hinges on the power of subalterns to forge their own world, they are strangely silent on social power. Perhaps this is because they openly accepted Glassie's view that society does not exist as a pyramid. Their avoidance of social power demonstrates the weakness of their approach and shows that they have made the subaltern speak from an artificial podium.

WHEN THE DISCOURSE BECOMES A SHOUTING MATCH

To discuss social power is to enter an extensive literature, a frequently contradictory and confusing intellectual landscape filled with many pitfalls (see Blau 1964; Boulding 1989; Lukes 1974). As Eric Wolf (1990:586) said, power "is certainly one of the most loaded and polymorphous words in our repertoire." Archaeologists discovered social power a few years ago, and since then important overviews have appeared (Miller and Tilley 1984; Paynter and McGuire 1991). Rather than to duplicate these efforts, I want to explore social power from a mutualist perspective as a network of relations that held men and women together through time and space. I take as my main premise the idea that "power—seeking it, using it, abusing it, decrying it, coveting it, contesting and overthrowing it—is central to the human condition" (Lipman-Blumen 1994:108).

Michael Carrithers (1992) did not expound upon social power in his mutualist tract on which I have relied so strongly in this book. A compatible concept of social power, however, can be found in the work of French philosopher Michel Foucault (1980). Foucault (1980:93, 98) argued that "there are manifold relations of power which permeate, characterise, and constitute the social body," and that "power is employed and exercised through a net-like organisation." Foucault said that power does not simply descend from on high, but that it is implemented through a discourse. This is, in fact, precisely the point made by Beaudry, Cook, and Mrozowski (1991) and by Hall (1992). I would highlight, however, Foucault's (1980:99) explicit view that social power was not evenly distributed in a society; "when I say that power establishes a network through which it freely circulates, this is true only up to a certain point." And, while he made it clear that some kind of power resides in all human beings, "one should not conclude from that that power is the best distributed thing in the world" (Foucault 1980:99). Also, from a methodological standpoint, Foucault did not espouse an inside-out perspective. On the contrary, he argued that scholars "need to investigate historically, and *beginning at the lowest level,* how mechanisms of power have been able to function" (Foucault 1980:100, emphasis added).

Scholars now generally recognize that power has both a negative and a positive side. They refer to "power to" as the ability to get something accomplished, and "power over" as coercive domination (French 1994:15; Miller and Tilley 1984:6). In an enlightening essay, Wolf (1990:586) proposed that four different modes of power can be envisioned in social life. The first mode involves power as a personal endowment, focusing on an individual's place in the enactment of power. The second mode is where power is a social relation, where one person imposes his or her will on someone else. The third mode is where power controls the settings in which people can bring forth their strengths and interact with other people. Wolf called this kind of power "tactical or organizational power." And finally, Wolf (1990:586) identified a power that not only operates within social settings but also "organizes and orchestrates the settings themselves" and specifies the distribution and direction of resources. Wolf termed this "structural power," and said that both Marx and Foucault studied it, albeit it with a different terminology and focus.

Power and social relations are inextricably linked. In an important study of power relations, feminist scholar Jean Lipman-Blumen (1994:110) argued that social power is a set of processes whereby one party gains a capacity to impose its will on another by its potential to contribute or to withhold critical resources and rewards or by threatening or inflicting punishment. The dominance that results from the access to resources can eventually become formally institutionalized. The balance of power, however, is constantly negotiated because of the changing content, quantity, and value of each party's resources. The changing nature of the resources is rooted in two sources. In the first place, the resources are not valued necessarily for any inherent "worth" or quality, but by the way they are defined. Individual groups can define a resource differently and what becomes important is which group can most forcefully promote its definition. The example cited by Lipman-Blumen (1994:111) is an office meeting where a female staff member's suggestion may be disregarded, while the same suggestion by a male staff member is accepted. In this case, the definition of male superiority was accepted as most appropriate. Second, the value of the resources is situational, or rooted in the social context. Different social situations can cast varying amounts of value over any particular resource. Circumstances can change drastically when one party attempts to appropriate the resources of another party. Because no individual or group is ever totally powerless, no other group or individual is ever completely omnipotent. As Lipman-Blumen (1994:113) said, "Even the most downtrodden and disenfranchised control some measure of resources, from personal, to social, political, financial and/or institutional, or some combination thereof."

Lipman-Blumen's (1994) focus on power as a set of processes that is definitionally and situationally malleable helps us to understand structural power and has significant implications for archaeological research. Archaeologists can never see power relationships in progress. Instead, they are restricted to the material aspects of power relations. As Robert Paynter and Randall McGuire (1991:7) pointed out, archaeologists have been fond of perceiving "power behind architectural splendors and material riches, mute testaments to the strength of centralized formal leaders—chiefs, priests, and lords." As they correctly indicated, archaeologists must look for the effects of power relations in the cabins of peasants as well as in palatial estates and temples.

This is all true enough. Historical archaeologists, however, face a problem Paynter and McGuire (1991) did not mention. Because of the presence of written records, historical archaeologists can often precisely identify the powerful while only having vague notions of the less powerful. William Paca's garden provides a perfect example. We know a great deal about Paca because he was able to define the importance of his resources within Annapolis and the United States. What we do not know is who actually built Paca's garden. We can assume, with some assurance, that Paca did not do the work himself, any more than Thomas Jefferson actually excavated prehistoric mounds in Virginia. In her study of Charles Carroll's garden—a tract much like Paca's—Elizabeth Kryder-Reid (1994) adeptly explained the many subtle meanings Carroll inserted into his garden, and she showed how these meanings were reshaped over time. What she did not explore were the gardeners themselves, though her title was "As Is the Gardener, So Is the Garden." Did she ignore the gardeners because she accepted the coarsest reading of the dominant ideology thesis? I doubt it. In fact, I would argue that Paca and Carroll consciously attempted to make their gardeners disappear. Probably, perhaps even more insidiously, neither Paca nor Carroll even considered mentioning the people who built and maintained their precious gardens. I would guess that the gardeners' names appear in a faded bill or account hidden within a pile of documents somewhere. Even if we knew their names and something of their life histories, we would still have to admit that the gardens would nonetheless invoke the messages intended by Paca and Carroll. The gardeners have no clearly active voice in the gardens. The gardens were situationally controlled by their owners. As situations, they structured the relations of power that were enacted within them.

In their inside-out examination of Boott Mills, Beaudry, Cook, and Mrozowski (1991) made it seem that the discourse between the workers and the owners was on a fairly equal footing, even though they fully acknowledged the existence of corporate paternalism. The owners decreed that no one was permitted to drink on the premises, but the workers drank anyway. This was the discourse. Beaudry et al. provided a picture of how the mill hands built lives for themselves in an environment of corporate paternalism, but the picture they present is unsatisfying. In attempting their inside-out way of making the subalterns speak, they downplayed the voice of the elites. In effect, they subtracted the oppressive, paternalist situation from their analysis. Also, because of their theoretical stance, they discredited cases where the superordinates—men like William Paca and Charles Carroll—spoke with an indisputably clear and loud voice, largely unhushed in the discourse.

The mill hands at Boott Mills were not as powerless as gardeners. The owners could suppress the workers but they could not erase them. The situations of the two relations of power were different because the owners needed the workers to provide their wealth. The mansion owners needed the gardeners only for a specific, ostensibly noneconomic purpose. Though the mill hands could not be erased, we must admit that in the discourse noted by Beaudry et al. (1991) the owners' voices were much louder than the replies. At most times, the discourse was a shouting match that the owners won. The reason for their victory was simple: the owners could have easily found more workers if they had to fire several of them for public drinking. At the same time, though, the owners realized that they did not wish to slow production and decrease their profits by having to train a new cadre of mill hands (Bond 1989a). The true power of the workers rested in the capitalist urges of the owners.

Historical archaeologists must be constantly aware of the manipulation of the four haunts by a society's more powerful members. Historical archaeologists can often attribute particular artifacts, and thereby conscious action, to a specific member of the elite, while only being able to relate groups of artifacts to groups of nonelites. We may know the names of the Boott Mills workers from census rolls, but the way the owners housed them under the strictures of corporate paternalism makes it forever impossible (except in the rarest of cases) to correlate excavated artifacts with specific individuals. This inequality cannot be described as a discourse, no matter how badly we may wish to empower the powerless. Drinking in the tenements may not have been an example of defiance (Beaudry et al. 1991:168–169), but only an effort to cope with a degrading and largely intolerable condition.

SPEAKING WITH POWER AT PALMARES AND GORTTOOSE

I do not wish to suggest by my critique of Beaudry, Cook, and Mrozowski (1991) that I believe that the subaltern cannot speak through historical archaeology. On the contrary, I believe that giving voice to the otherwise voiceless is the rightful destiny of historical archaeology. In this sense, I see historical archaeology as a probing, questioning field that can minutely investigate the domination gendered by the four haunts in the modern world. Historical archaeologists can shed the strong light of modern inquiry on the efforts of elites to make subalterns disappear at the same time that they illustrate the ability of subalterns to fight erasure. The problem I see with Beaudry, Cook, and Mrozowski's study is that they diluted the force exerted on the Boott Mills hands by the owners. Though they repeatedly mentioned corporate paternalism, their study made the workers' actions seem unheroic because the workers were simply building a culture, not fighting oppression. The root cause for giving this impression stems for Beaudry, Cook, and Mrozowski's passionate acceptance of the inside-out perspective.

Without doubt, "Power relationships are virtually ubiquitous" (Lipman-Blumen 1994:114). Men and women created numerous, complex power relationships everywhere around the globe and certainly at Palmares and Gorttoose. Modern researchers are left initially with much more information about the activities of the powerful at both places. The Portuguese and the Dutch attackers of Palmares and the landowners of Gorttoose left records of their experiences, and it is from these accounts that our initial impressions emerge. Archaeologists are left to make visible the runaway slaves and the rural peasants. Throughout the research, we must never forget that the ongoing dialogues between the colonial Portuguese and Dutch and the people of Palmares, and between the peasants of Gorttoose and Major Mahon and his agents, were in reality shouting matches. In both cases, the elites had the upper hand, even to the point of being able to appropriate history by attempting to make the subalterns disappear, to erase their history.

Saying that the elite articulates had the upper hand at both places may strike many as odd, particularly in the case of Palmares. After all, the Palmaristas were true revolutionaries in the strictest sense of the word. They openly fought two powerful colonial superpowers and they forged a defiant kingdom that lasted for almost 100 years. The men and women of Palmares were courageous and brave, and the colonial governments well understood their strength. In a letter dated February 18, 1694, the Portuguese governor of Pernambuco, Caetano de Melo e Castro, made this abundantly clear: "the Negroes were so powerful that, hidden in the Serra da Barriga, they awaited our army" (Ennes 1938:194). The governor defined power in terms of population, defensive strategy, and commitment to freedom. And, though they controlled the coast, the Portuguese did not control the Brazilian interior and they knew it. In this part of the empire, the Palmaristas were indeed powerful. But we must also not forget the eventual fate of Palmares. In a very public display of strength, the Portuguese funded, assembled, and outfitted an assault force to attack and destroy Palmares. Official Portuguese dispatches unambiguously called for the "extinction of the Negroes of Palmares" (Ennes 1938:171). The power of the Palmaristas ultimately was short lived. And, though their spirit is still strong in modern-day Brazil, most would agree that it would have been better had Palmares continued to thrive as an African kingdom in the New World. We must examine and understand the way the Palmaristas created and distributed power relationships within Palmares and comprehend how the shifting process of power changed with each new situation. As subaltern members of colonial Brazilian society, the Palmaristas have the ability to speak to us today through their archaeological remains, but we must never forget that their discourse with the colonial Europeans was a shouting match. This shouting match grew in intensity and then became quiet over the course of time.

Across the Atlantic, the peasants of Gorttoose had little real power to exert over the landlords or even over the head tenants. In 1840, Major Mahon became alarmed by the theft of timber from his estate. In Chapter 6, I mentioned the care Mahon took with his trees and the great amount of money he spent on them. In response to the thefts, he commanded his agents secretly to begin marking the timber so that he could catch the culprits with the stolen goods. Only a year later, Mahon began an investigation to discover who was also pilfering his wool. His agents searched many tenants' homes, finding wool in several of them (Pakenham-Mahon Papers). We could conceive of these transgressions as part of the constant conflict between Mahon and the tenants, as the men and women of the townlands expressed themselves through their material culture. We must admit, though, that Mahon held most of the cards. Ultimately, it was he who had the peasants evicted. He paid their passage out of Ireland; he had their homes demolished. A tenant could steal his timber or wool, but he best not get caught. Though not corporate paternalism in name, this situation was largely identical with that faced by the mill hands at Boott Mills who wished to drink in the tenements. Certain behaviors not accepted by the owners brought forth stern, repressive measures. The peasants' acts of defiance were "arts of resistance" used against powerful landlords (J. Scott 1985, 1990; see also Orser 1991). These expressions of tenant dissatisfaction could be short or long term and of varying degrees of severity, Mahon's murder being the extreme example.

It would be nice if archaeologists could obtain an intimate insider's view of all the interpersonal relations the Palmaristas and the

Irish peasants created, maintained, negotiated, and refashioned without reference to the Portuguese, the Dutch, and Major Mahon. Unfortunately, this is an unrealistic goal. Like it or not, historical archaeologists usually must begin with those in control, those men and women in power. This beginning often includes an actual name: Governor Caetano de Melo e Castro, Major Denis Mahon, Domingos Jorge Velho, John Ross Mahon. At Palmares and Gorttoose, these individuals won both the definitional and the real battles by manipulating the four haunts, the very framework of modern life. At the same time, though, these elites permitted us to glimpse the names of those they dominated: Zumbi, Farrel O'Garra, Aqualtune, the Widow Murray. The elites could suppress these men and women, but they could not erase them. The archaeologists' probing trowel has a way of finding these forgotten men and women. We have no reason to think that Mahon would symbolize the peasants in his formal garden any more than Paca or Carroll would have done. The subalterns only speak in the gardens, and in the other domains of the elite, as a negation.

Ultimately, archaeology is about all the people who lived in the past, elite and subaltern alike. Historical archaeologists are both blessed and cursed by the bold visibility of the elites and the quiet invisibility of the nonelites. In my critique of Beaudry, Cook, and Mrozowski's (1991) study of Boott Mills I argued against the inside-out perspective largely because I do not believe that archaeologists can ever obtain this viewpoint, even when confronted by a large body of written and archaeological information. At the same time, though, I argue against the bottom-up view, just as I also agree with Beaudry, Cook, and Mrozowski in rejecting the top-down perspective. Historical archaeologists do indeed confront the overwhelming presence of the elites in the past. They cannot avoid them, because the elites wrote memoirs, letters, and reports. They penned their accounts along the coast of colonial South America, in the green fields of central Ireland, and at a thousand other places around the world.

Historical archaeologists will find social hierarchies in most research situations because the four haunts created and maintained societal levels. Both haves and have-nots coexist in the historical archaeologist's pasts as a given. But if I reject the inside-out perspective as unrealistic, and dispute both the top-down and the bottom-up perspectives, how do I propose to make the subaltern speak? Am I really saying that historical archaeologists should throw up their hands and go back to measuring the size and shape of cannon balls and forget the more complex social issues? Is the study of the subaltern out of our reach?

I most certainly do not believe that the subalterns are outside the reach of historical archaeology. On the contrary, making them speak is our most serious challenge. I do believe, however, that the best way to listen to them is by using a dialectical approach that, in effect, allows us to see a past society from the top down and from the bottom up at the same time. This is a truly mutualist way in which to study the past. Such an approach will permit historical archaeologists to make a real contribution to scholarship. At the same time, it will permit us to situate our sites in truly global contexts.

Think Globally, Dig Locally | 8

I argue in this book that historical archaeologists study the creation and constant re-creation of the modern world. To make this study, I contend that historical archaeologists should adopt a global perspective that unambiguously understands the significance of past networks of interaction. On one level, my position is difficult to argue against. Few practicing historical archaeologists would ever propose that they should unfairly restrict their investigations. In fact, I suspect that most historical archaeologists would readily acknowledge the need to think in big terms when examining the past. Not many would chose to turn a blind eye to any body of information that would help them to establish the contexts of the sites they study. Historical archaeology is blessed with a wide array of potential source materials, and most historical archaeologists readily embrace the variety. Nonetheless, many archaeologists also may argue that they can focus only on individual communities when they conduct excavations. In many cases, the very specificity of these excavations can cause the exclusion of the wider contexts that extend far beyond the site's perceived boundaries (Chapter 2).

I am not alone in calling for analyses that extend beyond a site's immediate boundaries. For example, Anne Yentsch (1990) said that archaeologists should learn to focus first on one topic and then move to another until they obtain a broad understanding of the entire historical and cultural contexts of the men and women who lived at the site. Her idea was rooted in the concept "that one cannot understand the parts of an entity without some sense of the whole which they comprise nor can one comprehend the whole until one has seen the parts from which it is made" (Yentsch 1990:24). This is sound and reasonable thinking. Focusing on Lot 83 in Annapolis, Maryland, Yentsch traveled from one "hermeneutic circle" to another, beginning with the soil layers, artifacts, and features and ending with "Anglo-American culture and its English counterpart in that era" (Yentsch 1990:25; see also Hodder 1991). Each circle was progressively larger and encompassed a greater segment of past life. Even the largest circle provided a context for interpreting Lot 83.

At a base level, Yentsch's (1990) perspective and mine are compatible. I choose, however, to hang my interpretations on a wholly different framework than the one Yentsch has chosen. I replace the subtle mysticism of hermeneutic circles with historically based understandings of the four haunts. Where Yentsch (1990:25) chose to minimize the impact of capitalism in favor of cognitive models and mind-sets, I argue that capitalism and the other haunts have a central place in historical archaeological research. I do not believe that mind-sets and cognitive models have much to offer unless they are firmly contextualized within one of the four haunts. But specifically, how can historical archaeologists create the contextualizations, especially since the four haunts are so complex and fluid through time? I believe that historical archaeologists can produce these complex interpretations by adopting a dialectical research program.

MULTISCALED DIALECTICS, OR MOVING FROM SITE TO WORLD

My views on how historical archaeologists can move from site to world have been shaped by the ideas of prehistorian William Marquardt (1989, 1992), who has made detailed studies of sixteenth-century south Florida, and, in collaboration with Carole Crumley, pre-Roman Burgundy (Crumley and Marquardt 1987, 1990). In two important essays, Marquardt provided an elegant way for archaeologists to conduct the kind of analysis that can move them from the sites they study to the wider worlds within which these sites are situated. Marquardt called his approach "dialectical anthropological archaeology." He said that most modern archaeologists have remained interested in cultural dynamics, as a legacy from the New Archaeology, but most of them have not been able to match their interests with what they can archaeologically demonstrate. As a result, the many criticisms of their efforts have been largely justified. To rectify this situation, Marquardt proposed a dialectical approach that would be "a critical method of inquiry and exposition applicable to entities and the relationships between entities, past, present, and future" (Marquardt 1992:103).

At first glance, Marquardt's dialectical approach does not sound much different from the hermeneutic circles advocated by Yentsch and others. The two perspectives do share similarities. Rather than to rely on vague notions of cognition, Marquardt rooted his approach on four concepts: agency, contradiction, structure, and power.

By "agency," Marquardt (1992:104) simply meant "the purposeful activity of individual human beings." He saw the individual as a decision maker and an active member of a larger social group. Some of an individual's decisions will have only a personal impact, while others will have wider consequences. Archaeologists generally have considered individuals as members of social groups because of the anonymity of most archaeological remains. The urge to consider individuals as members of social groups is common to all archaeology, but perhaps prehistorians face greater temptation in this endeavor than historical archaeologists. But historical archaeologists obviously do the same thing, particularly where "inarticulate" peoples are concerned (see Chapter 7). I would never wish to diminish the significance of social groups, but we can easily understand the impact of individuals on the modern world. We know from history that prominent men and women, working alone or enforced by a mass of supporters, can affect events and change history. All we must do is to think of Zumbi at Palmares or Denis Mahon at Strokestown. Each man, by his actions, had an immense impact on the men and women with whom he was in contact. And, the activities of each were felt far beyond either Palmares or Strokestown. Zumbi affected Portugal; Mahon affected England and America.

By "contradiction," Marquardt meant that opposing elements make up the whole. Contradiction is not synonymous with conflict, though conflicts may arise from contradictions. Examples of contradictions would be embodied in masters and slaves (at a slave plantation), factory owners and workers (at an industrial plant), landlords and tenants (on a rural landscape). Conflicts that could arise from these contradictions would include fleeing the plantation, being fired from a job because of public drinking, and stealing the landlord's wool. Contradictions are rife in the modern world because of the structures of the four haunts.

Marquardt (1992:105) said that physical and sociohistorical structures "determine human potentialities." He meant that men and women are embedded within two environments, one natural and one social. The close relationship between physical structure and human potential is easy to understand. Humans cannot shape stone tools or fashion pottery in places that have neither rock outcroppings nor clay deposits. The sociohistorical structure is more complex because it includes men and women forging relations with one another within the economic, legal, political, social, and religious institutions they create. The relations are not separate from the institutions, but are integral to their meaning. Also, the sociohistorical structures are historically linked to the past and cannot be separated from it. Many of the relations forged in the sociohistorical structure will be relations of power.

For Marquardt (1992:106), "power" is "the ability to alter events or achieve desired goals, with or without the consent of other individuals who may be affected." "Authority" is an individual's capacity to influence the outcome of events (Marquardt 1992:106). Thus, his power is "power to," whereas authority is "power over" (see Chapter 7).

Marquardt was careful to point out that scholars who think dialectically conduct multiscalar analyses, because individual men and women conduct their daily lives along a number of different scales. As used in this sense, "scale" refers to a slice of space and time, and is like the geographer's "level of resolution" (Haggett 1990:23). People make decisions based both on spatial arenas of various sizes (regions) and on tiny or great amounts of time. An action may have immediate consequences or it may have long-term effects. It may affect only a few people living side by side or it may affect far-distant people. Out of the infinite variety of scales that may exist, men and women "comprehend patterns, recognize homogeneity, plan for the future, and operate in the present at specific scales" (Marquardt 1992:107; see also Marquardt 1985). For each conscious decision, though, there exists an "effective scale," or the level at which a pattern or meaning may be discerned (Crumley 1979:166).

Similar to their subjects, researchers think along a number of different scales. They can choose to conduct microlevel or macrolevel spatial analyses (Clarke 1977), or to focus on narrow or large segments of time (Braudel 1966:16). In any case, an analysis at one scale may contradict that conducted at another scale. Rather than showing the inadequacy of either analysis, however, the contradiction only demonstrates the complexities of daily life. For archaeologists, contradictions of this sort only enforce the difficulties of unravelling an entangled past. Archaeologists attempt to interpret past decisions that have left their imprints on the landscape and perceive patterns and regularities at effective scales. Research shows that the best analyses are multiscalar (Ames 1991; Crumley and Marquardt 1987; Little and Shackel 1989).

Multiscalar, dialectical analysis proceeds through a process Marquardt (1992:108) described as "suspension, preservation, and transcendence." A researcher begins at one effective scale and seeks to obtain understanding of it. Once the analysis is satisfactorily completed, the knowledge is preserved but transcended as the analyst moves to another scale. This process is repeated until all available information has been exhausted. As one moves on to a new scale of analysis, it usually becomes clear that the social entities of one scale cannot be separated from other entities. In other words, the dialectical approach is mutualist in that it acknowledges the significance of netlike connections across space and time. In the modern world, the effective scales are crosscut by the four haunts of historical archaeology. Historical archaeologists must always remember the haunts when attempting to comprehend agency, contradiction, structure, and power relations. Individual and group decisions were made in the past about the four haunts based on a series of effective scales that grew geographically wider and temporally deeper as they expanded outward from a particular archaeological site.

In Chapter 2, using Palmares as an example, I explained the need for historical archaeologists to adopt a global perspective. I wish to return to Palmares now and to expand my analysis as a way of further explaining Marquardt's multiscalar, dialectical approach.

The topography and other natural characteristics of the Brazilian backlands helped to create Palmares. The dense forests and the mountains sheltered the Palmaristas from the invading coastal, European forces. The mountain heights provided both a refuge and a way for the Palmaristas to spot the marauders at great distances. Historical documents make it clear that the environment sustained the Palmaristas while it restricted their enemies' approach. As I stated in Chapter 2, the Palmaristas grew a wide variety of crops, caught fish, and domesticated foul. They used the surrounding foliage for their homes, defensive works, and basketry. Historical accounts and archaeological surveys indicate that they used local clays to make a variety of pottery vessels. Thus, the word "Palmares," though overtly referring to the palm trees in the area, also provided the message that these same palms helped to sustain Palmares. As a result, the physical structure of Palmares was rich in resources and alive with meaning.

I detailed Palmares' complex sociohistorical structure in Chapter 2. As I said then, the Palmaristas maintained an intricate set of connections that stretched to Africa and to Europe. To suggest that Palmares was isolated is to overlook its history. The role of individual agency at Palmares is abundantly obvious. Ganga Zumba was a king of Palmares and Gana Zona, his brother, ruled Subupira. Andalaquituche was Ganga Zumba's nephew, and Aqualtune was his mother. Zumbi, the last great king of Palmares, was Ganga Zumba's nephew. Andalaquituche, Aqualtune, and Zumbi all ruled villages named for them, and through sheer force of ability and intellect, each one helped to build and maintain Palmares for almost 100 years. Bartholomeus Lintz, Jürgens Reijmbach, Rodolfo Baro, Fernão Carrilho, and Domingos Jorge Velho led assaults against Palmares with varying degrees of success. Remembering only one of these individuals causes us to consider many more people and to think about the complex web of political relations within which each moved. In considering human agency, we must also not forget the hundreds of Palmaristas whose names we do not know today. They were the people who daily re-created Palmares and who also had their own webs of interaction within which they moved.

If we choose to restrict our examination to Palmares as a discrete site, we can envision a maroon kingdom that lived in open defiance of colonial European authority (Orser 1994b). The Palmaristas appear to have been busy growing and harvesting crops, making pottery and weaving baskets, and seining fish in the river near the base of the Serra da Barriga. Occasionally, they were forced to run into the forests, fleeing the attacking Portuguese and Dutch. Two effective scales for the Palmaristas were undoubtedly the individual villages and the kingdom itself. When we consider the contradictions, we can move to a new scale of analysis and confront some of the most intriguing aspects of Palmares. One of the most significant contradictions existed inside the kingdom between the Palmaristas who saw their ultimate survival linked to accommodation to the Portuguese and those who argued for armed resistance. This is the crisis that thrust Zumbi into leadership. At the same time, another contradiction showed the cracks in the colonial empire. Numerous colonial Portuguese *moradores* found it advantageous to support the Palmaristas against their European homeland's colonial government. Europeans like Lintz once even lived in Palmares and then turned against it, only to lead an assault in 1640. In the light of these historical realities, we may conclude that Palmares incorporated many internal and external contradictions that helped to define it. The presence of the four haunts in northeastern Brazil during the late seventeenth century—often in incipient form, but there nonetheless—created other effective scales that the Palmaristas had to comprehend fully in order to function as a powerful, nationalist force. This understanding would have included Africa, both as a homeland—a place with displaced meaning—and as a source of new Palmaristas, men and women who could help the kingdom achieve lasting independence.

Understanding the importance of increasing the scale of analysis at Palmares allows me to ask an important question that otherwise may not be apparent. Why did the Dutch attack Palmares? At first glance, the answer seems apparent. Caspar Barleus (1923:315, 370), a Dutch contemporary of the maroon kingdom, described the Palmaristas as a "collection of united robbers and fugitive slaves preoccupying themselves with thefts and robberies." He said that Rodolfo Baro decided to attack these "thieving and poaching" fugitives, apparently to make them stop their depredations on the colonial Europeans. Thus, the reason for the Dutch attack seems painfully obvious: the Palmaristas were thieves who robbed the plantations and they had to be stopped. We must remember, though, that the Dutch, like their Portuguese rivals, were in Brazil to obtain the New World's wealth and to build a global empire. Based on this reality, and if we adopt a mutalist view, we must ask why the Dutch did not form an alliance with the Palmaristas to create a united front against the Portuguese. Can we, on the one hand, conclude that the Dutch were so deeply offended by the attacks of the Palmaristas on the coastal plantations that they rose in indignation against them? Were the Dutch simply offended by the Palmaristas' boldness, or can we say that they were motivated by racism and simply wished to see the rebellious Africans crushed? Was their decision to attack Palmares some complex combination of these factors? On the other hand, was it the connections the Palmaristas maintained that bothered the Dutch? Palmarista ties with the Portuguese living in the coastal towns and plantations, the *moradores* settled in the inland valleys, and the native Indians would have been a significant obstacle to Dutch control of the Brazilian northeast. If the Portuguese on the coast purchased foodstuffs from the Palmaristas, then it would have made sense for the Dutch to attack the food supply and thus to harry their Portuguese enemies from the interior. Though this scenario is simply a supposition, the Portuguese themselves did not begin their major assaults against Palmares until after the Dutch left Brazil in 1654. Also, if the Dutch were truly offended by the outrages of the Palmaristas or were simply racist, then it seems that they should have worked in concert with the Portuguese to destroy the detested maroon kingdom. In any case, one effective scale perceived by the Dutch clearly included the Palmaristas, which in turn undoubtedly included a certain segment of the colonial Portuguese population as well.

To understand the history of northeastern Brazil in the seventeenth century requires knowledge of both the colonial Portuguese and the people of Palmares. Between 1605 and 1694, and especially between 1670 and 1694, it is virtually impossible to explain Palmares without reference to the Portuguese, just as Portuguese colonial Brazil cannot be fully understood without reference to Palmares. Famed historian of Brazil, E. Bradford Burns (1980:55) said that during the entire colonial period, the threat of slave rebellion "hung ominously in the air, causing the plantation owners and even the city dwellers endless uneasy hours." Without doubt, Palmares contributed much to the unease. Understanding the process of creating and maintaining Palmares, therefore, requires a mutualist perspective and a dialectical analysis that allows comparison between the Portuguese and the Palmaristas and a firm grasp of their interconnections.

In Chapter 2, I also made reference to the significance of Portugal in reaching an understanding of Palmares. My inclusion of Europe may strike many as odd, particularly since Palmares was so far from Europe. But, I proposed in Chapter 6 that the colonial connections between Brazil and Portugal essentially put the two places in the same region. As such, Europe cannot be removed from my perception of global historical archaeology, especially when historical archaeologists investigate the earliest colonial history of the modern world. On the contrary, Europe has prime importance and it must be reattached to historical archaeology.

REATTACHING EUROPE

In 1967, the prominent anthropological journal *Current Anthropology* announced the formation of the Society for Historical Archaeology ("Institusions," 1967). The author of the announcement said that the primary geographic concern of the new organization would be "the Western Hemisphere." The society would also include "Oceanic, African, and Asian archaeology during the relatively late periods," but Europe would only be considered a part of the new discipline's focus if the subject had "a definite bearing upon problems in the non-Western world." Thus, the intent of the Society for Historical Archaeology from the beginning seems to have been to examine issues *of* Europe but not *European.* In other words, historical archaeologists would examine the same places traditionally studied by cultural anthropologists. The intent of the founding members of the Society for Historical Archaeology was clearly on exploration, colonization, and acculturation in the non-European world (Jelks 1993; Pilling 1967:6).

About three years before the organizational meeting of the Society for Historical Archaeology, K. J. Barton and John Hurt launched the "Post-Medieval Ceramic Research Group" in Bristol, England (Barton 1968:102). The goal of the research group was to develop and exchange information about English ceramics manufactured between 1450 and 1750. Interest in the group grew so large that in 1966, at the same time archaeologists in the United States were thinking about founding the Society for Historical Archaeology, the members dissolved the ceramics group and created the Society for Post-Medieval Archaeology ("Editorial," 1968). The new society kept its focus on the years from 1450 to 1750 because "there is something distinctive about the years between the impact of the Renaissance and Reformation at one end and the onset of the Industrial Revolution at the other" (Society for Post-Medieval Archaeology 1993:93). Postmedieval archaeology appears as the logical extension of medieval archaeology. The historical and cultural trends of the European Middle Ages seem to blend into the postmedieval period in an easy and straightforward way. And in general, postmedieval archaeologists are interested in the same sorts of questions as their medievally focused colleagues (Addyman 1989; Austin et al. 1989; Ayers 1991; Broberg 1992; Crossley 1990; Kajzer 1991; Martins 1992).

The gradation from medieval to postmedieval is not easily imagined outside Europe. When Europeans took their cultural institutions around the world, they and the indigenous peoples they met created a new world. The new ways of life were unlike anything that had existed before, and represented nothing less than a "decisive break in world history" (Amin 1989:1). The New World was not just a reinvented version of the Old World; it was a unique creation, woven from diverse strands of culture and tradition.

When considered in these terms, it seems that historical archaeology and postmedieval archaeology really are two distinct kinds of archaeologies. Historical archaeologists investigate the creation of new ways of life that bound together diverse cultures. Postmedieval archaeologists seem to study the continuation of a way of life that had thousands of years to develop. Thus, it seems that when archaeologists study the English at Jamestown they are historical archaeologists, but when they turn their attention to the seventeenth-century English at Southampton they are postmedieval archaeologists.

At first consideration, I would argue that any distinction between historical archaeology and postmedieval archaeology is trivial. The only difference between them is that one is practiced in Europe, while the other is practiced outside Europe. Still, I am compelled by experience to believe that the two archaeologies really are distinct. Robert Schuyler (1977:5) recognized years ago that the difference revolved around the issue of cultural context. His implication was that historical archaeologists are more interested in cultural contexts, while postmedieval archaeologists tended to focus on historical contexts. Though serious attempts have been made to link postmedieval and historical archaeology (see M. Johnson 1993), the two fields generally stay apart and aloof from one another.

I believe that the perceived distinction between postmedieval archaeology and historical archaeology stems from an understanding that the history of Europe and of the many non-Europes around the globe are uniquely different. The parts of the world examined by historical archaeologists have histories that are so different from the history of Europe that it appears natural that the archaeology of each is inherently distinct. We might argue that postmedieval archaeologists ask different questions than historical archaeologists by virtue of the realities of the past. The root cause of the apparent distinction may be laid at the feet of the overwhelming presence of the four haunts in the non-European world. Writing as I am from the United States, this reasoning all seems to make sense. But does it? Is postmedieval archaeology really different from historical archaeology, as I define it, just because postmedievalists tend not to examine the four haunts? The answer to this question can be found in Robert Bartlett's (1993) *The Making of Europe: Conquest, Colonization, and Cultural Change, 950–1350*.

Bartlett's book is amazing and enlightening. As an undergraduate majoring in history, I had studied medieval history with relish and excitement. In fact, my interest in the medieval past is what drew me to archaeology in the first place, and I had hoped for a career excavating castles and peasant villages. After years of studying the archaeology and anthropology of the New World, however, I slowly lost touch with the medieval world. Bartlett snapped me back to the history of premodern Europe and opened my eyes.

Bartlett's approach to European medieval history relies on a network model that is compatible with the mutualist approach I advocate in this book. Rather than to describe the tortured rise of Europe's nation-states or to chart the turbulent history of the medieval Church, Bartlett showed how medieval Europe was multicultural and international. And surprisingly, Bartlett built a convincing case that the four haunts gained European expression during the 950–1350 period. He argued, for example, that colonialism was in full swing during this period. The Germans moved into Pomerania, the Castilians settled Andalusia, and the Anglo-Normans invaded Ireland. The intent of these colonies was to replicate the life of the homeland on foreign soil, not to subjugate the people in a push toward economic dependency as during the modern age (Bartlett 1993:306). Nonetheless, their efforts were clearly colonialist. Bartlett showed how thirteenth-century knights in the Austrian countryside acted like budding capitalists as they looked at quiet, unproductive marshlands and swamps and envisioned bountiful fields of swaying corn raised by rent-paying tenant farmers (Bartlett 1993:121). Notions of Eurocentrism and modernity were not absent in Bartlett's Europe, either. For example, Bartlett argued that "Frank" was a generic term that gained widespread usage to refer to men from Western Europe who went outside Europe either to settle or to conduct warfare. By the twelfth and the thirteenth centuries, however, the term had become synonymous with forward-looking, progressive thought. As Bartlett (1993:105) said, "to be a Frank implied modernity and power." It seems, therefore, that many medieval Europeans were as concerned with modernity as their descendants would be many years later. It appears that race relations were also a central issue during the Late Middle Ages because so many diverse ethnic groups lived adjacent to one another (Bartlett 1993:197). The medieval conception of race did not mirror the modern understanding based on the often-vague concepts of blood, heritage, or national affiliation. Instead, medieval race was rooted in overt cultural difference. For example, perceived racial distinctions between Germans and Slavs gained expression in customs, dress, language, and law. According to Bartlett (1993:313–314), when European explorers sailed out of European ports in large numbers

beginning in 1492, they came from places that already had generations of experience with colonization and cultural transformation. In
other words, they had experienced the incipient forms of the four
haunts.

Bartlett's brilliant analysis opens up exciting possibilities for
archaeology because he provided the commonalities of topics that
can unite postmedieval and historical archaeologies. I share Bartlett's (1993:156) view that historical archaeology in Europe has
enormous future potential, particularly if it is focused on the issues
presented in this book. The goals should be not only to chart the
transition from feudalism to capitalism in Europe (see Chapter 3),
but also to investigate the beginnings of the modern world among
the castles, peasant villages, and cathedrals of the feudal world.
Once historical archaeologists fully accept the connection between
Europe and non-Europe in more than a tangential way, they will
encounter new vistas for research. By then, whether they choose to
term their research "historical archaeology" or "postmedieval archaeology" will be beside the point.

I feel at this time that I must anticipate some of the criticisms I
may receive from European archaeologists. Both from personal discussions with respected Europeanists and in reading, I have realized that many archaeologists may stubbornly wish to define historical archaeology simply as an archaeology that makes frequent and
abundant reference to written, or textual, sources of information. As
Marshall Becker (1995:6) recently noted, "The unifying theme for
historical archaeology simply seems to me to be 'history.'" Becker,
like many others, would classify Mayan archaeology, for example, as
historical archaeology. This is an old theme in historical archaeology
that unfortunately cannot be put to rest. I have tried to show in this
book, and elsewhere (Orser and Fagan 1995:14–22), why historical
archaeology is so much more than just a method. I have argued in
the clearest possible terms why I do not believe Mayanists are historical archaeologists. I encourage all doubters to read Bartlett
(1993) with care.

LOOKING BEYOND EUROPE

Historical archaeologists including Europe will broaden their
understanding of modern-world connections across time and
through space, and will be compelled to frame their research ques-

tions in global terms. Though the reattachment of Europe is important, it will accomplish only part of the broadened perspective that I believe is important in reshaping historical archaeology as a global study. Another place that must be considered is the rim of land around the Mediterranean Sea.

In an important paper presented at the annual meeting of the Society for Historical Archaeology in January 1995, Neil Silberman (1995:1) argued that "the recognition and intellectual integration of the 'old' world to the 'new' world could fundamentally challenge and redirect historical archaeology's quest to understand colonialism, capitalism, and the genesis of the modern world." The "old world" to which he referred was the Near East and the Mediterranean. Within the long and venerable history of the Mediterranean, Silberman specifically pointed historical archaeologists toward the Ottoman Empire. To him, historical archaeologists who continue to ignore the Mediterranean will never truly understand the motivations and designs of oceangoing Europeans.

Silberman said that American historical archaeologists do not think too much about the Ottoman Empire. Even archaeologists who investigate the earliest colonial expressions of European expansion find it easy to overlook the East. As Silberman (1995:3) noted, no less an important figure in historical archaeology than Ivor Noël Hume (1994) completely disregarded the Middle East in his otherwise captivating book on the early history of Virginia. Before he arrived on the banks of the James River, the famous Captain John Smith—who figures prominently in Noël Hume's book—had hair-raising experiences in the Balkans. According to Noël Hume (1994:126–127), Smith fought for the Austrians against the Ottoman Empire in Hungary, and was captured. Smith was sold as a slave, had his head shaved, and was forced to wear an iron ring around his neck. Eventually able to escape this torment, Smith reappeared in England during the winter of 1604–1605. Smith's experiences with the Ottomans are indeed colorful and interesting, but Noël Hume (1994:127) concluded that they had "no relevance to the Virginia story." Smith's epic tribulations and eventual triumph were merely a novelty, something totally separate from his experiences along the humid shores of the James River. The events among the Turks and those among the Powhatans were two parts of a long and interesting career, but they were unrelated, occurring in two distant worlds.

At first, Noël Hume's reasoning makes sense. The Ottoman

Turks had no knowledge of the Powhatans, and vice versa. We have no reason to imagine that either could have had anything to do with the other. But on second thought, must we necessarily accept the separation between the two? Do the Ottomans have any significance to the story of early Virginia and will knowledge of them aid in understanding American history and culture?

The Ottoman Empire was at its zenith during the sixteenth and seventeenth centuries and controlled what is today Turkey, the Mediterranean fringe of North Africa, and southwestern Asia. The Ottomans knocked on Europe's back door by holding the lands that today comprise Greece, Bulgaria, Albania, Croatia, Bosnia-Herzegovina, and part of Hungary, where Captain Smith met them. For Europe, the Ottoman Empire, with its Islamic religion, was a "lasting trauma" (Said 1978:59) and "an ever-present and fascinating or terrifying spectacle" (Heywood 1972:33). Europeans could not forget Islam; for them it was "a powerful and threatening Other" (Silberman 1995:4). They saw it and the Ottoman advances as a united, constant peril, a danger to the European way of life. In response to the perceived dangers of Islam, European Christendom had fought the Crusades (1096–1291) and had chased the Muslims from the Iberian Peninsula in 1492 as part of the Reconquista. In fact, Columbus made his first voyage at a time when many Europeans believed that Christendom was in a life-and-death struggle with infidel Moslems (Litvinoff 1991:47; Sale 1990:191). Bernard Lewis (1982:34), a prominent historian of the Middle East, said that all "the great voyages of discovery were seen as a religious war, a continuation of the Crusades and of the Reconquest, and against the same enemy." In short, Islam became the very antithesis of Europe (Said 1978:60). Some scholars say, in fact, that the Europeans' shift in terminology from "Christendom" to "Europe" in the fifteenth century was a direct result of the need to present a united front to the Ottoman Empire (Coles 1968:148–149).

The prominence of the Ottomans in the minds of many Europeans, including most of the great scholars of the day (Heywood 1972:33–34), indicates that historical archaeologists wishing to understand European expansion should not overlook them. For Silberman (1995:4), historical archaeologists cannot fully grasp the modern world without also comprehending the Islamic world. He said more forcefully that to ignore the Mediterranean world makes historical archaeologists accomplices to a process of Eurocentrism that most historical archaeologists openly reject (Silberman 1995:4).

In another essay, though, Silberman (1989) made it abundantly clear that historical archaeologists would face severe obstacles when attempting to conduct research in the Mediterranean. Most of the modern nations in the Mediterranean look back on the period of Ottoman domination as a time of degradation and gloom. When numerous epochs of glory can be easily recalled, many of today's Mediterranean peoples see no reason to dredge up the often-painful Ottoman past. Compounding this problem is the simple reality that many archaeologists find it impossible to overlook the ancient "golden ages" of Mediterranean history. Many fieldworkers are reluctant to investigate the modern past when Mediterranean antiquity has so much to offer. Many of the ancient walled cities and towering fortresses harken back to the very cradle of civilization. As acknowledgment of this honored history, the antiquity laws of most Mediterranean countries do not apply to sites dating after A.D. 1700 (Silberman 1989:232). This temporal boundary nearly separates the ancient from the modern, and legislatively imparts importance to the earlier period. Ironically, however, the passionate nationalisms of today's Middle East often make it impossible to separate the painful past from the violent present. The senseless murder of Professor Albert E. Glock in January 1992 made this abundantly clear (Seeden and Watson 1992). Glock, who was researching the historical nature of the Arab–Israeli conflict, "had a vision of using historical archaeology not only as an intellectual exercise, but as an active tool of identity and political consciousness for both Westerners and Middle Easterners as they interact politically, economically, and culturally *today* (Silberman 1995:4, emphasis in original). The stakes of doing historical archaeology in politically volatile environments can often extend far beyond the often trivial controversies of academia. Glock's tragic murder shows that archaeological research can have dire consequences. (For similar comments from Brazil, see Funari 1989.)

A consideration of the Muslim world will often deepen a historical archaeologist's understanding of cultural connections. This knowledge may help to explain many of the Europeans' actions and motivations. A brief example will suffice. A man named Vasif was an Ottoman ambassador who lived in Spain in 1787 and 1788. During his stay on the Iberian Peninsula, he observed that the Spanish Crown had the annual duty of sending five or six thousand workers to the gold and silver mines of New Spain. The reason for this huge transfer of labor, said Vasif, stemmed from the inability of the previous year's workers to tolerate the intense heat and humidity of the strange New World. Unused to such conditions, the Iberian laborers quickly perished from disease, heat exhaustion, and overwork. As a result, the work force had to be replenished yearly. But the exportation of so many able-bodied workers put a significant drain on Spanish agriculture. The strain on Iberian agriculture meant that the Spaniards were forced to import food from Islamic Morocco. These were basically the same people the Spanish had chased from their peninsula during the Reconquista. As Vasif cleverly observed, though, the potential shortage of food "is why they seek the good will of the Moroccan ruler" (B. Lewis 1982:197). Vasif's tale clearly shows that the modern world has always contained many webs of entangled relations that are neatly sewn together by history, tradition, and circumstance.

GLOBAL HISTORICAL ARCHAEOLOGY IN AN UNKNOWABLE FUTURE

Archaeologists admittedly love the past. In addition to loving the pasts of now dead cultures, many archaeologists also love the history of their discipline. Many excavators take a special pleasure in writing about the theoretical maturation of their discipline and in explaining the often subtle nuances of past debates and controversies. In fact, so many articles and books have been written about the history of archaeological theory that any elaborate comment and citation I might make would require another volume. Interested readers should start their odyssey through this literature with Bruce Trigger's (1989) brilliant review.

The archaeologists' interest in their discipline's past is not really all that surprising. Maybe British prehistorian David Clarke (1973) was correct when he said that self-consciousness occurs when a discipline comes of age. Still, in any case, we would imagine, perhaps, that any self-respecting archaeologist should be interested in the past. But in addition to looking backward, many archaeologists cannot help looking forward as well. For many, "What is the future of archaeology?" is a question of burning significance.

Ideas about archaeology's future are as variable as archaeologists themselves. For Clarke (1979:84–86), the development of a fully scientific archaeology would put an end to regional distinctions and lead to a truly united archaeology. For feminist archaeologist

Suzanne Spencer-Wood (1992), the abandonment of androcentric terms and conceptions would lead to a nonsexist archaeology that could transform the field and place it in the forefront of transdisciplinary, intellectual thought. Behavioral archaeologist Michael Schiffer (1992) believed that archaeology could make a tremendous contribution to understanding such contemporary human issues as technological innovation and competitiveness. Critical archaeologists Mark Leone and Robert Preucel (1992) argued that archaeology can be used by living peoples to help them understand their present situations. Each one of these well-trained, thoughtful archaeologists were committed, in one way or another, to taking archaeology out of dusty laboratories of academia and situating it firmly in the modern world.

Clearly, no one can precisely predict archaeology's future. We should not expect even the brightest theoretician to have this capability. One important thought to emerge from the many discussions of the future, however, is that archaeologists must make their discipline relevant and responsible. Part of this understanding is rooted in the notion that archaeology can provide powerful knowledge for living peoples. Archaeological knowledge has a direct bearing on the present. The understanding of archaeology's potential impact largely derives from "self-reflection." Some archaeologists see self-reflection as indispensable. As Michael Shanks and Christopher Tilley (1987:66) said, "Archaeology must become reflexive: archaeology needs to consider itself as much as the past." Their basic point is that to know the past we must also know ourselves. We must understand why we depict the past one way and not another. Walter Taylor (1948:35) said long ago that archaeologists must realize that they construct the past, not reconstruct it. In all cases, archaeological interpretation incorporates a strong measure of the archaeologist.

All archaeologists do not agree that self-reflection is important. As Shanks said, "I am angry that many sections of the archaeological community seem blissfully innocent, uncritically unreflective of what they are doing" (Mackenzie and Shanks 1994:38). The problem with self-reflection is that it often can appear as self-serving rhetoric, intended only to help an archaeologist support an interpretation or establish his or her credentials. But self-reflection is much more than personal anecdotes. In archaeology, self-reflection should empower readers "with the knowledge to draw their own conclusions or form their own positions" (Potter 1991a:232). In its essence, self-reflection permits archaeologists to think about the contemporary social contexts of their research and to understand that the results of today's archaeology can have an impact on living men and women. This self-understanding has the power to make the research more insightful because it challenges archaeologists' interpretations and motivations (Potter 1994:37–38). It makes an archaeologist wonder, "Why am I choosing this interpretation instead of another?" and "Are the data leading me, or am I leading the data?" Self-reflection consciously links past and present.

In North America, much of the debate about the relationship between archaeology and the present has centered around Native Americans (see, for example, Blancke and Slow Turtle 1990). Native peoples in other places also have caused archaeologists to rethink their discipline (see, for example, Creamer 1990; Layton 1989; O'Regan 1990). Given the nature of historical archaeology, we should not be surprised that some of its practitioners have examined the relationship of their field to living men and women (see, for example, Leone 1981; Potter 1991b, 1994).

In an important critique, Parker Potter (1991b) examined an article by William Adams and Sarah Boling (1989), in which they assessed the relationship between social position and ceramics at three slave plantations along the Georgia coast. Potter's analysis centered upon the article's final two sentences, in which Adams and Boling (1989:94) argued that slaves had more economic freedom than most people today realize. They said, in fact, that in terms of economics, plantation slaves, though held in bondage, were more like peasants or serfs. Potter (1991b:95) argued that Adams and Boling's interpretation was dangerous because it could innocently provide ammunition "for a social and political position they no doubt find repugnant." In appearing to make slavery a system with some latitude and freedom for slaves, Adams and Boling seemed to say that slavery was not so bad. But if Adams and Boling had imagined delivering their paper to an audience of African Americans, Potter believed that they would have thought more about the contemporary implications of their interpretations. Potter said that they should have realized that plantation archaeology could be used by today's African Americans both to understand their history and to empower them. In the final analysis, Potter (1991b:104) argued that self-reflection makes for better archaeological analysis because it forces archaeologists to frame their interpretations in multiple contexts.

Potter's point about the need for archaeologists to appreciate the impact of their interpretations was made abundantly clear to

Mark Leone's archaeological research team at Annapolis, Maryland. In 1986, while excavating at the Gott's Court site, a homesite inhabited by African Americans from about 1906 until the early 1950s, the fieldworkers unearthed a steel-shanked comb with large steel teeth (Leone et al. 1995:113). The researchers tried in vain to ascertain the past function and meaning of this comb, but it took an African-American informant to explain that the object was a "hot" or "straightening" comb. The archaeologists assumed that African Americans at Gott's Court used this comb to straighten their hair in an effort to assimilate into white America. African Americans, however, quickly rejected this interpretation, arguing instead that the comb was a conscious social strategy intended only to give the appearance of assimilation. African Americans living in Annapolis perceived the archaeologists' inability to see this usage as an example of racism (Leone et al. 1995:114).

In truth, it remains to be seen whether archaeology can have an impact outside the sheltered halls of academia. It may very well be the case that the public is only interested in unfamiliar cultures and valuable finds. Their interest in the use of archaeology to understand the modern world may be quite small. In any case, and regardless of the public's response to archaeological research, it surely will not harm historical archaeologists to consider the wider impacts of their research, as they learn to situate their studies in a world that extends far beyond the confines of the university.

Self-reflection is a necessary part of this book. I fully understand that my perspective about global historical archaeology as examining interlaced webs of interaction and association is a product of the growing awareness of the so-called global community. Electronic mail, facsimile machines, overnight mail, supercomputers, and supersonic aircraft really do seem to be making the world smaller. As I wrote this book, I used the telephone, electronic mail, the fax machine, and the airmail postal service to correspond with colleagues around the world. In the middle of the writing, one valued colleague, Professor Anders Andrén, went on leave and travelled from the University of Lund, Sweden, to the Swedish Institute in Athens, Greece. His move from the cold North to the sunny South had no effect on my ability to contact him. These marvels of modern technology were unthinkable even 30 years ago when the founders of the Society for Historical Archaeology first discussed the new organization. Modern historical archaeologists, along with everyone else, truly do seem to live in a global village.

More importantly, perhaps I fully understand that my research at Palmares and at Gorttoose exists in the present, though it focuses on the past. Both projects are firmly tied to the politics of the present. The year I write these lines, 1995, has deep significance to both places.

The year 1995 marks the 300th anniversary of Zumbi's death at the hands of his Portuguese captors. This historical landmark is not lost on the people of Brazil, and in November 1994, the Brazilian Ministry of Culture held a conference in São Paulo entitled "Palmares: 300 Years." The image of Zumbi is forever before the people of Brazil. He is considered to be the "first great Negro of Brazil" (Souza 1963:15), and men and women in today's Brazilian northeast are surrounded by Zumbi and Palmares. At coastal Maceió, planes land at Palmares Field, and cars and busses pass the Zumbi Auto Parts store on the road that links the airport and the city. In União dos Palmares, a mural of Zumbi points to the Serra da Barriga from the side of the bus depot. If you stop in town, you can have your film developed at the Foto Zumbi. In 1969, a leftist group took the name "Armed Revolutionary Vanguard—Palmares" (Dassin 1986:94), and the maroon community has been the subject of two full-length, feature films (*Gunga Zumba,* 1964; *Quilombo,* 1984). To be conducted, all archaeological research at Palmares must be approved by the governmental Palmares Cultural Foundation and be accepted by the local black rights groups. Local African-Brazilian leaders are immensely interested in the results of the archaeological research at Palmares, and they do not consider the work to be only an exercise in knowing the past. They see the archaeology in the dual light of empowerment and cultural pride. To think that archaeology at Palmares is only about the past is to overlook the modern world at the base of the Serra da Barriga; it is to be blind to reality.

The year 1995 also marks the 150th anniversary of the beginning of the Great Irish Famine. Other famines have been more costly in human terms than the Irish Famine of 1845–1849. For example, the famine in China in 1877–1878 is said to have killed between 9 and 13 million people, and the Bengali famine of 1940–1943 may have killed as many as 10 million (Ó Gráda 1989). Though exact figures on the Great Irish Famine will never be known with certainty, it is thought to have been responsible for around one million deaths. And though historians disagree about whether the Great Famine was a true watershed in modern Irish history (Foster 1989:319), it did provide a strong impetus for emigration. Historians estimate that between 1845 and 1855, almost 1.5 million Irish men,

women, and children left for the United States, 340,000 sailed for
Canada, as many as 300,000 settled across the Irish Sea in Great
Britain, and several thousand went to Australia. In all, about one-
quarter of the prefamine population left Ireland during the famine
years (K. A. Miller 1985:291). In addition to the sheer size of emigration, the Great Irish Famine also presents a frightening specter: it
occurred in Western Europe in modern times on the very doorstep of
one of the world's richest empires. Numerous conferences and museum exhibits are planned in Ireland, the United States, England, and
Australia as part of the commemoration of the Great Irish Famine.
Several books will undoubtedly be published about this terrible
event. Within this atmosphere, the project at Gorttoose will be closely watched for at least two reasons. In the first place, Irish archaeologists have yet to focus on the Great Famine. Many of them are
waiting to see whether it has validity as a serious research endeav-
or. Second, though the Gorttoose project investigates one tiny corner
of Ireland, many modern Irish men and women can see the wider
political significance of studying Irish poverty and famine. For millions of Irish descendants, it is difficult to maintain ambivalence
about famine research. Farrell O'Gara (see Chapter 4) perceives a
strong continuity between himself and his ancestors who lived
where he lives now.

The question of self-reflection brings me to one final question:
what do I envision for a global historical archaeology? Surely, I must
imagine that the adoption of a global perspective will be advantageous to historical archaeologists or I would not have spent these
pages examining it. I do not expect that historical archaeologists
will ever be able to excavate an entire global network, or even a
large percentage of one. In this respect, I completely agree with
Robert Schuyler (1988). Archaeologists cannot be expected to bring
to light all of the many manifestations of past cultural networks.
The modern world is simply too complex, too interwoven to submit
to facile analysis. Any archaeologist who sets out to study every
representation of even one web of interaction will soon become intellectually frustrated and physically exhausted (even if provided with
unlimited time and funding). Let me make it clear that I am not
calling for the creation of large-scale archaeological expeditions
whose members will blanket the globe, seeking intercontinental
explanation and truth. What I am proposing, though, is that historical archaeologists—regardless of where they conduct their
investigations—couch their research questions mutualistically in

broadly conceived terms that fully incorporate the netlike complexities of modern life. This approach will yield more interesting and insightful analyses than studies that are narrowly conceived and minutely focused. In short, historical archaeologists must think globally and dig locally. Having said that, I can imagine some readers may misconstrue my message about the four haunts. My focus on colonialism, Eurocentrism, capitalism, and modernity is not meant to restrict research by historical archaeologists. On the contrary, I see my perspective as liberating the field. By making the haunts explicit, historical archaeologists can proceed to examine the significant social relations that men and women created, manipulated, and redesigned as part of their daily existence. Some historical archaeologists may find sites that they argue were not affected by any one of the four haunts. If such sites can be located, they will be truly interesting, and I look forward to learning more about them. Of course, sites unaffected by the four haunts are widespread throughout prehistory. Their presence in the modern world, however, is another matter entirely.

Without doubt, global analyses will be difficult to conduct, and in many cases the archaeologist may initially miss the mutualist connections or fail to understand them. In the light of such difficulty, however, we must take solace in the knowledge that the modern world historical archaeologists examine was the complex, interwoven precursor of today's world. Since we have the complexities of our world impressed upon us at every turn, we can appreciate the challenge and the promise of the approach I have outlined in this book.

References

Aalen, F.
1989   Imprint of the Past. In *The Irish Countryside: Landscape, Wildlife, History, People,* edited by D. Gillmor, pp. 83–119. Wolfhound Press, Dublin.
Abercrombie, N., S. Hill, and B. S. Turner
1980   *The Dominant Ideology Thesis.* George Allen and Unwin, London.
Abu-Lughod, J. L.
1989   *Before European Hegemony: The World System, A.D. 1250–1350.* Oxford University Press, New York.
Adams, G.
1994   *Free Ireland: Towards a Lasting Peace.* Roberts Rinehart, Niwot, Colorado.
Adams, R. McC.
1974   Anthropological Perspectives on Ancient Trade. *Current Anthropology* 15:239–258.
Adams, S. H.
1912   *The Great American Fraud: Articles on the Nostrum Evil and Quackery Reprinted from Collier's.* American Medical Association, Chicago.
Adams, W. H.
1977   *Silcott, Washington: Ethnoarchaeology of a Rural American Community.* Reports of Investigation 54. Laboratory of Anthropology, Washington State University, Pullman.
Adams, W. H., and S. J. Boling
1989   Status and Ceramics for Planters and Slaves on Three Georgia Coastal Plantations. *Historical Archaeology* 23(1):69–96.
Addyman, P. V.
1989   The Archaeology of Public Health at York, England. *World Archaeology* 21:244–264.
Alcock, N. W.
1993   *People at Home: Living in a Warwickshire Village, 1500–1800.* Phillimore, Chichester, England.
Allen, K.M.S., S. W. Green, and E.B.W. Zubrow (editors)
1990   *Interpreting Space: GIS and Archaeology.* Taylor and Francis, London.
Allibone, S. A.
1890   *Prose Quotations from Socrates to Macaulay.* J. B. Lippincott, Philadelphia.
Ames, K. M.
1991   The Archaeology of the *Longue Duree:* Temporal and Spatial Scale in the Evolution of Social Complexity on the Southern Northwest Coast. *Antiquity* 65:935–945.
Amin, S.
1989   *Eurocentrism.* Translated by R. Moore. Monthly Review Press, New York.
Anderson, K. and F. Gale
1992   Introduction. In *Inventing Places: Studies in Cultural Geography,* edited by K. Anderson and F. Gale, pp. 1–12. Longman Cheshire, Melbourne.

Andrade Lima, T.
    1993   Arqueologia História no Brasil: balanço bibliográfico (1960–1991). *Anais do Museu Paulista* 1:225–262.
Antonelli, C., P. Petit, and G. Tahar
    1992   *The Economics of Industrial Modernization.* Academic Press, London.
Arnold, B.
    1990   The Past as Propaganda: Totalitarian Archaeology in Nazi Germany. *Antiquity* 64:464–478.
Asad, T.
    1987   Are There Histories of Peoples without Europe? A Review Article. *Comparative Studies in Society and History* 29:594–607.
Ascher, R.
    1974   Tin Can Archaeology. *Historical Archaeology* 8:7–16.
Ascher, R., and C. H. Fairbanks
    1971   Excavation of a Slave Cabin: Georgia, U.S.A. *Historical Archaeology* 5:3–17.
Aston, T. H., and C.H.E. Philpin
    1985   *The Brenner Debate: Agrarian Class Structure and Economic Development in Pre-Industrial Europe.* Cambridge University Press, Cambridge.
Austin, D., G.A.M. Gerrard, and T.A.P. Greeves
    1989   Tin and Agriculture in the Middle Ages and Beyond: Landscape Archaeology in St. Neot Parish, Cornwall. *Cornish Archaeology* 28:5–251.
Ayes, B.
    1991   Post-Medieval Archaeology in Norwich: A Review. *Post-Medieval Archaeology* 25:1–23.
Bach, R. L.
    1982   On the Holism of a World-System Perspective. In *World-Systems Analysis: Theory and Methodology,* edited by T. K. Hopkins and I. Wallerstein, pp. 145–158. Sage, Beverly Hills, California.
Bahn, P.
    1989   *Bluff Your Way in Archaeology.* Ravette, West Sussex, England.
Baker, S. G.
    1972   Colono-Indian Pottery from Cambridge, South Carolina with Comments on the Historic Catawba Pottery Trade. *Notebook* (of the South Carolina Institute of Archaeology and Anthropology) 4(1):3–30.
Balandier, G.
    1968   *Daily Life in the Kingdom of the Kongo: From the Sixteenth Century to the Eighteenth Century.* Translated by H. Weaver. Pantheon, New York.
Barleus, C.
    1647   *Rerum Per Octennium in Brasilia.* Joannis Blaeu, Amsterdam.
    1923   *Nederlandsch Brazilie Onder Het Bewind von Johan Maurits, Grave van Nassau, 1637–1644.* Martinus Nijhoff, 's Gravenhage.
    1974   *História dos Feitas Recentemente Practicados Durante Oito Anos no Brasil.* Livraria Italaia Editora, Belo Horizonte.
Barnard, T.
    1975   *Cromwellian Ireland: English Government and Reform in Ireland, 1649–60.* Oxford University Press, Oxford.
Barnes, J. A.
    1954   Class and Committees in a Norwegian Island Parish. *Human Relations* 7:39–58.

Bartlett, R.
  1993 *The Making of Europe: Conquest, Colonization, and Cultural Change, 950–1350*. Princeton University Press, Princeton.
Barton, K. J.
  1968 Origins of the Society for Post-Medieval Archaeology. *Post-Medieval Archaeology* 1:102–103.
Beames, M.
  1975 Cottiers and Conacre in Pre-Famine Ireland. *Journal of Peasant Studies* 2:352–354.
Beaudry, M. C.
  1987 The Boott Cotton Mills Corporation Mill Yard and Housing: Material Expressions of Industrial Capitalism. In *Interdisciplinary Investigations of the Boott Mills, Lowell, Massachusetts, Volume I: Life at the Boarding Houses,* edited by M. C. Beaudry and S. A. Mrozowski, pp. 9–14, National Park Service, Boston.
  1989 Introduction. In *Interdisciplinary Investigations of the Boott Mills, Lowell, Massachusetts, Volume III: The Boarding House System as a Way of Life,* edited by M. C. Beaudry and S. A. Mrozowski, pp. 1–5. National Park Service, Boston.
Beaudry, M. C., L. J. Cook, and S. A. Mrozowski
  1991 Artifacts and Active Voices: Material Culture as Social Discourse. In *The Archaeology of Inequality,* edited by R. H. McGuire and R. Paynter, pp. 150–191. Basil Blackwell, Oxford.
Becker, M. J.
  1995 Letter to the Editor. *Society for American Archaeology Bulletin* 13(2):6.
Befu, H.
  1977 Social Exchange. *Annual Review of Anthropology* 6:255–281.
Bell, E. L.
  1987 A Preliminary Report on Health, Hygiene, and Sanitation at the Boott Mills Boarding Houses: An Historical and Archaeological Perspective. In *Interdisciplinary Investigations of the Boott Mills, Lowell, Massachusetts, Volume I: Life at the Boarding Houses,* edited by M. C. Beaudry and S. A. Mrozowski, pp. 57–68. National Park Service, Boston.
Bennett, N. R.
  1975 *Africa and Europe: From Roman Times to the Present.* Africana, New York.
Bennett, W. J.
  1984 *To Reclaim a Legacy: A Report on the Humanities in Higher Education.* National Endowment of the Humanities, Washington.
Billet, B. L.
  1993 *Modernization Theory and Economic Development: Discontent in the Developing World.* Praeger, Westport, Connecticut.
Binford, L. R.
  1972 *An Archaeological Perspective.* Seminar Press, New York.
  1977 Historical Archaeology: Is It Historical or Archaeological? In *Historical Archaeology and the Importance of Material Things,* edited by L. Ferguson, pp. 13–22. Society for Historical Archaeology, Tucson, Arizona.
Birmingham, D.
  1965 *The Portuguese Conquest of Angola.* Oxford University Press, London.

Black, C. E., L. Dupree, E. Endicott-West, D. C. Matuszewski, E. Naby, and A. N. Waldron
  1991   *The Modernization of Inner Asia.* M. E. Sharpe, Armonk, New York.
Blades, B. S.
  1986   English Villages in the Londonderry Plantation. *Post-Medieval Archaeology* 20:257–269.
Blancke, S., and C.J.P. Slow Turtle
  1990   The Teaching of the Past of the Native Peoples of North America in U.S. Schools. In *The Excluded Past: Archaeology in Education,* edited by P. Stone and R. MacKenzie, pp. 109–133. Unwin Hyman, London.
Blanton, R. E., S. A. Kowalewski, G. Feinman, and J. Appel
  1981   *Ancient Mesoamerica: A Comparison of Change in Three Regions.* Cambridge University Press, Cambridge.
Blanton, R. E., and Gary Feinman
  1984   The Mesoamerican World System. *American Anthropologist* 86:673–682.
Blassingame, J. W. (editor)
  1979   *The Frederick Douglass Papers, Series One: Speeches, Debates, and Interviews, Volume 1, 1841–46.* Yale University Press, New Haven.
Blau, P. M.
  1964   *Exchange and Power in Social Life.* John Wiley, New York.
Blaut, M.
  1970   Geographic Models of Imperialism. *Antipode* 2:65–85.
Bloom, A.
  1987   *The Closing of the American Mind: How Higher Education Has Failed Democracy and Impoverished the Souls of Today's Students.* Simon and Schuster, New York.
Boggs, G. L.
  1990   Beyond Eurocentrism. *Monthly Review* 41(9):12–18.
Bond, K. H.
  1987   A Preliminary Report on the Demography of the Boott Mills Housing Units #33–48, 1838–1942. In *Interdisciplinary Investigations of the Boott Mills, Lowell, Massachusetts, Volume I: Life at the Boarding Houses,* edited by M. C. Beaudry and S. A. Mrozowski, pp. 35–55. National Park Service, Boston.
  1989a "That We May Purify Our Corporation by Discharging the Offenders": The Documentary Record of Social Control at the Boott Mills. In *Interdisciplinary Investigations of the Boott Mills, Lowell, Massachusetts, Volume III: The Boarding House System as a Way of Life,* edited by M. C. Beaudry and S. A. Mrozowski, pp. 23–35. National Park Service, Boston.
  1989b The Medicine, Alcohol, and Soda Vessels from the Boott Mills Boardinghouses. In *Interdisciplinary Investigations of the Boott Mills, Lowell, Massachusetts, Volume III: The Boarding House System as a Way of Life,* edited by M. C. Beaudry and S. A. Mrozowski, pp. 121–139. National Park Service, Boston.
Boorstin, D. J.
  1987   *Hidden History.* Harper and Row, New York.
Borgmann, A.
  1992   *Crossing the Postmodern Divide.* University of Chicago Press, Chicago.

Boulding, K.
1989 *Three Faces of Power.* Sage, Newbury Park, California.
Boxer, C. R.
1973a *Salvador de Sá e a Luta pelo Brasil e Angola, 1602–1686.* Translated by O. M. de Oliveira Pito. Companhia Editora Nacional, São Paulo.
1973b *The Dutch Seaborne Empire, 1600–1800.* Penguin, London.
Brady, C., and R. Gillespie (editors)
1986 *Natives and Newcomers: Essays on the Making of Irish Colonial Society, 1534–1641.* Irish Academic Press, Bungay, Suffolk.
Brannon, N. F.
1984 Excavation at a Farmyard in the Bonn Townland, Country Tyrone. *Ulster Journal of Archaeology* 47:177–181.
1990 Excavations at Brackfield Bawn, County Londonderry. *Ulster Journal of Archaeology* 53:8–14.
Braudel, F.
1966 *La Méditerranée et la Monde Méditerranéen a L'époch de Philippe II* (2nd ed.). Librairie Armand Colin, Paris.
1973 *Capitalism and Material Life, 1400–1800.* Translated by M. Kochan. Harper and Row, New York.
1977 *Afterthoughts on Material Civilization and Capitalism.* Translated by P. M. Ranum. Johns Hopkins University Press, Baltimore.
1984 *The Perspective of the World.* Translated by S. Reynolds. Harper and Row, New York.
Breen, T. H.
1989 *Imagining the Past: East Hampton Histories.* Addison-Wesley, Reading, Massachusetts.
British Parliamentary Papers
1970 *1851 Census Ireland, Part I: Ulster and Connacht, Area Population and Housing.* Irish University Press, Shannon.
Broberg, A.
1992 Archaeology and East-Swedish Agrarian Society, A.D. 700–1700. In *Rescue and Research: Reflections of Society in Sweden, 700–1700 A.D.,* edited by L. Ersgård, M. Holmström, and K. Lamm, pp. 273–309. Riksantikvarieämbetet, Stockholm.
Brooks, S. T., and R. H. Brooks
1980 Cranial Deformation: Possible Evidence of Pochteca Trading Movements. *Transactions of the Illinois Academy of Science* 72(4):1–12.
Brown, I. W.
1979 Historic Artifacts and Sociocultural Change: Some Warnings from the Lower Mississippi Valley. *The Conference on Historic Site Archaeology Papers* 13:109–121.
Browne, G.J.P.
1848 The Mahon Evictions. *The Freeman's Journal,* April 29.
Bullen, A. K., and R. P. Bullen
1945 Black Lucy's Garden. *Bulletin of the Massachusetts Archaeological Society* 6:17–28.
Burns, E. B.
1980 *A History of Brazil* (2nd ed.). Columbia University Press, New York.

Burton, R. F.
    1874   Preface and Introduction. In *The Captivity of Hans Stade of Hesse, in A.D. 1547–1555. Among the Wild Tribes of Eastern Brazil.* Translated by A. Tootal, pp. i–xciv. The Hakluyt Society, London.
Caldwell, J. R.
    1964   Interaction Spheres in Prehistory. In *Hopewellian Studies,* edited by J. R. Caldwell and R. L. Hall, pp. 133–143. Illinois State Museum, Springfield.
Cameron, R.
    1989   *A Concise Economic History of the World.* Oxford University Press, New York.
Campbell, G.
    1879   *White and Black: The Outcome of a Visit to the United States.* Chatto and Windus, London.
Campbell, S. J.
    1990   The Strokestown Famine Papers: The Mahon Family and the Strokestown Estate, 1845–1848. Unpublished paper on file, Strokestown Park House, Strokestown, County Roscommon, Republic of Ireland.
    1994   *The Great Irish Famine: Words and Images from the Famine Museum, Strokestown Park, County Roscommon.* The Famine Museum, Strokestown.
Canny, N.
    1976   *The Elizabethan Conquest of Ireland: A Pattern Established, 1575–76.* Harvester Press, Sussex.
    1989   Early Modern Ireland, c. 1500–1700. In *The Oxford Illustrated History of Ireland,* edited by R. F. Foster, pp. 104–160. Oxford University Press, Oxford.
Cardoso, G.
    1983   *Negro Slavery in the Sugar Plantations of Veracruz and Pernambuco, 1550–1680: A Comparative Study.* University Press of America, Washington.
Carneiro, E.
    1988   *Os Quilombo dos Palmares* (4th ed.). Companhia Editora Nacional, São Paulo.
Carrithers, M.
    1992   *Why Humans Have Cultures: Explaining Anthropology and Social Diversity.* Oxford University Press, Oxford.
Carvalho, A. de (translator)
    1902   Diario da viagem de Capitão João Blaer aos Palmares em 1645. *Revista do Instituto Arqueología e Geográfico Pernambuco* 10:87–96.
Caulfield, M. D.
    1974   Culture and Imperialism: Proposing a New Dialectic. In *Reinventing Anthropology,* edited by D. Hymes, pp. 182–212. Random House, New York.
Cawley, M.
    1989   Rural People and Services. In *The Irish Countryside: Landscape, Wildlife, History, People,* edited by D. Gillmor, pp. 197–225. Wolfhound Press, Dublin.
Chahon, S.
    1995   O espaço social nas igrejas do Rio de Janeiro imperial. *Historical Archaeology in Latin America* 6:27–43.
Champion, T. C. (editor)
    1989   *Centre and Periphery: Comparative Studies in Archaeology.* Unwin Hyman, London.

Charlton, T. H., and D. L. Nichols
  1992 Late Postclassic and Colonial Period Elites at Otumba, Mexico: The Archae-
    ological Dimensions. In *Mesoamerican Elites: An Archaeological Assess-
    ment,* edited by D. Z. Chase and A. F. Chase, pp. 242–258. University of
    Oklahoma Press, Norman.
Chaunu, P.
  1979 *European Expansion in the Later Middle Ages.* Translated by K. Bertram.
    North-Holland, Amsterdam.
Childe, V. G.
  1946 *Scotland before the Scots.* Methuen, London.
  1947 *History.* Cobbett Press, London.
  1951 *Man Makes Himself.* New American Library, New York.
Clarke, D. L.
  1968 *Analytical Archaeology.* Methuen, London.
  1973 Archaeology: The Loss of Innocence. *Antiquity* 47:6–18.
  1977 Spatial Information in Archaeology. In *Spatial Archaeology,* edited by D. L.
    Clarke, pp. 1–32. Academic Press, London.
  1979 *Analytical Archaeologist: Collected Papers of David L. Clarke.* Academic
    Press, London.
Cleland, C. E.
  1988 Questions of Substance, Questions that Count. *Historical Archaeology*
    22(1):13–17.
Cleland, C. E., and J. E. Fitting
  1968 The Crisis of Identity: Theory in Historic Sites Archaeology. *Conference on
    Historic Site Archaeology Papers* 2(2):124–138.
Coe, M. D.
  1994 *Mexico from the Olmec to the Aztecs* (4th ed.). Thames and Hudson, London.
Cohen, G. A.
  1978 *Karl Marx's Theory of History: A Defence.* Princeton University Press,
    Princeton.
Coles, P.
  1968 *The Ottoman Impact on Europe.* Harcourt, Brace, and World, New York.
Collins, A. (editor)
  1992 *Fodor's 93: Ireland.* Fodor's Travel, New York.
Combes, J. D.
  1968 A Comment on Clyde Dollar's Paper. *Conference on Historic Site Archaeol-
    ogy Papers* 2(2):162–165.
Condren, M.
  1989 *The Serpent and the Goddess: Women, Religion, and Power in Celtic Ireland.*
    HarperCollins, New York.
Connolly, J.
  1922 *Labour in Ireland: Labour in Irish History, The Re-Conquest of Ireland.*
    Maunsel and Roberts, Dublin.
Conrad, R. E.
  1986 *World of Sorrow: The African Slave Trade to Brazil.* Louisiana State Univer-
    sity Press, Baton Rouge.
Conway, D.
  1987 *A Farewell to Marx: An Outline and Appraisal of His Theories.* Penguin,
    Middlesex, England.

Cooney, G.
   1993   A Sense of Place in Irish Prehistory. *Antiquity* 67:632–641.
Cooter, W. S.
   1977   Preindustrial Frontiers and Interaction Spheres: Prolegomenon to a Study
          of Roman Frontier Regions. In *The Frontier: Comparative Studies,* edited by
          D. H. Miller and J. O. Steffen, pp. 81–107. University of Oklahoma Press,
          Norman.
Cosgrove, A.
   1995   The Gaelic Resurgence and the Geraldine Supremacy (c. 1400–1534). In
          The Course of Irish History, edited by T. W. Moody and F. X. Martin, pp. 158–
          173. Roberts Rinehart, Niwot, Colorado.
Cotter, J. L.
   1967   Progress on a Chapbook and Bibliography for Historical Sites Archaeology.
          Conference on Historic Site Archaeology Papers 1:15–18.
   1977   Continuity in Teaching Historical Archaeology. In *Teaching and Training in
          American Archaeology: A Survey of Programs and Philosophies,* edited by
          W. P. McHugh, pp. 100–107. University Museum and Art Gallies, Southern
          Illinois University, Carbondale.
   1994   Beginnings. In *Pioneers in Historical Archaeology: Breaking New Ground,*
          edited by S. South, pp. 15–25. Plenum, New York.
Crawford, I. A.
   1968   The Divide between Medieval and Post-Medieval in Scotland. *Post-Medieval
          Archaeology* 1:84–89.
Creamer, H.
   1990   Aboriginal Perceptions of the Past: The Implications for Cultural Resource
          Management. In *The Politics of the Past,* edited by P. Gathercole and D.
          Lowenthal, pp. 130–140. Unwin Hyman, London.
Crossley, D.
   1990   *Post-Medieval Archaeology in Britain.* Leicester University Press, London.
Crumley, C. L.
   1979   Three Locational Models: An Epistemological Assessment for Anthropology
          and Archaeology. In *Advances in Archaeological Method and Theory,* volume
          2, edited by M. B. Schiffer, pp. 141–173. Academic Press, New York.
Crumley, C. L., and W. H. Marquardt
   1987   (editors) *Regional Dynamics: Burgundian Landscapes in Historical Perspec-
          tive.* Academic Press, San Diego.
   1990   Landscape: A Unifying Concept in Regional Analysis. In *Interpreting Space:
          GIS and Archaeology,* edited by K.M.S. Allen, S. W. Green, and E.B.W.
          Zubrow, pp. 73–79. Taylor and Francis, London.
Csikszentmihalyi, M., and E. Rochberg-Halton
   1981   *The Meaning of Things: Domestic Symbols and the Self.* Cambridge Univer-
          sity Press, Cambridge.
Curtin, P. D.
   1984   *Cross-Cultural Trade in World History.* Cambridge University Press, Cam-
          bridge.
   1990   *The Rise and Fall of the Plantation Complex: Essays in Atlantic History.*
          Cambridge University Press, Cambridge.
Daly, M. E.
   1986   *The Famine in Ireland.* The Dublin Historical Association, Dublin.

Dames, M.
1992 *Mythic Ireland*. Thames and Hudson, London.

Daniel, G.
1976 *A Hundred and Fifty Years of Archaeology*. Harvard University Press, Cambridge, Massachusetts.

Danks, P.
1977 Some Observations on Medieval and Post-Medieval Artefact Distributions: A Spatial Model at the Regional Scale (Macro). In *Spatial Archaeology,* edited by D. L. Clarke, pp. 353–381. Academic Press, London.

Dassin, J. (editor)
1986 *Torture in Brazil: A Report by the Archdioceses of São Paulo*. Translated by J. Wright. Vintage, New York.

Davidson, B.
1966 *African Kingdoms*. Time, New York.

Davidson, J. W., and M. H. Lytle
1982 *After the Fact: The Art of Historical Detection*. Alfred A. Knopf, New York.

Deagan, K.
1988 Neither History nor Prehistory: The Questions that Count in Historical Archaeology. *Historical Archaeology* 22(1):7–12.
1991 Historical Archaeology's Contributions to Our Understanding of Early America. In *Historical Archaeology in Global Perspective,* edited by L. Falk, pp. 97–112. Smithsonian Institution Press, Washington.

Deagan, K., and M. Scardaville
1985 Archaeology and History on Historic Hispanic Sites: Impediments and Solutions. *Historical Archaeology* 19(1):32–37.

Deetz, J.
1967 *Invitation to Archaeology*. The Natural History Press, Garden City, New York.
1977 *In Small Things Forgotten: The Archaeology of Early American Life*. Anchor Press/Doubleday, Garden City, New York.
1983 Scientific Humanism and Humanistic Science: A Plea for Paradigmatic Pluralism in Historical Archaeology. *Geoscience and Man* 23:27–34.
1988 History and Archaeological Theory: Walter Taylor Revisited. *American Antiquity* 53:13–22.
1990 Landscapes as Cultural Statements. In *Earth Patterns: Essays in Landscape Archaeology,* edited by W. M. Kelso and R. Most, pp. 1–4. University Press of Virginia, Charlottesville.
1991 Introduction: Archaeological Evidence and Sixteenth- and Seventeenth-Century Encounters. In *Historical Archaeology in Global Perspective,* edited by L. Falk, pp. 1–9. Smithsonian Institution Press, Washington.

Demmy, G. G.
1968 Comment on Clyde Dollar's Paper. *Conference on Historic Site Archaeology Papers* 2(2):103.

Desai, M.
1983 Capitalism. In *A Dictionary of Marxist Thought,* edited by T. Bottomore, pp. 64–67. Harvard University Press, Cambridge, Massachusetts.

Dietler, M.
1989 Greeks, Etruscans, and Thirsty Barbarians: Early Iron Age Interaction in the Rhône Basin of France. In *Centre and Periphery: Comparative Studies*

in Archaeology, edited by T. C. Champion, pp. 127–141. Unwin Hyman, London.

Dirks, N. B.
  1992   Introduction: Colonialism and Culture. In *Colonialism and Culture,* edited by N. B. Dirks, pp. 1–25. University of Michigan Press, Ann Arbor.

Dixon, R. (editor)
  1972   *Ireland and the Irish Question: A Collection of Writings by Karl Marx and Frederick Engels.* International, New York.

Dollar, C. D.
  1968   Reply to Demmy. *Conference on Historic Site Archaeology Papers* 2(2):104.

Donnelly, J. S., Jr.
  1975   *The Land and the People of Nineteenth-Century Cork: The Rural Economy and the Land Question.* Routledge and Kegan Paul, London.
  1993   The Great Famine: Its Interpreters, Old and New. *History Ireland* 1(3): 27–33.

Douglas, M., and B. Isherwood
  1979   *The World of Goods.* Basic, New York.

Dowd, G. E.
  1992   *A Spirited Resistance: The North American Indian Struggle for Unity, 1745– 1815.* Johns Hopkins University Press, Baltimore.

Dowdle, J. E.
  1987   Road Networks and Exchange Systems in the Aeduan *Civitas,* 300 B.C.–A.D. 300. In *Regional Dynamics: Burgundian Landscapes in Historical Perspective,* edited by C. L. Crumley and W. H. Marquardt, pp. 265–294. Academic Press, San Diego.

Drummond, C.
  1859   Relação das Guerras Feitas aos Palmares de Pernambuco no Tempo de Governador D. Pedro de Almeida de 1675 a 1678. *Revista do Instituto Histório e Geográfico Brasileiro* 22:303–329.

Duffy, J.
  1962   *Portugal in Africa.* Harvard University Press, Cambridge.

Duffy, S.
  1993   Pre-Norman Dublin: Capital of Ireland? *History Ireland* 1(4):13–18.

Dufour, R. P.
  1987   *Modernization in Colonial Massachusetts, 1630–1763.* Garland, New York.

Durkheim, E.
  1915   *The Elementary Forms of the Religious Life: A Study in Religious Sociology.* Translated by J. W. Swain. G. Allen and Unwin, London.

Dussel, E.
  1993   Eurocentrism and Modernity. *Boundary 2* 20:65–76.

Dymond, D. P.
  1974   *Archaeology and History: A Plea for Reconciliation.* Thames and Hudson, London.

Earle, T. K., and R. W. Preucel
  1987   Processual Archaeology and the Radical Critique. *Current Anthropology* 28:501–538.

Edens, C.
  1992   Dynamics of Trade in the Ancient Mesopotamian "World System." *American Anthropologist* 94:118–139.

Edgeworth, M.
1992   *Castle Rackrent and Ennui,* edited by M. Butler. Penguin, London.
Editorial
1968   *Post-Medieval Archaeology* 1:1–2.
Edwards, R. D.
1973   *An Atlas of Irish History.* Methuen, London.
Edwards, R. D., and T. D. Williams
1957   *The Great Famine: Studies in Irish History, 1845–52.* New York University Press, New York.
Ellis, P. B.
1988   *Hell or Connaught! The Cromwellian Colonisation of Ireland, 1652–1660.* Blackstaff Press, Belfast.
Elster, J.
1985   *Making Sense of Marx.* Cambridge University Press, Cambridge, and Editions de la Maison des Sciences de l'Homme, Paris.
Emerson, M. C.
1988   *Decorated Clay Tobacco Pipes from the Chesapeake.* Doctoral dissertation, Department of Anthropology, University of California, Berkeley.
1994   Decorated Clay Tobacco Pipes from the Chesapeake: An African Connection. In *Historical Archaeology of the Chesapeake,* edited by P. A. Shackel and B. J. Little, pp. 35–49. Smithsonian Institution Press, Washington.
Emerson, R. M.
1976   Social Exchange Theory. *Annual Review of Sociology* 2:335–362.
Ennes, E.
1938   *As Guerras nos Palmares (Subsídios para a sua História).* Companhia Editora Nacional, São Paulo.
1948   The Palmares "Republic" of Pernambuco: Its Final Destruction, 1697. *The Americas* 5:200–216.
Erickson, P.
1992   What Multiculturalism Means. *Transition* 55:105–114.
Evans, E. E.
1957   *Irish Folk Ways.* Routledge, London.
1992   *The Personality of Ireland: Habitat, Heritage, and History.* Lilliput Press, Dublin.
Fairbanks, C. H.
1974   The Kingsley Slave Cabins in Duval County, Florida, 1968. *Conference on Historic Site Archaeology Papers* 7:62–93.
1983   Historical Archaeological Implications of Recent Investigations. *Geoscience and Man* 23:17–26.
1984   The Plantation Archaeology of the Southeastern Coast. *Historical Archaeology* 18(1):1–14.
Fairbanks, C. H., and S. A. Mullins-Moore
1980   How Did Slaves Live? *Early Man,* summer, pp. 2–6.
Fanon, F.
1968   *The Wretched of the Earth.* Translated by C. Farrington. Grove Press, New York.
Feenberg, A.
1980   The Political Economy of Social Space. In *The Myths of Information: Tech-*

nology and Postindustrial Culture, edited by K. Woodward, pp. 111–124. Coda Press, Madison, Wisconsin.

Ferguson, L.
1978 Looking for the 'Afro-' in Colono-Indian Pottery. *Conference on Historic Site Archaeology Papers* 12:68–86.
1991 Struggling with Pots in Colonial South Carolina. In *The Archaeology of Inequality,* edited by R. H. McGuire and R. Paynter, pp. 28–39. Basil Blackwell, Oxford.
1992 *Uncommon Ground: Archaeology and Early African America, 1650–1800.* Smithsonian Institution Press, Washington.

Fish, S. K., and S. A. Kowalewski (editors)
1990 *The Archaeology of Regions: A Case for Full-Coverage Survey.* Smithsonian Institution Press, Washington.

Flanagan, L.
1992 *A Dictionary of Irish Archaeology.* Gill and Macmillan, Dublin.

Fontana, B. L.
1965 On the Meaning of Historic Sites Archaeology. *American Antiquity* 31: 61–65.
1968 A Reply to "Some Thoughts on Theory and Method in Historical Archaeology." *Conference on Historic Site Archaeology Papers* 2(2):75–78.
1978 Artifacts of the Indians of the Southwest. In *Material Culture and the Study of American Life,* edited by I.M.G. Quimby, pp. 75–108. W. W. Norton, New York.

Ford, J. A.
1954 The Type Concept Revisited. *American Anthropologist* 56:42–53.

Foster, R. F.
1989 *Modern Ireland, 1600–1972.* Penguin, London.

Foucault, M.
1980 *Power / Knowledge: Selected Interviews and Other Writings, 1972–1977.* Edited by C. Gordon. Pantheon, New York.

Frame, R.
1981 *Colonial Ireland, 1169–1369.* Helicon, Dublin.

Frank, A. G.
1978 *World Accumulation, 1492–1789.* Monthly Review Press, New York.

Fraser, A. C. (editor)
1871 *The Works of George Berkeley, D.D.* Clarendon, Oxford.

Freitas, D.
1984 *Palmares: O Guerra dos Escravos* (5th ed.). Movimento, Porto Alegre.

French, M.
1994 Power/Sex. In *Power / Gender: Social Relations in Theory and Practice,* edited by H. L. Radtke and H. J. Stam, pp. 15–35. Sage, London.

Fry, M. (editor)
1992 *Adam Smith's Legacy: His Place in the Development of Modern Economics.* Routledge, London.

Funari, P.A.A.
1989 Brazilian Archaeology and World Archaeology: Some Remarks. *World Archaeological Bulletin* 3:60–68.
1991a A arqueologia e a cultura africana nas Américas. *Estudos Ibero-Americanos* 17(2):61–71.

1991b Archaeology in Brazil: Politics and Scholarship at a Crossroads. *World Archaeological Bulletin* 5:122–132.
1994 South American Historical Archaeology. *Historical Archaeology in Latin America* 2:1–14.
1995 The Archaeology of Palmares and Its Contribution to the Understanding of the History of African-American Culture. *Historical Archaeology in Latin America* 7:1–41.
Gailey, C. W.
1983 Categories without Culture: Structuralism, Ethnohistory, Ethnocide. *Dialectical Anthropology* 8:241–250.
García Arévalo, M. A.
1986 El Maniel de José Leta: Evdencias arqueológicas de un posible asentamiento cimarrón en la región sudoriental de la Isla de Santo Domingo. *Cimmaron*, pp. 33–76.
Garlake, P.
1978 *The Kingdoms of Africa*. Elsevier, Oxford.
Gathercole, P., and D. Lowenthal
1990 The Heritage of Eurocentrism: Introduction. In *The Politics of the Past*, edited by P. Gathercole and D. Lowenthal, pp. 7–9. Unwin Hyman, London.
Genovese, E. D., and L. Hochberg (editors)
1989 *Geographic Perspectives in History*. Oxford University Press, Oxford.
Gerbi, A.
1973 *The Dispute of the New World: The History of a Polemic, 1750–1900*. Translated by J. Moyle. University of Pittsburgh Press, Pittsburgh.
Ghani, A.
1987 A Conversation with Eric Wolf. *American Ethnologist* 14:346–366.
Gibbon, G.
1984 *Anthropological Archaeology*. Columbia University Press, New York.
1989 *Explanation in Archaeology*. Basil Blackwell, Oxford.
Gibbons, L.
1991 Race against Time: Racial Discourse and Irish History. *Oxford Literary Review* 13:95–113.
Giddens, A.
1984 *The Constitution of Society: Outline of the Theory of Structuration*. University of California Press, Berkeley.
Gilroy, P.
1993 *The Black Atlantic: Modernity and Double Consciousness*. Harvard University Press, Cambridge.
Giorgadze, G. G.
1991 The Hittite Kingdom. In *Early Antiquity*, edited by I. M. Diakonoff, pp. 266–285. University of Chicago Press, Chicago.
Glassie, H.
1975 *Folk Housing in Middle Virginia: A Structural Analysis of Historic Artifacts*. University of Tennessee Press, Knoxville.
1982 *Passing the Time in Ballymenone: Culture and History of an Ulster Community*. University of Pennsylvania Press, Philadelphia.
Gless, D. L., and B. H. Smith (editors)
1992 *The Politics of Liberal Education*. Duke University Press, Durham, North Carolina.

Godelier, M.
  1975   Modes of Production, Kinship, and Demographic Structures. In *Marxist Analyses and Social Anthropology,* edited by M. Bloch, pp. 3–27. John Wiley, New York.
  1986   *The Mental and the Material: Thought, Economy, and Society.* Translated by M. Thom. Verso, London.
Goldfrank, W. L. (editor)
  1979   *The World-System of Capitalism: Past and Present.* Sage, Beverly Hills, California.
Gough, K.
  1968   Anthropology: Child of Imperialism. *Monthly Review* 19(11):12–27.
Gramsci, A.
  1971   *Selections from the Prison Notebooks.* Edited by Q. Hoare and G. N. Smith. International, New York.
Greenblatt, S.
  1991   *Marvelous Possessions: The Wonder of the New World.* University of Chicago Press, Chicago.
Griffith, R.
  1857   *Valuation of the Several Tenements Comprised in the Union of Strokestown, in the Country of Roscommon.* Thom and Sons, Dublin.
Guimarães, C. M.
  1990   O quilombo do Ambrósio: lenda, documentos e arqueologia. *Estudos Ibero-Americanos* 16:161–174.
Guimarães, C. M., and A.L.D. Lanna
  1980   Arqueologia de quilombos em Minas Gerais. *Pesquisas* 31:146–163.
Gutman, H. G.
  1976   *Work, Culture, and Society in Industrializing America: Essays in American Working Class and Social History.* Alfred A. Knopf, New York.
Haddix, C.
  1975   *Who Speaks for Appalachia?* Washington Square Press, New York.
Haggett, P.
  1965   *Locational Analysis in Human Geography.* Edward Arnold, London.
  1990   *The Geographer's Art.* Basil Blackwell, Oxford.
Haggett, P., and R. J. Chorley
  1969   *Network Analysis in Geography.* St. Martin's Press, New York.
Hahn, S., and J. Prude (editors)
  1985   *The Countryside in the Age of Capitalist Transformation: Essays in the Social History of Rural America.* University of North Carolina Press, Chapel Hill.
Hall, E. T.
  1963a   A System for the Notation of Proxemic Behavior. *American Anthropologist* 65:1003–1026.
  1963b   Proxemics: The Study of Man's Spatial Relations. In *Man's Image in Medicine and Anthropology,* edited by I. Galdston, pp. 422–445. International Universities Press, New York.
  1969   *The Hidden Dimension.* Doubleday, Garden City, New York.
Hall, F. H., W. F. Harrison, and D. W. Welker (editors and translators)
  1987   *Dialogues of the Great Things of Brazil, Attributed to Ambrósio Fernandes Brandão.* University of New Mexico Press, Albuquerque.

Hall, M.
  1992   Small Things and the Mobile, Conflictual Fusion of Power, Fear, and Desire. In *The Art and Mystery of Historical Archaeology: Essays in Honor of James Deetz,* edited by A. E. Yentsch and M. C. Beaudry, pp. 373–399. CRC Press, Boca Raton, Florida.
Handler, J. S.
  1983   An African Pipe from a Slave Cemetery in Barbados, West Indies. In *The Archaeology of the Clay Tobacco Pipe, VIII. America,* edited by P. Davey, pp. 245–254. B. A. R., Oxford, England.
Handler, J. S., and F. W. Lange
  1978   *Plantation Slavery in Barbados: An Archaeological and Historical Investigation.* Harvard University Press, Cambridge.
Handler, J. S., F. W. Lange, and C. E. Orser
  1979   Carnelian Beads in Necklaces from a Slave Cemetery in Barbados, West Indies. *Ornament* 4(2):15–18.
Handsman, R. G.
  1985   *Thinking about an Historical Archaeology of Alienation and Class Struggles.* Unpublished paper presented at the Annual Meeting of the Society for Historical Archaeology, Boston.
Hardy, T.
  1959   *The Return of the Native.* New American Library, New York.
Harrington, J. C.
  1952   Historic Site Archaeology in the United States. In *Archaeology of Eastern United States,* edited by J. B. Griffin, pp. 335–344. University of Chicago Press, Chicago.
  1955   Archaeology as an Auxillary Science of American History. *American Anthropologist* 7:1121–1130.
Haselgrove, C.
  1987   Culture Process on the Periphery: Belgic Gaul and Rome during the Late Republic and Early Empire. In *Centre and Periphery in the Ancient World,* edited by M. Rowlands, M. Larsen, and K. Kristiansen, pp. 104–124. Cambridge University Press, Cambridge.
Hemming, J.
  1978   *Red Gold: The Conquest of the Brazilian Indians, 1500–1760.* Harvard University Press, Cambridge.
Henderson, L. W.
  1979   *Angola: Five Centuries of Conflict.* Cornell University Press, Ithaca, New York.
Henry, S. L.
  1979   Terra-Cotta Tobacco Pipes in 17th Century Maryland and Virginia: A Preliminary Study. *Historical Archaeology* 13:14–37.
Herity, M., and G. Eogan
  1977   *Ireland in Prehistory.* Routledge and Kegan Paul, London.
Hersey, I.
  1974   The Traditional Art of Guinea-Bissau, Mozambique, and Angola. In *Cultural Resistance: Art from Guinea-Bissau, Mozambique, and Angola,* pp. 1–3. African-American Institute, New York.
Heslinga, M. W.
  1971   *The Irish Border as a Cultural Divide: A Contribution to the Study of Regionalism in the British Isles.* Royal Van Gorcum, Assen, Netherlands.

Heywood, C. J.
　　1972　Sir Robert Rycant, A Seventeenth-Century Observer of the Ottoman
　　　　　Empire: Notes for a Study. In *English and Continental Views of the Ottoman
　　　　　Empire, 1500–1800,* edited by E. K. Shaw and C. J. Heywood. William
　　　　　Andrews Clark Memorial Library, University of California, Los An-
　　　　　geles.
Hill, J.
　　1989　The Meaning and Significance of 'Protestant Ascendancy,' 1787–1840. In
　　　　　Ireland After the Union, introduced by Lord Blake, pp. 1–22. Oxford Univer-
　　　　　sity Press, Oxford.
Hill, J., and C. Ó Gráda (editors)
　　1993　*'The Visitation of God'? The Potato and the Great Irish Famine.* Lilliput
　　　　　Press, Dublin.
Hill, M. H.
　　1987　Ethnicity Lost? Ethnicity Gained? Information Functions of 'African
　　　　　Ceramics' in West Africa and North America. In *Ethnicity and Culture,*
　　　　　edited by R. Auger, M. F. Glass, S. MacEachern, and P. H. McCartney,
　　　　　pp. 135–139. Archaeological Association, University of Calgary, Calgary.
Hillier, B., and J. Hanson
　　1984　*The Social Logic of Space.* Cambridge University Press, Cambridge.
Hilton, R.
　　1976a　Capitalism: What's in a Name? In *The Transition from Feudalism to Cap-
　　　　　italism,* edited by R. Hilton, pp. 145–158. NLB, London.
　　1976b　Introduction. In *The Transition from Feudalism to Capitalism,* edited by R.
　　　　　Hilton, pp. 9–30. NLB, London.
　　1976c　(editor) *The Transition from Feudalism to Capitalism.* NLB, London.
Hindess, B., and P. Q. Hirst
　　1975　*Pre-Capitalist Modes of Production.* Routledge and Kegan Paul, London.
Hindley, R.
　　1990　*The Death of the Irish Language: A Qualified Obituary.* Routledge, London.
Hirsch, E. D., Jr.
　　1987　*Cultural Literacy: What Every American Needs to Know.* Houghton Mifflin,
　　　　　Boston.
Hodder, I.
　　1977　Some New Directions in the Spatial Analysis of Archaeological Data at the
　　　　　Regional Scale (Macro). In *Spatial Archaeology,* edited by D. L. Clarke,
　　　　　pp. 223–351. Academic Press, London.
　　1986　*Reading the Past: Current Approaches to Interpretation in Archaeology.*
　　　　　Cambridge University Press, Cambridge.
　　1991　Interpretive Archaeology and Its Role. *American Antiquity* 56:7–18.
Hodder, I., and C. Orton
　　1976　*Spatial Analysis in Archaeology.* Cambridge University Press, Cambridge.
Hodgen, M. T.
　　1974　*Anthropology, History, and Cultural Change.* University of Arizona Press, Tucson.
Hogarth, D. G.
　　1899　*Authority and Archaeology: Sacred and Profane.* John Murray, London.
Honderich, T.
　　1982　Against Teleological Historical Materialism. *Inquiry* 25:451–469.

Honerkamp, N.
  1988 Questions that Count in Historical Archaeology. *Historical Archaeology* 22(1):5–6.
Hopkins, T. K.
  1979 The Study of the Capitalist World-Economy: Some Introductory Considerations. In *The World-System of Capitalism: Past and Present,* edited by W. L. Goldfrank, pp. 21–52. Sage, Beverly Hills, California.
  1982 World-Systems Analysis: Methodological Issues. In *World-Systems Analysis: Theory and Methodology,* edited by T. K. Hopkins and I. Wallerstein, pp. 145–158. Sage, Beverly Hills, California.
Hopkins, T. K., I. Wallerstein, N. Bousquet, N. Dyson-Hudson, P. McMichael, and D. Tomich
  1982 Patterns of Development of the Modern World-System. In *World-Systems Analysis: Theory and Methodology,* edited by T. K. Hopkins and I. Wallerstein, pp. 41–82. Sage, Beverly Hills, California.
Howard, J. H.
  1974 Rejoinder to Thurman. *Conference on Historic Site Archaeology Papers* 7(3):224–225.
Huey, P. R.
  1991 The Dutch at Fort Orange. In *Historical Archaeology in Global Perspective,* edited by L. Falk, pp. 21–67. Smithsonian Institution Press, Washington.
Hughes, S. S.
  1992 Beyond Eurocentrism: Developing World Women's Studies. *Feminist Studies* 18:389–404.
Hutchings, M.
  1968 Hardy's Countryside. In *The Thomas Hardy Festival,* edited by C. E. Brooks, pp. 63, 65, 67. Thomas Hardy Festival Society, Dorchester.
Institutions
  1967 *Current Anthropology* 8:509.
Jelks, E. B.
  1968 Critique of Dollar's "Some Thoughts on Theory and Method in Historical Archaeology." *Conference on Historic Site Archaeology Papers* 2(2): 80–93.
  1993 The Founding Meeting of the Society for Historical Archaeology, 6 January 1967. *Historical Archaeology* 27(1):10–11.
Jennett, S.
  1970 *Connacht: The Counties of Galway, Mayo, Sligo, Leitrim and Roscommon in Ireland.* Faber and Faber, London.
Jhally, S.
  1987 *The Codes of Advertising: Fetishism and the Political Economy of Meaning in the Consumer Society.* Francis Pinter, London.
Johnson, M.
  1992 Meanings of Polite Architecture in Sixteenth-Century England. In Meanings and Uses of Material Culture, edited by B. J. Little and P. A. Shackel. *Historical Archaeology* 26(3):45–56.
  1993 *Housing Culture: Traditional Architecture in an English Landscape.* Smithsonian Institution Press, Washington.

Johnson, S.
1760 *A Dictionary of the English Language* (2nd ed.). Knapton, Hitch, Hawes, Millar, Strahan, Dodsley, and Longman, London.

Jones Hughes, T.
1965 Society and Settlement in Nineteenth-Century Ireland. *Irish Geography* 5:79–96.

Kajzer, L.
1991 Recent Excavation and Survey at Zduny, Wrzaca and Kliczków Maly: Earthworks of the Modern Period. *Antiquity* 65:716–721.

Katz, C. J.
1989 *From Feudalism to Capitalism: Marxian Theories of Class Struggle and Social Change.* Greenwood Press, New York.

Kelly, P.
1939 *Irish Family Names.* O'Connor and Kelly, Chicago.

Kelso, W. M.
1990 Landscape Archaeology at Thomas Jefferson's Monticello. In *Earth Patterns: Essays in Landscape Archaeology,* edited by W. M. Kelso and R. Most, pp. 7–22. University Press of Virginia, Charlottesville.

Kemeny, J. G.
1959 *A Philosopher Looks at Science.* D. Van Nostrand, Princeton.

Kent, R. K.
1965 Palmares: An African State in Brazil. *Journal of African History* 6:161–175.

Kent, S. (editor)
1990 *Domestic Architecture and the Use of Space: An Interdisciplinary Cross-Cultural Study.* Cambridge University Press, Cambridge.

Keough, W.
1995 Mind You, I'll Say Everything: The Perils of Truth-Telling. *Irish Literary Supplement* 14(1):23–24.

Kimball, R.
1990 *Tenured Radicals: How Politics Has Corrupted Our Higher Education.* Harper and Row, New York.

Kinealy, C.
1995 *This Great Calamity: The Irish Famine, 1845–52.* Roberts Rinehart, Boulder, Colorado.

King, A. D.
1989 *Urbanism, Colonialism, and the World-Economy: Cultural and Spatial Foundations of the World Urban System.* Routledge, London.

Klingelhofer, E.
1992 The Renaissance Fortifications at Dunboy Castle, 1602: A Report on the 1989 Excavations. *Journal of the Cork Historical and Archaeological Society* 97:85–96.

Kloppenberg, J. T.
1989 Objectivity and Historicism: A Century of American Historical Writing. *American Historical Review* 94:1011–1030.

Knoke, D., and J. H. Kuklinski
1982 *Network Analysis.* Sage, Newberry Park, California.

Kohl, P. L.
1987a The Ancient Economy, Transferable Technologies, and the Bronze Age World-System: A View from the Northeastern Frontier of the Ancient Near

East. In *Centre and Periphery in the Ancient World,* edited by M. Rowlands, M. Larsen, and K. Kristiansen, pp. 13–24. Cambridge University Press, Cambridge.

1987b The Use and Abuse of World Systems Theory: The Case of the Pristine West Asian State. In *Advances in Archaeological Method and Theory,* edited by M. B. Schiffer, vol. 11, pp. 1–35. Academic Press, San Diego.

Kolakowski, L.
1990 *Modernity on Endless Trial.* University of Chicago Press, Chicago.

Kopytoff, I.
1986 The Cultural Biography of Things: Commodization as Process. In *The Social Life of Things: Commodities in Cultural Perspective,* edited by A. Appadurai, pp. 64–91. Cambridge University Press, Cambridge.

Kryder-Reid, E.
1994 "As Is the Gardener, So Is the Garden": The Archaeology of Landscape as Myth. In *Historical Archaeology of the Chesapeake,* edited by P. A. Shackel and B. J. Little, pp. 131–148. Smithsonian Institution Press, Washington.

Kulikoff, A.
1992 *The Agrarian Origins of American Capitalism.* University Press of Virginia, Charlottesville.

Lacy, B.
1979 The Archaeology of British Colonization in Ulster and America: A Comparative Approach. *The Irish-American Review* 1:1–5.

Lamberg-Karlovsky, C. C.
1972 Trade Mechanisms in Indus-Mesopotamian Interrelations. *Journal of the American Oriental Society* 92:222–229.

1975 Third Mellennium Modes of Exchange and Modes of Production. In *Ancient Civilization and Trade,* edited by J. A. Sabloff and C. C. Lamberg-Karlovsky, pp. 341–368. University of New Mexico Press, Albuquerque.

Larkin, E. (translator)
1990 *Alexis de Tocqueville's Journey in Ireland: July–August, 1835.* Catholic University of America Press, Washington.

Larrain, J.
1986 *A Reconstruction of Historical Materialism.* Allen and Unwin, London.

Larsen, M. T.
1987 Commercial Networks in the Ancient Near East. In *Centre and Periphery in the Ancient World,* edited by M. Rowlands, M. Larsen, and K. Kristiansen, pp. 47–56. Cambridge University Press, Cambridge.

Las Casas, B. de
1992 *A Short Account of the Destruction of the Indies.* Edited and translated by N. Griffin. Penguin, London.

Layton, R. (editor)
1989 *Conflict in the Archaeology of Living Traditions.* Unwin Hyman, London.

Lebow, R. N.
1976 *White Britain and Black Ireland: The Influence of Stereotypes on Colonial Policy.* Institute for the Study of Human Issues, Philadelphia.

Leed, E. J.
1991 *The Mind of the Traveler: From Gilgamesh to Global Tourism.* Basic, New York.

Lefebvre, H.
   1979   Space: Social Product and Use Value. In *Critical Sociology: European Per-spectives,* edited by J. W. Freiberg, pp. 285–295. Irvington, New York.
Leone, M. P.
   1978   Time in American Archaeology. In *Social Archaeology: Beyond Subsistence and Dating,* edited by C. L. Redman, M. J. Berman, E. V. Curtin, W. T. Langhorne, N. M. Versaggi, and J. C. Wanser, pp. 25–36. Academic Press, New York.
   1981   Archaeology's Relationship to the Present and the Past. In *Modern Material Culture: The Archaeology of Us,* edited by R. A. Gould and M. B. Schiffer, pp. 5–14. Academic Press, New York.
   1984   Interpreting Ideology in Historical Archaeology: Using the Rules of Perspective in the William Paca Garden, Annapolis, Maryland. In *Ideology, Power, and Prehistory,* edited by D. Miller and C. Tilley, pp. 25–35. Cambridge University Press, Cambridge.
   1987   Rule by Ostentation: The Relationship between Space and Sight in Eighteenth-Century Landscape Architecture in the Chesapeake Region of Maryland. In *Method and Theory for Activity Area Research: An Ethno-archaeological Approach,* edited by S. Kent, pp. 604–633. Columbia University Press, New York.
   1988   The Georgian Order as the Order of Merchant Capitalism in Annapolis, Maryland. In *The Recovery of Meaning: Historical Archaeology in the Eastern United States,* edited by M. P. Leone and P. B. Potter, Jr., pp. 235–261. Smithsonian Institution Press, Washington.
   1994   The Archaeology of Ideology: Archaeological Work in Annapolis Since 1981. In *Historical Archaeology of he Chesapeake,* edited by P. A. Shackel and B. J. Little, pp. 219–229. Smithsonian Institution Press, Washington.
   1995   A Historical Archaeology of Capitalism. *American Anthropologist* 97:251–268.
Leone, M. P., and P. B. Potter, Jr.
   1988   Introduction: Issues in Historical Archaeology. In *The Recovery of Meaning: Historical Archaeology in the Eastern United States,* pp. 1–22. Smithsonian Institution Press, Washington.
Leone, M. P., and R. W. Preucel
   1992   Archaeology in a Democratic Society: A Critical Theory Perspective. In *Quandaries and Quests: Visions of Archaeology's Future,* edited by L. Wandsnider, pp. 115–135. Center for Archaeological Investigations, Southern Illinois University, Carbondale.
Leone, M. P., P. R. Mullins, M. C. Creveling, L. Hurst, B. Jackson-Nash, L. D. Jones, H. J. Kaiser, G. C. Logan, and M. S. Warner
   1995   Can An African-American Historical Archaeology be an Alternative Voice? In *Interpreting Archaeology: Finding Meaning in the Past,* edited by I. Hodder, M. Shanks, A. Alexandri, V. Buchli, J. Carman, J. Last, and G. Lucas, pp. 110–124. Routledge, London.
Lesser, A.
   1961   Social Fields and the Evolution of Society. *Southwestern Journal of Anthropology* 17:40–48.
Lewis, B.
   1982   *The Muslim Discovery of Europe.* W. W. Norton, New York.

Lewis, S.
  1970 *A Topographical Dictionary of Ireland, Comprising the Several Counties, Cities, Boroughs, Corporate, Market, and Post Towns, Parishes, and Villages.* Kennikat, Port Washington, New York.
Lipman-Blumen, J.
  1994 The Existential Bases of Power Relationships: The Gender Role Case. In *Power / Gender: Social Relations in Theory and Practice,* edited by H. L. Radtke and H. J. Stam, pp. 108–135. Sage, London.
Little, B. J.
  1994 People with History: An Update on Historical Archaeology in the United States. *Journal of Archaeological Method and Theory* 1:5–40.
Little, B. J., and P. A. Shackel
  1989 Scales of Historical Anthropology: An Archaeology of Colonial Anglo-America. *Antiquity* 63:495–509.
Litton, H.
  1994 *The Irish Famine: An Illustrated History.* Wolfhound Press, Dublin.
Litvinoff, B.
  1991 *1492: The Decline of Medievalism and the Rise of the Modern Age.* Avon, New York.
Livermore, H. V.
  1973 *Portugal: A Short History.* Edinburgh University Press, Edinburgh.
Lowenthal, D.
  1985 *The Past Is a Foreign Country.* Cambridge University Press, Cambridge.
Lowie, R. H.
  1946 The "Tapuya." In *Handbook of South American Indians, Volume 1: The Marginal Tribes,* edited by J. H. Steward, pp. 553–556. U.S. Government Printing Office, Washington.
Lukacs, J.
  1970 *The Passing of the Modern Age.* Harper and Row, New York.
Lukes, S.
  1974 *Power: A Radical View.* Macmillan, London.
Mac Aodha, B. S.
  1965 Clachán Settlement in Iar-Chonnacht. *Irish Geography* 5:20–28.
MacDonagh, O.
  1994 Irish Emigration to the United States of America and the British Colonies during the Famine. In *The Great Famine: Studies in Irish History,1845–52,* edited by R. D. Edwards and T. D. Williams, pp. 317–388. Lilliput Press, Dublin.
MacKendrick, P. L.
  1960 *The Mute Stones Speak: The Story of Archaeology in Italy.* St. Martin's Press, New York.
Mackenzie, I. M., and M. Shanks
  1994 Archaeology: Theories, Themes, and Experience. A Dialogue between Iain Mackenzie and Michael Shanks. In *Archaeological Theory: Progress or Posture?,* edited by I. M. MacKenzie, pp. 19–40. Avebury, Aldershot, England.
MacLysaght, E.
  1969 *The Surnames of Ireland.* Barnes and Noble, New York.
  1972 *Irish Families: Their Names, Arms, and Origins.* Crown, New York.

Mahoney, R.
    1994   *Whoredom in Kimmage: Irish Women Coming of Age.* Anchor, New York.
Malins, E., and The Knight of Glin
    1976   *Lost Demesnes: Irish Landscape Gardening, 1660–1845.* Barrie and Jenkins, London.
Mandl, C.
    1979   *Applied Network Organization.* Academic Press, London.
Marcus, G. J.
    1980   *The Conquest of the North Atlantic.* Boydell, Suffolk.
Marins, P.C.G.
    1995   Queluz e o café: quotidiano e cultura material no séc. XIX através de inventários. *Historical Archaeology in Latin America* 6:45–65.
Marquardt, W. H.
    1985   Complexity and Scale in the Study of Fisher-Gatherer-Hunters: An Example from the Eastern United States. In *Prehistoric Hunter-Gatherers: The Emergence of Cultural Complexity,* edited by T. D. Price and J. A. Brown, pp. 59–98. Academic Press, Orlando.
    1989   Agency, Structure, and Power: Operationalizing a Dialectical Anthropological Archaeology. Presented at "Critical Approaches in Archaeology: Material Life, Meaning, and Power," Wenner-Gren Foundation for Anthropological Research, Symposium 108. Cascais, Portugal.
    1992   Dialectical Archaeology. In *Archaeological Method and Theory,* edited by M. B. Schiffer, vol. 4, pp. 101–140. University of Arizona Press, Tucson.
Marquardt, W. H., and C. L. Crumley
    1987   Theoretical Issues in the Analysis of Spatial Patterning. In *Regional Dynamics: Burgundian Landscapes in Historical Perspectives,* edited by C. L. Crumley and W. H. Marquardt, pp. 1–18. Academic Press, San Diego.
Marques, A. H. de Oliveira
    1971   *Daily Life in Portugal in the Late Middle Ages.* Translated by S. S. Wyatt. University of Wisconsin Press, Madison.
Martin, A. S.
    1989   The Role of Pewter as Missing Artifact: Consumer Attitudes toward Tablewares in Late 18th-Century Virginia. *Historical Archaeology* 23(2):1–27.
Martin, W. G. (editor)
    1990   *Semiperipheral State in the World-Economy.* Greenwood, New York.
Martins, M.
    1992   A arqueologia pós-medieval. *História* 14:84–89.
Marx, K.
    1954   *Communist Manifesto.* Henry Regnery, Chicago.
    1967   *Capital: A Critique of Political Economy,* Volume 1. International, New York.
    1970   *A Contribution to the Critique of Political Economy.* Edited by M. Dobb. International, New York.
Marx, K., and F. Engels
    1970   *The German Ideology, Part One.* Edited by C. J. Arthur. International, New York.
Mathien, F. J.
    1986   External Contact and the Chaco Anasazi. In *Ripples in the Chichimec Sea: New Considerations of Southwestern-Mesoamerican Interactions,* edited by F. J. Mathien and R. H. McGuire, pp. 220–242. Southern Illinois University Press, Carbondale.

Mathien, F. J., and R. H. McGuire (editors)
  1986 *Ripples in the Chichimec Sea: New Considerations of Southwestern-Mesoamerican Interactions.* Southern Illinois University Press, Carbondale.
Maxwell, M. S., and L. R. Binford
  1961 *Excavation at Fort Michilimackinac, Mackinac City, Michigan, 1959 Season.* The Museum, Michigan State University, East Lansing.
McCann, W. J.
  1990 'Volk und Germanentum': The Presentation of the Past in Nazi Germany. In *The Politics of the Past,* edited by P. Gathercole and D. Lowenthal, pp. 74–88. Unwin Hyman, London.
McCormack, W. J.
  1987 Vision and Revision in the Study of Eighteenth-Century Irish Parlimentary Rhetoric. *Eighteenth-Century Ireland* 2:7–35.
McCracken, G.
  1988 *Culture and Consumption: New Approaches to the Symbolic Character of Consumer Goods and Activities.* Indiana University Press, Bloomington.
McErlean, T.
  1983 The Irish Townland System of Landscape Organisation. In *Landscape Archaeology in Ireland,* edited by T. Reeves-Smyth and F. Hamond, pp. 315–339. B. A. R. British Series 116. B. A. R., Oxford, England.
McGee, T. G.
  1991 Eurocentrism in Geography: The Case of Asian Urbanization. *The Canadian Geographer* 35:332–344.
McGuire, R. H.
  1980 The Mesoamerican Connection in the Southwest. *Kiva* 46:3–38.
  1988 Dialogues with the Dead: Ideology and the Cemetery. In *The Recovery of Meaning: Historical Archaeology in the Eastern United States,* edited by M. P. Leone and P. B. Potter, Jr., pp. 435–480. Smithsonian Institution Press, Washington.
  1992 *A Marxist Archaeology.* Academic Press, San Diego.
McKay, J.
  1976 The Coalescence of History and Archaeology. *Historical Archaeology* 10:93–98.
McKendrick, N.
  1982 Commercialization and the Economy. In *The Birth of a Consumer Society: The Commoditization of Eighteenth-Century England,* edited by N. McKendrick, J. Brewer, and J. H. Plumb, pp. 7–194. Indiana University Press, Bloomington.
McMurty, J.
  1978 *The Structure of Marx's World-View.* Princeton University Press, Princeton.
Mead, M.
  1951 Anthropologist and Historian: Their Common Problems. *American Quarterly* 3:3–13.
Megenney, W. W.
  1978 *A Bahian Heritage: An Ethnolinguistic Study of African Influences on Bahian Portuguese.* Department of Romance Languages, University of North Carolina, Chapel Hill.
Menezes, J.L.M., and M. do R. R. Rodrigues
  1986 *Fortificações Portuguesas no Nordeste do Brasil: Séculos XVI, XVII, e XVIII.* Pool Editorial, Recife.

Messenger, J. C.
  1975   Montserrat: The Most Distinctively Irish Settlement in the New World.
          Ethnicity 2:281–303.
  1994   St. Patrick's Day in "The Other Emerald Isle." *Éire-Ireland* 29:12–23.
Métraux, A.
  1948   The Tupinamba. In *Handbook of South American Indians, Volume 3: The
          Tropical Forest Tribes,* edited by J. H. Steward, pp. 95–133. U.S. Govern-
          ment Printing Office, Washington.
Mikolajczyk, A.
  1990   Didactic Presentation of the Past: Some Retrospective Considerations in
          Relation to the Archaeological and Ethnological Museum, Lódz, Poland. In
          The Politics of the Past, edited by P. Gathercole and D. Lowenthal, pp. 247–
          256. Unwin Hyman, London.
Mill, J. S.
  1979   Editorials from the Morning Chronicle. In *John Stuart Mill on Ireland,*
          edited by R. N. Lebow, pp. 1–37. Institute for the Study of Human Issues,
          Philadelphia.
Miller, D., and C. Tilley
  1984   Ideology, Power, and Prehistory: An Introduction. In *Ideology, Power, and
          Prehistory,* edited by D. Miller and C. Tilley, pp. 1–15. Cambridge Univer-
          sity Press, Cambridge.
Miller, G. L.
  1980   Classification and Economic Scaling of 19th Century Ceramics. *Historical
          Archaeology* 14:1–40.
Miller, J. C.
  1976   *Kings and Kinsmen: Early Mbundu States in Angola.* Clarendon Press,
          Oxford.
  1982   The Significance of Drought, Disease, and Famine in the Agriculturally
          Marginal Zones of West-Central Africa. *Journal of African History* 23:
          17–61.
Miller, K. A.
  1985   *Emigrants and Exiles: Ireland and the Irish Exodus to North America.* Ox-
          ford University Press, New York.
Mintz, S. W.
  1986   *Sweetness and Power: The Place of Sugar in Modern History.* Penguin, New
          York.
Mitchell, F.
  1976   *The Irish Landscape.* Collins, London.
Mokyr, J.
  1983   *Why Ireland Starved: A Quantitative and Analytical History of the Irish
          Economy, 1800–1850.* George Allen and Unwin, Boston.
Monks, G. G.
  1992   Architectural Symbolism and Non-Verbal Communication at Upper Fort
          Garry. *Historical Archaeology* 26(2):37–57.
Moore, J. A., and A. S. Keene
  1983   Archaeology and the Law of the Hammer. In *Archaeological Hammers and
          Theories,* edited by J. A. Moore and A. S. Keene, pp. 3–13. Academic Press,
          New York.

Moser, G. M.
  1985   Grumbling Veterans of an Empire. In *Empire in Transition: The Portuguese World in the Time of Camões,* edited by A. Hower and R. A. Preto-Rodas, pp. 97–105. University Presses of Florida, Gainesville.
Mouer, L. D.
  1993   Chesapeake Creoles: The Creation of Folk Culture in Colonial Virginia. In *The Archaeology of 17th-Century Virginia,* edited by T. R. Reinhart and D. J. Pogue, pp. 105–166. Archaeological Society of Virginia, Courtland.
Mrozowski, S. A.
  1988   Historical Archaeology as Anthropology. *Historical Archaeology* 22(1): 18–24.
  1991   Landscapes of Inequality. In *The Archaeology of Inequality,* edited by R. H. McGuire and R. Paynter, pp. 79–101. Basil Blackwell, Oxford.
Mumford, L.
  1967   *The Myth of the Machine: Technics and Human Development.* Harcourt, Brace, and World, New York.
Nassaney, M. S.
  1989   An Epistemological Enquiry into Some Archaeological and Historical Interpretations of 17th Century Native American–European Relations. In *Archaeological Approaches to Cultural Identity,* edited by S. Shennan, pp. 76–93. Unwin Hyman, London.
Nichols, E.
  1988   *No Easy Run to Freedom: Maroons in the Great Dismal Swamp of North Carolina and Virginia, 1677–1850.* Master's thesis, University of South Carolina, Columbia.
Nieuhoff, J.
  1813   Voyages and Travels into Brazil. In *A General Collection of the Best and Most Interesting Voyages and Travels in All Parts of the World,* edited by J. Pinkerton, pp. 697–881. Longman, Hurst, Rees, Orme, and Brown, London.
Noël Hume, I.
  1962   An Indian Ware of the Colonial Period. *Quarterly Bulletin of the Archaeological Society of Virginia* 17:2–14.
  1964   Archaeology: Handmaiden to History. *North Carolina Historical Review* 41:215–225.
  1969   *The Wells of Williamsburg: Colonial Time Capsules.* Colonial Williamsburg, Williamsburg, Virginia.
  1972   *A Guide to Artifacts of Colonial America.* Alfred A. Knopf, New York.
  1994   *The Virginia Adventure: Roanoke to James Towne—An Archaeological and Historical Odyssey.* Alfred A. Knopf, New York.
Novick, P.
  1988   *That Noble Dream: The "Objectivity Question" and the American Historical Profession.* Cambridge University Press, Cambridge.
Nowak, L.
  1983   *Property and Power: Towards a Non-Marxian Historical Materialism.* D. Reidel, Dordrecht, Netherlands.
O'Brien, G.
  1921   *The Economic History of Ireland, From the Union to the Famine.* Longmans, Green, London.

Ó Corráin, D.
1989   Prehistoric and Early Christian Ireland. In *The Oxford Illustrated History of Ireland*, edited by R. F. Foster, pp. 1–52. Oxford University Press, Oxford.
O'Dowd, M.
1986   Gaelic Economy and Society. In *Natives and Newcomers: The Making of Irish Colonial Society, 1534–1641*, edited by C. Brady and R. Gillespie, pp. 120–147. Irish Academic Press, Bungay, Suffolk.
Ó Gráda, C.
1989   *The Great Irish Famine*. Gill and Macmillan, Dublin.
Ollman, B.
1971   *Alienation: Marx's Conception of Man in Capitalist Society*. Cambridge University Press, Cambridge.
Oppenheim, A. L.
1957   A Bird's-Eye View of Mesopotamian Economic History. In *Trade and Market in the Early Empires: Economies in History and Theory*, edited by K. Polanyi, C. M. Arensberg, and H. W. Pearson, pp. 27–37. The Free Press, Glencoe, Illinois.
O'Regan, S.
1990   Maori Control of the Maori Heritage. In *The Politics of the Past*, edited by P. Gathercole and D. Lowenthal, pp. 95–106. Unwin Hyman, London.
O'Rourke, C. J.
1989   *The Great Irish Famine*. Veritas, Dublin.
Orser, C. E., Jr.
1987   Plantation Status and Consumer Choice: A Materialist Framework for Historical Archaeology. In *Consumer Choice in Historical Archaeology*, edited by S. M. Spencer-Wood, pp. 121–137. Plenum Press, New York.
1988a *The Material Basis of the Postbellum Tenant Plantation: Historical Archaeology in the South Carolina Piedmont*. University of Georgia Press, Athens.
1988b Toward a Theory of Power for Historical Archaeology: Plantations and Space. In *The Recovery of Meaning: Historical Archaeology in the Eastern United States*, edited by M. P. Leone and P. B. Potter, Jr., pp. 313–343. Smithsonian Institution Press, Washington.
1990   Archaeological Approaches to New World Plantation Slavery. In *Archaeological Method and Theory*, edited by M. B. Schiffer, vol. 2, pp. 111–154. University of Arizona Press, Tucson.
1991   The Continued Pattern of Dominance: Landlord and Tenant on the Postbellum Cotton Plantation. *The Archaeology of Inequality*, edited by R. H. McGuire and R. Paynter, pp. 40–54. Basil Blackwell, Oxford.
1992   *Introdução à Arqueologia História*. Translated by P. P. A. Funari. Oficina de Livros, Belo Horizonte.
1993   *In Search of Zumbi: The 1993 Season*. Midwestern Archaeological Research Center, Illinois State University, Normal.
1994a Consumption, Consumerism, and Things from the Earth. *Historical Methods* 27:61–70.
1994b Toward a Global Historical Archaeology: An Example from Brazil. *Historical Archaeology* 28(1):5–22.
Orser, C. E., Jr., and B. M. Fagan
1995   *Historical Archaeology*. HarperCollins, New York.

Pailes, R. A.
1980   The Upper Rio Sonora Valley in Prehistoric Times. *Transactions of the Illinois Academy of Science* 72(4):20–39.
Pailes, R. A., and J. W. Whitecotton
1979   The Greater Southwest and the Mesoamerican "World" System: An Explanatory Model of Frontier Relationships. In *the Frontier, Volume 2: Comparative Studies,* edited by W. W. Savage, Jr., and S. I. Thompson, pp. 105–121. University of Oklahoma Press, Norman.
Parsons, J. R.
1990   Critical Reflections on a Decade of Full-Coverage Regional Survey in the Valley of Mexico. In *The Archaeology of Regions: A Case for Full-Coverage Survey,* edited by S. K. Fish and S. A. Kowalewski, pp. 7–31. Smithsonian Institution Press, Washington.
Paynter, R., and R. H. McGuire
1991   The Archaeology of Inequality: Material Culture, Domination, and Resistance. In *The Archaeology of Inequality,* edited by R. H. McGuire and R. Paynter, pp. 1–27. Basil Blackwell, Oxford.
Phillips, J.R.S.
1988   *The Medieval Expansion of Europe.* Oxford University Press, Oxford.
Pilling, A. R.
1967   Beginnings. *Historical Archaeology* 1:1–22.
Pinion, F. B.
1968   *A Hardy Companion: A Guide to the Works of Thomas Hardy and Their Background.* St. Martin's Press, New York.
Postman, N.
1993   *Technopoly: The Surrender of Culture to Technology.* Vintage, New York.
Potter, P. B., Jr.
1991a   Self-Reflection in Archaeology. In *Processual and Postprocessual Archaeologies: Multiple Ways of Knowing the Past,* edited by R. W. Preucel, pp. 225–234. Center for Archaeological Investigations, Southern Illinois University, Carbondale.
1991b   What Is the Use of Plantation Archaeology? *Historical Archaeology* 25(3):94–107.
1994   *Public Archaeology in Annapolis: A Critical Approach to History in Maryland's Ancient City.* Smithsonian Institution Press, Washington.
Power, D.
1991   The Archaeology of the Munster Plantation. In *The Illustrated Archaeology of Ireland,* edited by M. Ryan, pp. 198–201. Country House, Dublin.
Pred, A.
1990   *Making Histories and Constructing Human Geographies: The Local Transformation of Practice, Power Relations, and Consciousness.* Westview Press, Boulder.
Price, T. D., and G. M. Feinman
1993   *Images of the Past.* Mayfield, Mountain View, California.
Prous, A.
1991   *Arqueologia Brasileira.* Editora Universidade de Brasília, Brasília.
Quimby, G. I.
1966   *Indian Culture and European Trade Goods: The Archaeology of the Historic*

Period in the Western Great Lakes Region. University of Wisconsin Press, Madison.

Quimby, G. I., and A. Spoehr
  1951   Acculturation and Material Culture—I. *Fieldiana: Anthropology* 36:107–147.

Rabasa, J.
  1993   *Inventing America: Spanish Historiography and the Formation of Eurocentrism.* University of Oklahoma Press, Norman.

Rabinow, P. (editor)
  1984   *The Foucault Reader.* Pantheon, New York.

Radcliffe-Brown, A. R.
  1940   On Social Structure. *Journal of the Royal Anthropological Society of Great Britain and Ireland* 70:1–12.

Rader, M.
  1979   *Marx's Interpretation of History.* Oxford University Press, New York.

Ramos, A.
  1939   *The Negro in Brazil.* Translated by R. Pattee. Associated Publishers, Washington.

Ravenstein, E. G. (editor)
  1967   *The Strange Adventure of Andrew Battell of Leigh in Angola and the Adjoining Regions.* Klaus, Nendeln/Liechtenstein.

Riley, C. L., and B. C. Hedrick (editors)
  1980   New Frontiers in the Archaeology and Ethnohistory of the Greater Southwest. *Transactions of the Illinois Academy of Science* 72(4):1–96.

Riordan, T. B., and W. H. Adams
  1985   Commodity Flows and National Market Access. *Historical Archaeology* 19(2):5–18.

Rocha Pita, S. da
  1950   *História da América Portuguesa* (3rd ed.). Livaria Progresso Editora, Salvador.

Rodrigues, N.
  1945   *Os Africanos no Brasil* (3rd ed.). Companhia Editora Nacional, São Paulo.

Roemer, J. E.
  1988   *Free to Lose: An Introduction to Marxist Economic Philosophy.* Harvard University Press, Cambridge.

Rowlands, M., M. Larsen, and K. Kristiansen (editors)
  1987   *Centre and Periphery in the Ancient World.* Cambridge University Press, Cambridge.

Rubertone, P. E.
  1989   Archaeology, Colonialism, and 17th-Century Native America: Towards an Alternative Interpretation. In *Conflict in the Archaeology of Living Traditions,* edited by R. Layton, pp. 32–45. Unwin Hyman, London.

Russell, C. P.
  1967   *Firearms, Traps, and Tools of the Mountain Men.* Alfred A.Knopf, New York.

Russell, J.
  1994   Measuring Time. *Archaeology* 47(2):6.

Ryan, M. (editor)
  1991   *The Illustrated Archaeology of Ireland.* Country House, Dublin.

Sahagún, F. de
  1959 *Florentine Codex: General History of the Things of New Spain, Book 9—The Merchants.* Translated by C. E. Dibble and A. J. O. Anderson. School of American Research, Sante Fe, and University of Utah Press, Salt Lake City.
Said, E. W.
  1978 *Orientalism.* Pantheon, New York.
  1993 *Culture and Imperialism.* Alfred A. Knopf, New York.
Sale, K.
  1990 *The Conquest of Paradise: Christopher Columbus and the Columbian Legacy.* Penguin, New York.
Salmon, M. H.
  1982 *Philosophy and Archaeology.* Academic Press, New York.
Sanders, W. T.
  1992 Ranking and Stratification in Prehispanic Mesoamerica. In *Mesoamerican Elites: An Archaeological Assessment,* edited by D. Z. Chase and A. F. Chase, pp. 278–291. University of Oklahoma Press, Norman.
Saunders, A. C.
  1982 *A Social History of Black Slaves and Freedmen in Portugal, 1441–1555.* Cambridge University Press, Cambridge.
Scally, R. J.
  1995 *The End of Hidden Ireland: Rebellion, Famine, and Emigration.* Oxford University Press, New York.
Scammell, G. V.
  1981 *The World Encompassed: The First European Maritime Empires, c. 800–1650.* Methuen, London.
Scarre, C.
  1990 The Western World View in Archaeological Atlases. In *The Politics of the Past,* edited by P. Gathercole and D. Lowenthal, pp. 11–18. Unwin Hyman, London.
Schiffer, M. B.
  1992 Archaeology and Behavioral Science: Manifesto for an Imperial Archaeology. In *Quandaries and Quests: Visions of Archaeology's Future,* edited by L. Wandsnider, pp. 225–238. Center for Archaeological Investigations, Southern Illinois University, Carbondale.
Schmidt, P. R.
  1978 *Historical Archaeology: A Structural Approach in an African Culture.* Greenwood Press, Westport, Connecticut.
Schortman, E. M., and P. A. Urban
  1987 Modeling Interregional Interaction in Prehistory. In *Advances in Archaeological Method and Theory,* edited by M. B. Schiffer, vol. 11, pp. 37–93. Academic Press, San Diego.
Schrire, C.
  1991 The Historical Archaeology of the Impact of Colonialism in Seventeenth-Century South Africa. In *Historical Archaeology in Global Perspective,* edited by L. Falk, pp. 69–96. Smithsonian Institution Press, Washington.
Schuyler, R. L.
  1968 The Use of Historic Analogs in Archaeology. *American Antiquity* 33:390–392.

1970   Historical Archaeology and Historic Sites Archaeology as Anthropology:
       Basic Definitions and Relationships. *Historical Archaeology* 4:83–89.
1977   Parallels in the Rise of the Various Subfields of Historical Archaeology.
       Conference on Historic Site Archaeology Papers 10:2–10.
1988   Archaeological Remains, Documents, and Anthropology: A Call for a New
       Culture History. *Historical Archaeology* 22(1):36–42.
Schwartz, S. B.
1970   The Mocambo: Slave Resistance in Colonial Bahia. *Journal of Social History*
       3:313–333.
1985   *Sugar Plantations in the Foundation of Brazilian Society: Bahia, 1550–
       1835.* Cambridge University Press, Cambridge.
Scott, E. M.
1994   Through the Lens of Gender: Archaeology, Inequality, and Those "Of
       Little Note." In *Those of Little Note: Gender, Race, and Class in Historical
       Archaeology,* edited by E. M. Scott, pp. 3–24. University of Arizona Press,
       Tucson.
Scott, J. C.
1985   *Weapons of the Weak: Everyday Forms of Peasant Resistance.* Yale Univer-
       sity Press, New Haven.
1990   *Domination and the Arts of Resistance: Hidden Transcripts.* Yale Univer-
       sity Press, New Haven.
Seccombe, W.
1992   *A Millennium of Family Change: Feudalism to Capitalism in Northwestern
       Europe.* Verso, London.
Seeden, H., and P. J. Watson
1992   Albert Ernest Glock, 1925–1992. *World Archaeological Congress News*
       1(2):4.
Setzler, F. M.
1943   Archaeological Explorations in the United States, 1930–1942. *Acta Ameri-
       cana* 1:206–220.
Shackel, P. A.
1993   *Personal Discipline and Material Culture: An Archaeology of Annapolis,
       Maryland, 1695–1870.* University of Tennessee Press, Knoxville.
Shanks, M., and C. Tilley
1987   *Re-Constructing Archaeology.* Cambridge University Press, Cambridge.
1988   *Social Theory and Archaeology.* University of New Mexico Press, Albu-
       querque.
Shapiro, G., and J. J. Miller
1990   The Seventeenth-Century Landscape of San Luis de Talimali: Three Scales
       of Analysis. In *Earth Patterns: Essays in Landscape Archaeology,* edited by
       W. M. Kelso and R. Most, pp. 89–101. University Press of Virginia, Char-
       lottesville.
Sharer, R. J., and W. Ashmore
1987   *Archaeology: Discovering Our Past.* Mayfield, Palo Alto, California.
Silberman, N. A.
1989   *Between Past and Present: Archaeology, Ideology, and Nationalism in the
       Modern Middle East.* Henry Holt, New York.
1995   *Sultans, Merchants, and Minorities: The Challenge of Historical Archaeol-*

ogy in the Modern Middle East. Paper presented at the annual meeting of the Society for Historical Archaeology, Washington, D.C.

Simmel, G.
1978   *The Philosophy of Money.* Translated by T. Bottomore and D. Frisby. Routledge and Kegan Paul, London.

Skibo, J. M., M. B. Schiffer, and K. C. Reid
1989   Organic-Tempered Pottery: An Experimental Study. *American Antiquity* 54:122–146.

Slater, D.
1975   The Poverty of Modern Geographic Enquiry. *Pacific Viewpoint* 16:159–176.

Society for Post-Medieval Archaeology
1993   Prioridades de investigação em arqueologia pós-medieval. *Arqueologia Industrial* 1:87–93.

Soja, E. W.
1989   *Postmodern Geographies: The Reassertion of Space in Critical Social Theory.* Verso, London.

Solow, B. L.
1984   Why Ireland Starved. *Journal of Economic History* 44:839–843.
1991   (editor) *Slavery and the Rise of the Atlantic System.* Cambridge University Press, Cambridge.

South, S.
1964   Preface. *Florida Anthropologist* 17(2):34.
1968   Comment on "Some Thoughts on Theory and Method in Historical Archaeology" by Clyde Dollar. *Conference on Historic Site Archaeology Papers* 2(2):35–53.
1977   *Method and Theory in Historical Archaeology.* Academic Press, New York.
1988   Whither Pattern? *Historical Archaeology* 22(1):25–28.

Southey, R.
1822   *History of Brazil* (2nd ed.). Longman, Hurst, Rees, Orme, and Brown, London.

Souza, Y. de
1963   *Grandes Negros do Brasil.* Livraria São José, Rio de Janeiro.

Spaulding, A. C.
1953   Statistical Techniques for the Discovery of Artifact Types. *American Antiquity* 18:305–313.

Spencer-Wood, S. M.
1991   Toward a Feminist Historical Archaeology of the Construction of Gender. In *The Archaeology of Gender: Proceedings of the Twenty-Second Annual Conference of the Archaeological Association of the University of Calgary,* edited by D. Walde and N. D. Willows, pp. 234–244. Archaeological Association of the University of Calgary, Calgary.
1992   A Feminist Program for Nonsexist Archaeology. In *Quandaries and Quests: Visions of Archaeology's Future,* edited by L. Wandsnider, pp. 98–114. Center for Archaeological Investigations, Southern Illinois University, Carbondale.

Spriggs, M. (editor)
1984   *Marxist Perspectives in Archaeology.* Cambridge University Press, Cambridge.

Stewart-Abernathy, L. C.
1986   *The Moser Farmstead, Independent but Not Isolated: The Archaeology of a*

Late Nineteenth Century Ozark Farmstead. Arkansas Archaeological Survey, Fayetteville.

1992 Industrial Goods in the Service of Tradition: Consumption and Cognition on an Ozark Farmstead before the Great War. In *The Art and Mystery of Historical Archaeology: Essays in Honor of James Deetz,* edited by A. E. Yentsch and M. C. Beaudry, pp. 101–126. CRC Press, Boca Raton, Florida.

Stoltman, J. B.
1966 New Radiocarbon Dates for Southeastern Fiber-Tempered Pottery. *American Antiquity* 31:872–874.

Struever, S., and G. L. Houart
1972 An Analysis of the Hopewell Interaction Sphere. In *Social Exchange and Interaction,* edited by E. N. Wilmsen, pp. 47–79. Museum of Anthropology, University of Michigan, Ann Arbor.

Taylor, L. J.
1980 Colonialism and Community Structure in Western Ireland. *Ethnohistory* 27:169–181.

Taylor, W. W.
1948 A Study of Archaeology. *American Anthropological Association, Memoir* 69, Washington.

Thomas, N.
1991 *Entangled Objects: Exchange, Material Culture, and Colonialism in the Pacific.* Harvard University Press, Cambridge.

Thompson, E. P.
1978 Eighteenth-Century English Society: Class Struggle Without Class? *Social History* 3:133–165.

Thornton, J.
1992 *Africa and Africans in the Making of the Atlantic World, 1400–1680.* Cambridge University Press, Cambridge.

Thurman, M. D.
1974 Reply to Howard's Rejoinder. *Conference on Historic Site Archaeology Papers* 7(3):226–227.

Trigger, B. G.
1968 The Determinants of Settlement Patterns. In *Settlement Archaeology,* edited by K. C. Chang, pp. 53–78. National Press, Palo Alto, California.
1989 *A History of Archaeological Thought.* Cambridge University Press, Cambridge.

Trombold, C. D. (editor)
1991 *Ancient Road Networks and Settlement Hierarchies in the New World.* Cambridge University Press, Cambridge.

Vansina, J.
1963 The Foundation of the Kingdom of Kasanje. *Journal of African History* 4:355–374.
1966 *Kingdoms of the Savanna: A History of Central African States until European Occupation.* University of Wisconsin Press, Madison.

Vaughan, W. E.
1994 *Landlords and Tenants in Mid-Victorian Ireland.* Clarendon, Oxford.

Vernon, R.
1988 17th Century Apalachee Colono-Ware as a Reflection of Demography, Economics, and Acculturation. *Historical Archaeology* 22(1):76–82.

Vernon, R., and A. S. Cordell
  1993 A Distributional and Technological Study of Apalachee Colono-Ware from San Luis de Talimali. In *The Spanish Missions of La Florida,* edited by B. G. McEwan, pp. 418–441. University Press of Florida, Gainesville.
Voget, F. W.
  1975 *A History of Ethnology.* Holt, Rinehart, and Winston, New York.
Wagstaff, J. M. (editor)
  1987 *Landscape and Culture: Geographical and Archaeological Perspectives.* Basil Blackwell, Oxford.
Walker, I. C.
  1967 Historic Archaeology: Methods and Principles. *Historical Archaeology* 1: 23–34.
  1968 Comments on Clyde Dollar's "Some Thoughts on Theory and Method in Historical Archaeology." *Conference on Historic Site Archaeology Papers* 2(2):105–122.
  1970 The Crisis of Identity: History and Anthropology. *Conference on Historic Site Archaeology Papers* 3:62–69.
Wallace, I.
  1990 *The Global Economic System.* Unwin Hyman, London.
Wallerstein, I.
  1974 *The Modern World-System: Capitalist Agriculture and the Origins of the European World-Economy in the Sixteenth Century.* Academic Press, New York.
  1979 *The Capitalist World-Economy.* Cambridge University Press, Cambridge.
  1980 *The Modern World-System II: Mercantilism and the Consolidation of the European World-Economy, 1600–1750.* Academic Press, New York.
Walsh, C. M.
  1901 *The Measurement of General Exchange-Value.* Macmillan, New York.
Walthall, J. A. (editor)
  1991 *French Colonial Archaeology: The Illinois Country and the Western Great Lakes.* University of Illinois Press, Urbana.
Walthall, J. A., and T. E. Emerson (editors)
  1992 *Calumet and Fleur-de-Lis: Archaeology of Indian and French Contact in the Midcontinent.* Smithsonian Institution Press, Washington.
Washburn, D. K.
  1980 The Mexican Connection: Cylinder Jars from the Valley of Oaxaca. *Transactions of the Illinois Academy of Science* 72(4):70–85.
Watkins, C. M.
  1968 *The Cultural History of Marlborough, Virginia: An Archaeological and Historical Investigation of the Port Town for Stafford County and the Plantation of John Mercer.* United States National Museum Bulletin 253. Smithsonian Institution Press, Washington.
West, C., and B. Brown
  1993 Beyond Eurocentrism and Multiculturalism. *Modern Philology* 90 (supplement):142–166.
Whelan, K.
  1994 Settlement Patterns in the West of Ireland in the Pre-Famine Period. In *Decoding the Landscape,* edited by T. Collins, pp. 60–78. Centre for Landscape Studies, University College Galway, Galway.

White, J. R.
   1975   Historic Contact Sites as Laboratories for the Study of Culture Change. *The Conference of Historic Site Archaeology Papers* 9:153–163.
Wilcox, D. R.
   1986   A Historical Analysis of the Problem of Southwestern-Mesoamerican Connections. In *Ripples in the Chichimec Sea: New Considerations of Southwestern-Mesoamerican Interactions,* edited by F. J. Mathien and R. H. McGuire, pp. 9–44. Southern Illinois University Press, Carbondale.
Willey, G. R.
   1953   *Prehistoric Settlement Patterns in the Virú Valley, Perú.* Smithsonian Institution, Bureau of American Ethnology Bulletin 155. Government Printing Office, Washington.
Willey, G. R., and P. Phillips
   1958   *Method and Theory in American Archaeology.* University of Chicago Press, Chicago.
Wilson, D. J.
   1990   Full-Coverage Survey in the Lower Santa Valley: Implications for Regional Settlement Pattern Studies on the Peruvian Coast. In *The Archaeology of Regions: A Case for Full-Coverage Survey,* edited by S. K. Fish and S. A. Kowalewski, pp. 117–145. Smithsonian Institution Press, Washington.
Wolf, E. R.
   1982   *Europe and the People without History.* University of California Press, Berkeley.
   1984   Culture: Panacea or Problem? *American Antiquity* 49:393–400.
   1990   Facing Power: Old Insights, New Questions. *American Anthropologist* 92: 586–596.
Wolfe, L. M. (editor)
   1938   *John of the Mountains: The Unpublished Journals of John Muir.* Houghton Mifflin, Boston.
Wood, W. R., and T. D. Thiessen (editors)
   1985   *Early Fur Trade on the Northern Plains: Canadian Traders among the Mandan and Hidatsa Indians, 1738–1818.* University of Oklahoma Press, Norman.
Woodham-Smith, C.
   1991   *The Great Hunger: Ireland, 1845–1849.* Penguin, London.
Woodruff, W.
   1967   *Impact of Western Man: A Study of Europe's Role in the World Economy, 1750–1960.* St. Michael's Press, New York.
   1981   *The Struggle for World Power, 1500–1980.* St. Michael's Press, New York.
Woolley, L.
   1937   *Digging Up the Past.* Penguin, Harmondsworth, Middlesex.
Wright, B. W.
   1979   *A Proxemic Analysis of the Iroquoian Settlement Pattern.* Western, Calgary.
Wynn, T.
   1989   *The Evolution of Spatial Competence.* University of Illinois Press, Urbana.
Yentsch, A.
   1990   An Interpretive Study of the Use of Land and Space on Lot 83, Annapolis, Md. *Maryland Archaeology* 26(1–2):21–53.

Young, A.
 1780 *A Tour of Ireland with General Observations on the Present State of that Kingdom made in the Years 1776, 1777, and 1778.* T. Cadell and J. Dodsley, London.
Zanettini, P. E.
 1988 Canudos: memórias do fim do mundo. *Horizonte Geográfico* 1(3):28–38.
 1990 Calçada do Lorena: o primeiro caminho para o mar. *Memória* 3(7–9).
Zimmerman, L. J.
 1977 *Prehistoric Locational Behavior: A Computer Simulation.* Office of the State Archaeologist, Iowa City, Iowa.
 1987 The Impact on the Concept of Time and Past on the Concept of Anthropology: Some Lessons from the Reburial Issue. *Archaeological Review from Cambridge* 6(1):42–50.
Zinn, H.
 1970 *The Politics of History.* Beacon Press, Boston.

Index